2nd edition

Solutions

Upper-Intermediate Student's Book

Tim Falla Paul A Davies

OXFORD
UNIVERSITY PRESS

🎧 Listening (1.01 = disk 1, track 1 / 2.01 = disk 2, track 1)

Check your progress

Think about your progress as you work through *Solutions 2nd edition Upper-Intermediate*. After completing Skills Round-up 1–4 read each statement and write the number of ticks (✓) that is true for you. Do the same again after Skills Round-up 1–10.

✓ = I need more practice.   ✓✓ = I sometimes find this difficult.   ✓✓✓ = No problem!

In English I can …		Skills Round-up 1–4	Skills Round-up 1–10
Listening			
B1	… understand the main points of speech about familiar topics and follow the main points of an extended discussion. **1A, 2C, 10C**		
B2	… understand extended discussions on familiar topics and identify speaker viewpoints. **5C, 6C, 8A**		
B2	… understand and react to current affairs radio programmes. **4A, 5C, 6C**		
B2	… follow complex lines of argument on familiar topics. **2C, 4C, 5C, 6C**		
B2	… understand detailed and linguistically complex descriptive and narrative passages. **1C, 5D, 9C**		
C1	… understand a wide range of broadcast material and identify finer points of detail. **3B, 8A, 9A**		
Reading			
B1	… understand the description of events and feelings. **1C, 1D, 3D, 9D**		
B2	… scan quickly through long and complex texts, locating relevant detail. **5D, 6D, 7D, 8D, 9D**		
B2	… understand magazine articles about current issues in which writers adopt particular viewpoints. **2C, 3D, 6C, 8D**		
B2	… understand factual articles and reports. **1D, 2D, 2G, 4D, 8D, 10D**		
C1	… understand long and complex factual and literary texts. **4D, 6D, 7D, 8D**		
Speaking			
B1	… express personal views on familiar topics. **1A, 2A, 2E, 6F**		
B1	… give detailed accounts of events, real or imagined. **5E, 7E, 8B**		
B2	… present detailed descriptions on a variety of familiar topics. **5D, 7A**		
B2	… take an active part in a discussion on familiar topics. **1B, 2B, 3D**		
B2	… develop a clear argument, supporting my views at some length with relevant examples. **1G, 2D, 4A, 9E**		
B2	… explain a viewpoint on a topical issue giving the advantages and disadvantages. **3C, 7C, 8A, 10G**		
C1	… formulate ideas and opinions and present them skilfully and coherently to others. **5E, 6A, 6C, 7D**		
Writing			
B1	… write accounts of experiences, describing feelings and reactions in a simple text. **5G, 9G**		
B1	… write detailed descriptions on a range of familiar subjects. **1G, 6G, 10G**		
B2	… write a review of a film, book or play. **7G**		
B2	… write detailed descriptions of real or imaginary events in a clear connected text. **2G, 5G, 9G**		
B2	… write an essay which develops an argument, giving reasons in support of or against a particular point of view. **3G, 8G**		
B2	… write an essay which develops an argument, explaining the advantages and disadvantages of various options. **3G**		
C1	… expand and support views with subsidiary points, reasons and examples. **8G**		
C1	… write formally correct letters. **4G**		

THIS UNIT INCLUDES

Vocabulary ▪ personality traits ▪ synonyms and antonyms ▪ compound adjectives ▪ prepositions ▪ extra-curricular activities
Grammar ▪ present perfect simple and continuous ▪ state and dynamic verbs ▪ verb patterns
Speaking ▪ photo description ▪ interpreting pictures and giving opinions
Writing ▪ description of a person

Out of the ordinary | 1

1A VOCABULARY AND LISTENING Describing personality
I can talk about personality traits.

1 SPEAKING Describe the photos. What mental qualities do the people need for doing these activities? Which of those qualities do you have, in your opinion?

2 VOCABULARY Check the meaning of the adjectives below. Which could you use to describe the people in the photos? Why?

Personality traits ambitious argumentative assertive calm considerate conventional creative dedicated eccentric immature organised outgoing responsible selfish sensible serious sociable stubborn unconventional

▶▶▶ VOCABULARY BUILDER 1.1: PAGE 134 ◀◀◀

3 Complete the sentences with adjectives from exercise 2.
1 My brother is so _____ ! He screams like a baby if he loses at a game.
2 My aunt is very _____ . If a conversation isn't about her, she isn't interested.
3 You're so _____ ! If I give an opinion, you always disagree with it!
4 I suppose I'm quite _____ . If I don't want to go out, it's impossible to persuade me!
5 My best friend is very _____ . If her parents have to work late, she looks after her little brothers.

4 Choose four adjectives from exercise 2, then write more sentences like the ones in exercise 3. Can the class guess the adjectives?

5 SPEAKING Choose the three adjectives from exercise 2 which best describe you, in your opinion. Explain your choices to your partner.

6 🎧 1.02 Listen to six people discussing personality traits. Which question a–f is each person answering? Whose answer surprises you most?

Which personality trait:
a do you find most annoying? Why?
b do you most admire? Why?
c would you like but don't have? Give reasons.
d would you prefer not to have? Give reasons.
e is the most important to become rich? Why?
f is the most important in a friend? Why?

7 🎧 1.02 Listen again and complete the compound adjectives 1–6.
1 _____-motivated   4 _____-tempered
2 _____-meaning   5 _____-skinned
3 _____-minded   6 _____-pinching

8 SPEAKING Work in pairs. Ask and answer all the questions in exercise 6. Give your own ideas and reasons.

▶▶▶ VOCABULARY BUILDER 1.2: PAGE 134 ◀◀◀

1 **SPEAKING** Look at the photo below. What mental qualities do people need to climb mountains?

2 Read the text and find the name, age and nationality of the person it is describing. Then give your own answers to the two questions at the end of the text.

AT FIRST GLANCE, Jordan Romero appears to be a typical American teenager, but for the past three years he has not been leading an ordinary life. Since he was ten, he's had a single goal: to climb the highest mountain on every continent in the world.

Now thirteen, Jordan has already climbed seven of the eight mountains on his list, including Mount Everest; he is due to climb the last, Mount Vinson in Antarctica, next month. He's been using Facebook and Twitter to publicise his climbs and raise money. And recently, Jordan has been giving motivational talks to schoolchildren around the world via an online link. 'I've learned a lot about setting goals, healthy eating and living, and of course climbing mountains.' He has also been appearing on TV chat shows.

But some experts have been voicing concerns about the climbs. Have Jordan and his family been considering the risks? Or have they been thinking more about the publicity?

3 Read the *Learn this!* box. Then underline all the examples of the present perfect continuous in the text in exercise 2 and match them with uses 1, 2 and 3.

> **LEARN THIS!**
>
> **Present perfect simple and present perfect continuous**
> 1 We use the present perfect continuous form for an action **in progress** and, the simple form for a **completed** action.
> *I've been learning Russian, but I can't speak it well.*
> *I've learnt a new piece on the piano. I can play it now.*
> 2 We use the continuous form for something which has been happening **recently** and **repeatedly**:
> *I haven't been doing my homework this term.*
> But we use the simple form for one occasion or an exact number of occasions:
> *I haven't done my project/my last three projects.*
> 3 We can use the simple or continuous form with *for* or *since* to say **how long** a current action has been in progress. The continuous form is more frequent:
> *I've been waiting/I've waited for hours!*

>>> GRAMMAR BUILDER 1.1: PAGE 115 <<<

4 Complete each sentence in two ways: with the present perfect simple and continuous. Explain the difference.

1 I _____ (read) the new Stephenie Meyer novel.
2 We _____ (not play) football for a long time.
3 She _____ (do) well in her exams this year.
4 He _____ (finish) his science homework.
5 My parents _____ (go) to the new gym.
6 You _____ (eat) my crisps!

LOOK OUT!
State verbs are verbs which describe states, whereas dynamic verbs describe actions. We do not use state verbs in continuous tenses.
I've always been hating... ✗ *I've always hated dogs.*
Some verbs can be state or dynamic verbs, depending on the meaning: e.g. *taste* is a dynamic verb when it means *try*.
We've been tasting different cheeses.
Is it tasting funny? ✗ *Does it taste funny?*

5 Read the *Look out!* box. Then find a verb in the text in exercise 2 which is used once as a state verb and once as a dynamic verb. What is the difference in meaning?

>>> GRAMMAR BUILDER 1.2: PAGE 115 <<<

6 Complete the sentences about Jordan using the present perfect continuous, affirmative or negative, or the present perfect simple form when the continuous is not correct.

1 His dad and step-mum _____ (help) him.
2 He _____ (like) mountain-climbing since he was nine.
3 He _____ (climb) the highest mountain in Australia.
4 He _____ (not climb) the highest mountain in Antarctica yet.
5 He _____ (not go) to school very regularly this year.
6 He _____ (appear) on TV a lot recently.

7 Look at the prompts below and write questions using the present perfect continuous if possible. If it is a state verb, use the present perfect simple.

1 what / you / watch on TV / recently?
2 how long / you / learn / English?
3 you / work hard / recently?
4 how long / you / know / your teacher?
5 your best friend / seem / happy / recently?
6 how much / it / rain / this month?
7 what time / you / go to bed / recently?
8 how well / you / understand / this grammar lesson?

8 **SPEAKING** Work in pairs. Ask and answer the questions in exercise 7.

I can talk about fictional depictions of adolescence.

1 SPEAKING In pairs, make a list of books, films or TV shows about adolescents. How many can you think of in three minutes?

2 🎧 1.03 Listen to a radio programme about two writers. Think of at least two things they have in common.

EXAM TIP

When you do a multiple choice listening task, mark the answers you know after the first listening. When you listen again, focus mainly on the answers you still need.

3 🎧 1.03 Read the Exam tip and mark the answers which you think you know for questions 1–5. Then listen again and choose the best answers.

1 The novelist J. D. Salinger went to university but
   a was asked to leave.
   b received poor grades in his first year.
   c left before finishing the first year.
   d did not regard getting a degree as 'success'.
2 Salinger's famous novel about adolescence was
   a popular mainly because it was controversial.
   b only popular with younger readers.
   c extremely popular but condemned by some people.
   d not taught in many schools at first.
3 Because Salinger refused to be in the public eye,
   a people stopped asking him for interviews.
   b nobody was even sure what religion he was.
   c he was rarely talked about.
   d his fame actually increased.
4 Harper Lee's education was
   a not as successful as she had hoped.
   b more successful than Salinger's.
   c not as successful as Salinger's.
   d very similar to Salinger's.
5 How did Harper Lee find time to write her first novel?
   a A friend paid for her to take a year off work.
   b A friend got her work as a songwriter in New York.
   c She couldn't find a job in New York.
   d She wrote slowly for ten years in total.

4 VOCABULARY Complete the chart using a dictionary to help you if necessary. Which four religions did J. D. Salinger follow during his life, according to the radio programme?

Religion	Adjective	Follower
1_____	Buddhist	Buddhist
Christianity	2_____	3_____
Hinduism	4_____	Hindu
Islam	5_____ / Islamic	6_____
Judaism	7_____	Jew
8_____	Sikh	9_____

5 🎧 1.04 Read an extract from *To Kill A Mockingbird*, narrated by a girl called Scout. Find two separate implications in the text that Aunt Alexandra will be staying for a long time.

'Put my bag in the front bedroom, Calpurnia,' was the first thing Aunt Alexandra said. 'Jean Louise, stop scratching your head,' was the second thing she said. Calpurnia picked up Aunty's heavy suitcase and opened the door. 'I'll take it,' said Jem, and took it. I heard the suitcase hit the bedroom floor with a thump. The sound had a dull permanence about it. 'Have you come for a visit, Aunty?' I asked. Aunt Alexandra's visits from the Landing were rare, and she travelled in state. She owned a bright green square Buick and a black chauffeur, both kept in an unhealthy state of tidiness, but today they were nowhere to be seen.
'Didn't your father tell you?' she asked.
Jem and I shook our heads.
'Probably he forgot. He's not in yet, is he?'
'Nome, he doesn't usually get back till late afternoon,' said Jem.
'Well, your father and I decided it was time I came to stay with you for a while.'
'For a while' in Maycomb meant anything from three days to thirty years. Jem and I exchanged glances. 'Jem's growing up now and you are too,' she said to me. 'We decided that it would be best for you to have some feminine influence. It won't be many years, Jean Louise, before you become interested in clothes and boys.'
I could have made several answers to this: Cal's a girl; it would be many years before I would be interested in boys; I would never be interested in clothes ... but I kept quiet.

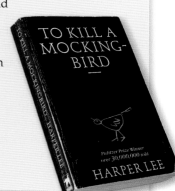

6 Find evidence in the text which implies that:
1 Aunt Alexandra is bossy.
2 Jem is considerate.
3 Scout and Jem's father is absent-minded.
4 Scout is a tomboy.

7 SPEAKING Work in pairs. Choose one book, film or TV show from your list in exercise 1. Give an example of how it deals with one or more of these topics:
• friendship and arguments between friends.
• the relationship between teenagers and adults.
• rebellion and breaking the rules.
• becoming an adult and taking responsibility for your life.

HIGH MATHS ABILITIES
BAD SCHOOL LIVES

1 SPEAKING Work in pairs. Discuss the quotation below. What personality adjectives could you use to describe this person? Does it sound like you?

I'm desperate to achieve, I'm desperate to get high marks. I'm too hard on myself.

Cameron Thompson, fourteen-year-old maths prodigy

2 🎧 1.05 Read the text opposite about Cameron Thompson. Do you think the adjectives you chose in exercise 1 are accurate? What others could you add to your description? Justify your answer with evidence from the text.

EXAM TIP

When you do a multiple choice reading task, read the options carefully and choose the one which matches the text in terms of *information*. Do not be distracted by specific words or phrases, focus on the *meaning*.

3 Read the Exam tip. Then choose the correct answers for the questions (1–5).

1 Between the ages of four and ten, Cameron
   a demonstrated outstanding ability in maths.
   b allowed his passion for numbers to dominate his life.
   c excelled at various school subjects.
   d didn't really fulfil his promise at maths.

2 Cameron's problems with communication
   a have been getting worse recently.
   b haven't been affecting his popularity at school.
   c are irrelevant when he's doing maths.
   d have been interfering with his ability to do maths work.

3 Cameron met a boy at his new school who
   a has something in common with him.
   b has even more severe problems with communication.
   c is even better at maths.
   d took a strong dislike to him from the first day.

4 Professor Leader thinks Cameron should
   a continue with his degree.
   b have a temporary break from his degree.
   c give up maths completely for a few years.
   d try to increase the speed of his progress.

5 Recently, Cameron has noticed
   a a deterioration in his relationship with his parents.
   b a loss of ambition academically.
   c an improvement in his social life.
   d a sudden improvement in his school life.

Teachers first noticed Cameron Thompson's talent for numbers when he was four years old and at pre-school. Throughout primary school, Cameron Thompson's best subject was maths. Then, when he was eleven, he took a maths test prior to entering secondary school. The test was out of 140; Cameron scored 141. 'I broke the system,' he recalls.

Since then, he has continued to progress quickly. He passed two GCSEs (maths and further maths) at the age of eleven and then got the highest grade in his maths A-level before the end of that same academic year. He is now fourteen years old and studying for a degree in maths, a remarkable achievement bearing in mind his age.

But his academic achievements have not always been matched by social success. 'I have the social ability of a talking potato,' he admits. In other words, he feels more at ease with numbers than among other teenagers. 'Most people my age do despise me. I've been like this for years.'

Communication is not one of Cameron's strong points and, aside from the problems this causes socially, it is now beginning to affect his marks in mathematics. This is because, at undergraduate level, he is expected to give

reasons for his answers alongside the answers themselves. Cameron's difficulty is that he often doesn't know how he has arrived at the answers, even though the answers are usually correct.

Cameron and his family have recently moved house and Cameron is due to start at a new school. He regards it as a chance to make a fresh start and make some friends. But his mother, Alison, has a few worries concerning his lack of social skills. While she describes Cameron as 'very sensitive', she also acknowledges that he is socially naive and often oblivious to signals from other people.

The new school specialises in dealing with students who, like Cameron, excel academically but find it difficult to relate to other students. And indeed, on his first day, Cameron did make a new friend – a boy called Tim – mainly owing to a shared dislike of Justin Bieber's music.

Recently, a maths professor from Cambridge University has been looking at Cameron's work. His advice to Cameron is perhaps surprising. Professor Imre Leader thinks Cameron should slow down, stop taking maths exams, and wait until he is eighteen before doing a degree. 'There's quite an important distinction,' he explains, 'between taking lots of exams as fast as you can, and relaxing and enjoying the level that you are at – what we call enrichment.' Professor Leader believes Cameron will do better in the long run if he stops trying to progress so quickly. And although Cameron does want to finish his current degree, he isn't making any academic plans beyond that. He goes to a weekly karate class after school. And recently, he went to a computer games convention with some friends from karate.

Since turning fourteen, Cameron's feelings towards girls have changed. As he puts it, 'I started to like them instead of being disgusted by them.' He's even been on a first date – without his parents. And in general, he feels less isolated and unusual than he did before. 'There are other people like me – high maths abilities, bad school lives – I am not alone. Spooky.'

4 **VOCABULARY** Look at the prepositions and prepositional phrases (1–10) below. Match them with the highlighted prepositions in the text.

1 considering
2 together with
3 about
4 with
5 before
6 apart from
7 past/further than
8 right through
9 because of
10 regarding

5 **VOCABULARY** Choose the correct preposition in these sentences. Then say if you agree or disagree.

1 It's better to maintain the same extra-curricular activities **right through / before** school.
2 Doing a hobby usually means spending more time **about / among** people your own age.
3 It's impossible to devote your energy to hobbies **alongside / aside from** schoolwork and exams.
4 It's essential to develop non-academic skills **prior to / regarding** starting your career.
5 Many teenagers can't pursue their hobbies easily **considering / owing to** a lack of facilities.
6 Doing hobbies can help develop useful skills **among / aside from** the ones you need for the hobby itself.

6 **SPEAKING** Work in pairs. Agree on three out-of-school activities which would be best for developing a person's social skills. Give reasons for your choices. Use the activities below or your own ideas.

Extra-curricular activities   doing drama   doing karate
doing yoga   going dancing   going shopping
joining a choir   jogging   learning an instrument
playing basketball   playing computer games
watching sport

7 **SPEAKING** Prepare a role-play.

Student A: You are a teenager who, like Cameron, has poor social skills. You want advice on how to improve them.
Student B: You are giving Student A advice on how to improve his/her social skills. Suggest activities to achieve this.

8 **SPEAKING** Perform your role-play to the class. Together, you should agree on one activity for Student A to try. Use the expressions below to help you.

Suggesting
How about taking up … ?   It's really good for (building confidence/meeting people/getting fit, etc.)
Or what about … ?   It's a great way to …
In that case, why don't you try … ?

Objecting
To be honest, I don't really like …/I'm not that keen on …/I don't feel happy about …/I don't think … (would be my thing/would suit me).

Agreeing
Maybe you've got a point./That's not a bad idea./I could try it, I suppose./I might give it a go.

1 **SPEAKING** Work in pairs. Discuss how strongly you agree with this statement: *I prefer to be in the background than in the spotlight.* Give it a mark between 5 (strongly agree) and 0 (strongly disagree).

2 Work in pairs. Do questions 1–3 of a personality quiz. Are the results so far similar to your ideas in exercise 1?

QUIZ

Fitting in or STANDING OUT: Which do YOU prefer?
Take the personality quiz and find out!
More a's than b's? You like to stand out!

1 Do you let your friends borrow your clothes?
  a Sure – and I help them choose!   **b** No way!
2 If you want your room decorated, do you
  a invite your friends to come for a 'painting party'?
  b decide to paint it by yourself one weekend?
3 If a stranger seems to be upset in the street, do you
  a offer to help immediately?
  b avoid helping because you feel shy?

3 Read the *Learn this!* box. Complete the second example of each pattern with phrases from the quiz in exercise 2.

LEARN THIS!

Verb patterns
1 **verb + infinitive**
  a *They failed to finish the race.*
  b _____
2 **verb + -*ing* form**
  a *I gave up doing karate after school.*
  b _____
3 **verb + object + infinitive**
  a *They forced him to get into the car.*
  b _____
4 **verb + object + infinitive without *to***
  a *She made me wait outside her office.*
  b _____
5 **verb + object + past participle**
  a *Let's get your bike repaired tomorrow.*
  b _____

4 Find three more examples of verb patterns in questions 1–3 of exercise 2. Which pattern does each one belong to?

5 Can you remember if the verbs below are followed by (A) an infinitive or (B) an -*ing* form? Label them A or B then check your answers in the Grammar Builder 1.3 on page 116.

agree   avoid   can't help   can't stand   consider   deny
enjoy   feel like   finish   hope   imagine   keep (on)
miss   practise   pretend   refuse   risk   spend (time)
suggest

LOOK OUT!
The verbs *remember*, *forget*, *stop* and *try* can be followed by an infinitive or -*ing* form, but with different meanings:
I remembered to vote. | *I don't remember voting (but I did).*
I'll never forget visiting the Tate. | *I forgot to visit the Tate.*
She's stopped smoking. | *She stopped to light a cigarette.*
I tried to stand up but I couldn't. | *I tried standing up but I still couldn't see the stage.*
The verbs *see*, *hear*, *watch* and *feel* are followed by an object + -*ing* form for ongoing actions, or an object + infinitive without *to* for completed actions:
I can felt him staring at me. | *I felt the ball brush my arm.*
I saw two cats fighting. | *Did you see him steal the car?*

6 Read the *Look out!* box. Then explain the difference in meaning between each pair of sentences.
  1 **a** I heard my neighbour shout.
    b I heard my neighbour shouting.
  2 **a** She tried smiling at the policeman.
    b She tried to smile at the policeman.
  3 **a** The busker stopped chatting with the crowd.
    b The busker stopped to chat with the crowd.
  4 **a** You must remember to speak to Sam.
    b You must remember speaking to Sam.

⟫⟫⟫ **GRAMMAR BUILDER 1.3: PAGE 116** ⟪⟪⟪

7 Complete questions 4–6 of the quiz. Use the infinitive (with or without *to*), past participle or -*ing* form of the verb in brackets. Then answer the questions.

4 If you forget _____ (wear) smart clothes for a special occasion, do you
  a enjoy _____ (look) different?
  b spend all day _____ (feel) embarrassed?
5 If you see a group of teenagers _____ (look) at you, do you
  a consider _____ (chat) to them?
  b avoid _____ (make) eye contact?
6 If you're working in a group at school and the teacher wants _____ (know) how it's going, do you
  a immediately offer _____ (speak) on behalf of the group?
  b delay _____ (offer) and let somebody else _____ (speak)?

QUIZ

8 **SPEAKING** In pairs, write two more questions for the quiz. Include at least one verb pattern from the *Learn this!* or *Look out!* box. Swap with another pair and answer their questions.

1 **SPEAKING** Look at the photo. Choose three adjectives below to describe the couple's overall appearance. Then compare your ideas in pairs. Do you agree?

attention-seeking   cool
fashionable   individual
intriguing   messy
outlandish   unattractive

2 **VOCABULARY** Work in pairs. Add the words below to the mind map. Then add as many other words as you can in two minutes.

bracelet   crouching   dyed   eye-liner   mascara   moody
piercing   spiky   tie   tights

```
        hair
clothes         make-up



expression/posture    jewellery
```

3 🎧 1.06 Listen to a candidate describing the photo in exercise 1. How many of the words in exercise 2 does she mention?

EXAM TIP

When you describe a photo, talk about what you can see and also what you can guess or deduce. For guesses and deductions, avoid repeating *I think* and instead use phrases like:
I should think they are … Maybe/Perhaps …
They look as if … They look like …
They look as though … They are obviously …
I'd say they are …
They could be/may be/might be …

4 🎧 1.06 Read the first Exam tip. Then listen to the candidate again. Which of the phrases in the box does she use?

EXAM TIP

The examiner's first question in the picture description task usually asks you to interpret the picture, the second usually requires you to give a more general opinion. Listen carefully to each question and make sure you really answer them.

5 Read the second Exam tip. Then read the phrases below and decide if each one would be more useful in answering question 1 or question 2 in the exam.

a Judging by … , I reckon … ____
b By and large, … ____
c Looking at … , I'd say that … ____
d Personally, I think … ____
e In my experience, … ____
f It's clear from the photo that … ____

6 Look at the examiner's first two questions for the photo in exercise 1. Discuss them in pairs and note down your ideas.

1 Do you think the boy in the photo cares about his appearance? Why do you think so?
2 How much can you tell about a teenager's personality just from looking at their appearance?

7 🎧 1.07 Now listen to the candidate answering the questions. Do you agree with her answers? Why?/Why not?

8 🎧 1.07 Listen again. Which phrases from exercise 5 does the candidate use?

9 **SPEAKING** In pairs, describe the photo below. Then take turns to ask and answer the examiner's first two questions. Include at least two phrases from exercise 5.

1 What impression do you think these women want to give other people?
2 Why do some young people want to dress in a way that older people find shocking?

1 **SPEAKING** Read the saying below and its definition. Do you agree or disagree? Give examples to support your opinion.

Opposites attract.
People who are very different tend to get on well together.

2 Read the text. Can you explain the title?

CHALK and CHEESE

Connor and Bess are completely different from each other. They're both seventeen years old, but that's about all they've got in common!

For a teenager, Connor comes across as very confident. He finds it easy to talk to people and is never lost for words. He's got a good sense of humour and really enjoys making people laugh.

As far as clothes go, Connor dresses in quite an unusual way and buys a lot of his outfits in second-hand markets and charity shops. He often changes his hairstyle too.

Connor is really good fun to be with. He's up for anything, and when you go out with him, you end up doing some crazy things. Having said that, he isn't that reliable. We often make plans to go out at the weekend, but he's always phoning me at the last minute to change the arrangement.

Unlike Connor, Bess hates being the centre of attention and isn't particularly interested in fashion. When it comes to clothes, Bess usually plays it safe. And whilst Connor regularly changes his hairstyle, Bess's hair has looked the same since I first met her.

When Bess is with close friends, she tends to be very talkative, but she often gets tongue-tied in social situations. However, she's a very good friend. She always thinks of others and she never lets you down.

Connor and Bess are complete opposites. Nevertheless, I get on well with both of them – and surprisingly, perhaps, they get on well together.

3 Match four adjectives from the words below with Connor and four with Bess. Justify your answers using phrases from the text.

conformist   considerate   dependable   funny
outgoing   shy   unconventional   unreliable

4 **VOCABULARY** Complete these contrasting pairs of phrases for describing character and behaviour. Use the verbs below. Which phrases are in the text in exercise 2?

count   get   give   keep   let   look   play   take   wear

Describing character and behaviour
be up for anything / ¹_____ it safe
(always) ²_____ on the bright side / expect the worst
speak your mind / ³_____ your opinions to yourself
⁴_____ things in your stride / get stressed
⁵_____ your heart on your sleeve / not ⁶_____ much away
never be lost for words / ⁷_____ tongue-tied
you never ⁸_____ me down / I can't ⁹_____ on you

5 **USE OF ENGLISH** Complete the second sentence so that it means the same as the first. Write 2–5 words, including the word in brackets.

1 a She takes everything in her stride.
   b She _____ about anything. (stressed)
2 a You can always count on me.
   b I'll _____ down. (never)
3 a Suddenly, I got tongue-tied.
   b I was _____ words. (lost)
4 a He doesn't give much away.
   b He doesn't _____ his sleeve. (heart)
5 a I usually expect the worst.
   b I rarely _____ side. (bright)

6 Read the *Look out!* box below. Find an example of this use of the present continuous in the text in exercise 2.

LOOK OUT!
We normally use the present simple for describing regular actions. However, we can use the present continuous with *always* or *forever* to express disapproval.
*Tom **always goes** home by bus.* (fact)
*Lucy **is always asking** me for money.* (disapproval)

7 **SPEAKING** In pairs, discuss which person in the text, Connor or Bess, is more like you, in your opinion. Who would you rather be friends with? Give reasons.

1 You are going to do the following exam writing task. Look at the list of topics you might include in the description. Which ones are mentioned in the text on page 12?

Write a description of two people you know who are very different. Write 200–250 words.

annoying habits   clothes   hair   hobbies
likes and dislikes   personal traits   talents

2 Choose the two people you are going to write about. Make notes about them in the chart. Use four topics from exercise 1 or your own ideas.

	Name: _____	Name: _____
Topic 1: _____		
Topic 2: _____		
Topic 3: _____		
Topic 4: _____		

3 Read the *Learn this!* box below. Underline examples of these words and phrases in the text on page 12.

Contrast
You can use a variety of phrases for making contrasts, not just **but** and **however**.
Unlike Sara, Jade is tall.
In contrast to Sara, Jade is tall.
Sara is short, **but/whereas** her sister Jade is tall.
While/Whilst Sara is short, Jade is tall.
Sara is short. Jade, **on the other hand,** is tall.
Jade is tall, **and yet** her sister Sara is short.
Jade is tall. **However,** Sara is short.

4 Choose the correct words in these sentences.
1 Luke is eccentric, **unlike / whereas** his sister is conventional.
2 **Whilst / In contrast to** my brother is hard-working, I'm quite lazy.
3 Ryan is very popular, **and yet / while** he's quite shy.
4 Sam is easy-going, **but / however** his brothers aren't.
5 Charlie is quite generous. His cousin, **whereas / on the other hand,** is very penny-pinching.

5 Write four sentences using information from your chart in exercise 2. To make your writing more sophisticated, include four different ways to make contrasts from the *Learn this!* box.

EXAM TIP

Make your descriptions of people's personalities more subtle by using the phrases below:
She tends to … + verb
He has a tendency to … + verb
She has a habit of … + *-ing* form
He comes across as … + adjective
People regard her as … + adjective
People consider her … + adjective
Some people find her … + adjective
She can be (adjective) *at times.*

6 Read the Exam tip. Find two of the phrases in the model text on page 12. Then suggest two other places in the text where you could use phrases from the tip.

7 Rewrite these sentences in a more subtle way. Include the word in brackets.
1 My dad is immature. (across)
2 My neighbour talks too much. (tendency)
3 My friend George is an ambitious student. (regard)
4 Lucy's brother offends people. (tends)
5 My best friend is argumentative. (find)
6 My mum is unconventional. (can)
7 I'm trustworthy. (consider)
8 He says the wrong thing. (habit)

8 Do the writing task in exercise 1.

CHECK YOUR WORK

Have you:
- [ ] followed the writing plan?
- [ ] written 200–250 words?
- [ ] used different phrases for making contrasts?
- [ ] included phrases from the tip box?
- [ ] checked your spelling and grammar?

Listening

1 Get ready to LISTEN Look at the summer courses below and decide which you would most like to attend. Then explain your choice to your partner.

  a an intensive English course in the USA
  b a survival course in the Arctic
  c a meditation and martial arts course
  d a performing arts course (music, dance, drama, etc.)

2 Do the exam task.

LISTENING exam task

🎧 1.08 **You will hear information about various summer courses. Match each extract to the correct summary sentence (A–F). There is one extra sentence.**

Speaker 1		Speaker 2		Speaker 3	
Speaker 4		Speaker 5			

A Exercising your mind could be the answer to your everyday problems.
B Join the fast track to personal safety.
C Go back to the beginning to discover the true meaning.
D This year, exciting fun in the water is available to all.
E If you know the basics, refine your skills and train with the best.
F Spend your days outdoors and learn to move at speed.

Use of English

3 Do the exam task.

USE OF ENGLISH exam task

Read the text. Fill in the gaps with best word from a–j below. There is one item you do not need.

A	complex	F	off-beat
B	hand-to-hand	G	sensitive
C	heart-stopping	H	supervised
D	latter	I	watchful
E	newly-learned	J	weekly

SUMMER ☀ CAMP

If you're looking for a really ¹_____ summer camp, then Pali Adventures in California offers a chance to learn the ²_____ skills of a Hollywood stunt performer in a safe and closely-³_____ environment. You can learn swordplay, ⁴_____ combat, high falls and safe landing techniques, all under the ⁵_____ eye of professional stuntmen.

One-week and two-week courses are available, with the ⁶_____ offering the chance to do a ⁷_____ fall from a ten-metre tower! The camp includes other specialities, including dance, circus skills, watersports and fashion. Each Friday night, the ⁸_____ Pali Showcase gives campers from different specialities the opportunity to demonstrate their ⁹_____ skills to each other.

Speaking

4 Get ready to SPEAK **Which benefits of a summer activity course are most important? Put the ideas below in order from 1 (most important) to 4 (least important).**

  a having the chance to mix and make new friends
  b improving fitness and/or strength
  c learning a new skill or improving an existing one
  d having fun and avoiding boredom

5 Do the exam task.

SPEAKING exam task

Compare and contrast the advertisements for summer camps. Answer the questions.

1 What activities can you do at each camp?
2 Which of the two camps is more appealing. Why?
3 What personal qualities would these camps help to develop? How do the advertisements show this?

Florida Standard

Your Creative Side

THIS UNIT INCLUDES
Vocabulary ▪ value and price ▪ buying and renting ▪ extreme adjectives ▪ comment adverbs
Grammar ▪ *used to* and *would* ▪ past perfect simple and past perfect continuous
Speaking ▪ photo description
Writing ▪ story

Rich and poor 2

2A VOCABULARY AND LISTENING Value and price

I can talk about money and value.

1 SPEAKING Work in pairs. Tell your partner about:

1 something you'd like to buy but can't afford.
2 something you bought but don't need.
3 something you regret buying.
4 something you bought at a bargain price.

2 Complete the money management tips with the words below.

afford   allowance   budget (v)   debt   expenses
financial   income   repay   save   waste (v)

Money Management

Tips for teens

1 Work out your total ¹_____ (i.e. your ²_____ and/or money earned). Take responsibility for your ³_____ decisions.
2 Don't get into ⁴_____ . Try to ⁵_____ up for costly items.
3 Don't borrow money if it might be difficult to ⁶_____ it.

Tips for parents

4 Don't worry if your child ⁷_____ a lot of his/her money. What might seem a poor decision to you can sometimes be a valuable lesson for the child.
5 Involve teenagers in family finances. Discuss big decisions (e.g. Can we ⁸_____ to take a holiday this year?) and weekly or monthly ⁹_____ like food and power bills.
6 Teach teenagers how to ¹⁰_____ wisely but allow them the freedom to make mistakes.

3 Which two tips do you think are most useful? Give reasons.

4 VOCABULARY Complete the chart with the adjectives below.

careless   dear   extortionate   hard up   mean
valuable   well off   worthless

Money		
value		
precious	priceless	worth a fortune
¹_____	²_____	

price and cost		
costly	dirt cheap (*informal*)	pricey (*informal*)
reasonable	a rip-off (*informal*)	³_____	⁴_____

attitudes to money		
careful (with money)	stingy (*informal*)	generous
⁵_____	⁶_____ (with money)	

rich or poor?		
affluent	broke (*informal*)	comfortably off
⁷_____	⁸_____	

5 Complete the sentences with the words in red from the chart. Say if you agree or disagree, and why.

1 You get what you pay for. If something is _____ , it probably isn't worth having.
2 Friendship is _____ .
3 The more _____ you are, the easier your life is.
4 Being _____ will help you to get rich.

6 🎧 1.09 Listen and match each speaker with a statement (A–E). There is one statement you don't need.

This person:

A won't spend money just to have nice things. ☐
B has been raised to be careful with his/her money. ☐
C should probably be more careful with his/her money. ☐
D thinks that having a bank account isn't necessary. ☐
E is good with his/her finances but likes spending, too. ☐

7 SPEAKING Discuss in pairs. Give reasons and examples.

1 Does money burn a hole in your pocket?
2 Do you keep some money back for a rainy day?
3 When you buy something, do you shop around?

⟫⟫⟫ **VOCABULARY BUILDER 2.1: PAGE 135** ⟪⟪⟪

1 Do you know anyone who has won money on the lottery? Do you think buying a lottery ticket is a good idea? Give reasons.

2 Read the text and answer the questions.
   1 Has Molly always been well off?
   2 What was her life like in Bristol?
   3 Why didn't Molly check whether she'd won the lottery?

LUCKY NUMBERS!

Molly Higgins is a very rich woman and the proud owner of a ten-bedroom mansion near London. But she didn't use to be rich. She used to live in a small flat in a run-down area of Bristol and get by on state benefits. Every Thursday evening Molly would buy a *EuroMillions* lottery ticket. She'd always choose the same numbers but she didn't usually look at the winning numbers the following evening. 'I never used to win anything, and I'd sometimes forget to look at the results,' says Molly. But one Friday, when she checked the results she couldn't believe her eyes. She'd won the jackpot – €10 million!

3 Read the *Learn this!* box. Then underline all the examples of *used to* and *would* in the text.

used to and **would**
1 We use **used to** and **would** to talk about habits and situations that are now finished.
   We used to live in London. But now we live in Brighton. When I was at primary school I'd always play football after school.
2 We don't use **would** with state verbs.
   I would have a cat. ✗ I used to have a cat.
3 We don't use **used to** or **would** to say how long a situation or habit continued. We use the past simple.
   She used to work/would work in a bank for six years. ✗ She worked in a bank for six years.
4 **Never used to** and **would never** are common negative forms.
   I never used to save any money.
   He would never admit he was wrong.

4 Some of these sentences are incorrect. Correct them.
   1 Dan use to work in a bank. ✗
      Dan used to work in a bank.
   2 I'm not used to wear glasses, but I do now.
   3 Did you use to have long hair?
   4 My dad would have a beautiful old sports car.
   5 Sally used to be a teacher for ten years.
   6 Joe used to smoke. He'd smoke 30 a day.

5 Complete the sentences with *would*, *used to* or the past simple. Sometimes more than one answer is possible.
   1 My dad _____ (have) a credit card. He _____ (use) it for buying expensive things. But two years ago he _____ (get) rid of it. The credit card company _____ (charge) a very high rate of interest and he _____ (end) up deep in debt.
   2 My grandad _____ (be) a factory worker. He _____ (work) in a car factory for 30 years. He _____ (have to) work long hours and he _____ (not earn) very much money. But he _____ (do) the lottery every week and eventually he _____ (win) enough money to buy a car.

>>> GRAMMAR BUILDER 2.1: PAGE 117 <<<

LOOK OUT!
If we stress *would*, it suggests irritation and criticism. In this case, we don't use the contracted form *'d*.
He would wear those old jeans to school every day.

6 🎧 1.10 PRONUNCIATION Read the *Look out!* box. Then listen, repeat, and say if the speaker is irritated.

7 USE OF ENGLISH Complete the second sentence so that it has the same meaning as the first. Use no more than five words including the word in brackets.
   1 It was typical of Sue to interrupt all the time!
      Sue _____ all the time! (would)
   2 I was in the habit of spending all my pocket money.
      I _____ all my pocket money. (used)
   3 In the '90s my dad always drove to work.
      In the '90s my dad _____ work. (would)
   4 In the past was your hair much longer?
      _____ much longer hair? (use)
   5 There wasn't a bank at the end of the street.
      There _____ a bank at the end of the street. (never)

8 SPEAKING Work in pairs. Think about when you were younger. Using *would* or *used to*, tell your partner about:
   1 something ridiculous you often wore when you were little.
   2 something boring you did at weekends.
   3 something you did that annoyed other people.

Get out of my HOUSE!

In July property developer Jim Lock bought a large, detached, ten-bedroom building in Bath with plans to convert it into three luxury flats. He's planning to sell the flats for £400,000 and expects to ¹___ a profit of about £250,000. However, before building work started, a group of twenty squatters moved into the house and claimed they were 'looking ²___' the empty property. They climbed into the building, which ³___ be a nursing home, through a downstairs window that had been left open. The group, ⁴___ includes three small children, is sleeping on the floor in sleeping bags. There's no heating or furniture. Mr Lock went to the police but they said they could do nothing. Squatting in commercial properties isn't a criminal offence in England ⁵___ squatters don't actually break into an empty property or cause criminal damage. 'I was astonished that the police ⁶___ evict them,' said an exasperated Mr Lock. 'They're just a bunch of lazy hippies. I'll have to go to court to get them evicted. It'll cost me thousands in legal fees.'

1 **SPEAKING** Work in pairs. Describe the photo and answer the questions.

1 Are there a lot of homeless people in your country? What about in your town or city?
2 Why do people become homeless, do you think?
3 Think of five problems homeless people face.

2 🎧 1.11 **USE OF ENGLISH** Choose the correct words (a, b, c or d) to complete the text. Then listen and check.

1	**a** do	**b** take	**c** bring	**d** make
2	**a** for	**b** after	**c** at	**d** into
3	**a** was to	**b** would	**c** used to	**d** had to
4	**a** that	**b** which	**c** it	**d** whose
5	**a** as long as	**b** although	**c** as much as	**d** apart from
6	**a** can't	**b** shouldn't	**c** didn't use to	**d** wouldn't

3 🎧 1.12 Listen to a radio reporter interviewing one of the squatters. Are the sentences true (T) or false (F)?

1 Listeners can hear the interview on the radio as it takes place.
2 The squatters can't afford both rent and living expenses.
3 According to the squatter, there aren't enough properties in the UK to house everybody.
4 The squatters were certain that the house was unoccupied when they first saw it.
5 The squatters have improved the house since moving in.
6 The squatters won't move out under any circumstances.

4 🎧 1.12 Decide which opinion is not expressed by the squatter in the interview. Then listen again and check exactly what she says.

1 Rented accommodation is too expensive.
2 Property developers are wrong to leave houses empty and wait for prices to rise before selling them.
3 Private property is wrong.
4 Everybody has the right to shelter.
5 Squatters are using something that would otherwise go to waste.
6 Squatters contribute to society.

5 **VOCABULARY** Complete these buying and renting collocations with the verbs in the box.

become   do   get   make   make   pay   rent   take

1	_____ a flat	5	_____ possession (of)
2	_____ the rent	6	_____ maintenance
3	_____ a profit	7	_____ improvements
4	_____ homeless	8	_____ evicted

6 **SPEAKING** Discuss this question in pairs: *Who do you feel more sympathy with, Jim Lock or the squatters?* Give reasons. Then take a class vote.

7 **SPEAKING** Work in pairs. Prepare this role-play. Make notes.

Student A: You have been homeless for two years and have recently joined a squat with some friends. Explain to the owner of the property why you should be allowed to stay there.

Student B: You are the property owner. Explain to the squatter why you think he/she should move out immediately.

8 **SPEAKING** Work in pairs. Have a conversation using your notes from exercise 7. Include as many phrases as you can from exercise 5. Student B starts the conversation.

>>> **VOCABULARY BUILDER 2.2: PAGE 135** <<<

1 Look at the text title and the photos only. What is happening in the photos? What do you think the text will be about? Then look quickly through the text to check your ideas.

2 Read the introduction to the text and mark the sentences true (T) or false (F).

1 The people who meet the millionaires know that they are rich straight away.
2 The millionaires have to live differently for a while.
3 The millionaires have to donate lots of money.
4 The socially disadvantaged people benefit more than the rich people in the programme.
5 The millionaires don't stay in touch with the people they meet.

EXAM TIP

For multiple matching tasks, look quickly through the texts to get a general idea of their meaning. Then read the questions that you have to match with them. It may be easier to work through texts A–D in order, matching the questions to them as you go, and underlining the relevant parts of the text, rather than working through the questions in order and searching through all four texts each time.

In the programme, millionaires go undercover to deprived areas of Britain, where they volunteer in the local community. For a fortnight they give up their affluent lifestyle and live with little money in substandard accommodation. Their experiences often prompt them to hand over life-changing sums of money to deserving individuals and institutions. At the end, they reveal who they actually are.

There have been eight series of the programme in the UK so far, with millions of pounds being given away to good causes. While watching the programmes, it's sometimes hard to tell who is benefiting most from the relationship. All of the people involved have talked about how it has changed their lives. But interestingly, it seemed that it was the millionaires who found their experiences the most rewarding. Some discovered that there are more important things in life than making money, and forged lasting relationships with the people they met.

A HILARY DEVEY, who, as a single mother, risked everything to start up a now hugely successful transport company, lives on her own in her enormous mansion. She returned incognito to the place she grew up in, and one of the projects she got involved in was a local community support centre which was in danger of closing.

SECRET MILLIONAIRE

Secret Millionaire **is a reality TV show with a difference. The participants come on the programme to possibly give away thousands of pounds.**

The centre provides marriage counselling, support for single parents and homeless people and so on. She funded the centre and provided more facilities for it. Hilary is still a regular visitor to the centre, and feels she now has friends who value her for the person she is, not her money.

B **NICK LESLAU** is one of Britain's wealthiest property tycoons and lives in luxury with his family in London. He went to Glasgow and worked in a poor area with severely disabled people. He was astonished at how friendly and kind everyone was, even though they didn't know anything about him. Although he has always donated money to various charities, he found it immensely rewarding to get involved directly for once. He said he felt privileged to have met some of society's genuine heroes – people who work tirelessly to help others.

C **KAVITA OBEROI** is a 38-year-old IT millionaire whose sole interest in life, apart from her family, was making money. Her views completely changed when she went to a centre for disadvantaged girls in Manchester. She used to believe that people were poor because they didn't try to improve their lives. When she got involved with the girls' centre, she realised that people often need help and support to do their best. She realised that her own mother had sacrificed a lot so that Kavita could have a good education. Kavita became a director of the group and is helping it to go national to support more young women.

D **JAMES BENAMORE**, a tough financial dealer now worth £77 million, used to have a drug problem himself. He waved goodbye to his wife and children and went to a crime-ridden area of Manchester. He worked in a centre for teenagers who were excluded from mainstream education and found that they had no confidence in themselves, nor any belief that any effort they made would make any difference. James donated money to the centre so that children who worked hard earned rewards in the form of trips and outings. He also offered some teenagers a month's work experience at his company. He was delighted to see how their attitudes changed, and has set up the scheme permanently.

3 🎧 **1.13** Read the Exam tip. Then read questions 1–10 below. Finally, read texts A–D and match them to the questions.

Which millionaire ...
1 met young people who believed they were unable to improve their lives?
2 had changed his/her opinions by the end of the programme?
3 presently lives on his/her own?
4 was really impressed by the charity workers he/she met?
5 found it was better to get involved rather than just donate money?
6 went back to his/her hometown?
7 gave people the chance to work for him/her?
8 had been greatly helped by a member of his/her own family?
9 was surprised that people who didn't know him/her were so nice to him/her?
10 had to overcome addiction problems in his/her youth?

4 **VOCABULARY** Complete the phrases with the prepositions below. They are all in the text.

for   from   in   in   in   of   to   to   with

1 benefit _____   5 value sb/sth _____
2 forge a relationship _____   6 donate money _____
3 get involved _____   7 wave goodbye _____
4 be _____ danger _____   8 have confidence _____

5 **SPEAKING** Work in pairs. Each choose one of the millionaires. Read the relevant text again for one minute, then cover it and tell your partner as much about the millionaire as you can remember.

6 **SPEAKING** What do you think about the programme? Is it a good idea? Are there any bad aspects to it? Decide on at least two positive and two negative things with your partner.

7 Read the *Learn this!* box and complete the rule.

> **LEARN THIS!**
>
> **Second conditional**
> 1 We use the second conditional to talk about unreal situations and events.
> *If I was a secret millionaire, I'd visit a homeless charity.*
> *Perhaps he wouldn't be so stingy if he had more money.*
> 2 We use the _____ in the *if* clause and _____ + the base form of the verb in the main clause.

⟫ GRAMMAR BUILDER 2.2: PAGE 117 ⟪

8 **SPEAKING** Discuss this question in pairs: *If you had €50,000 to give away, who would you give it to, and why?* Use the second conditional. Agree on three good causes and make notes.

9 **SPEAKING** Report your ideas to the class. The class votes on the best ideas.

> We'd give money to ... because ...

2E GRAMMAR Past perfect simple and continuous

I can talk about actions and events and their consequences in the past.

1 Read the text. Underline the examples of the past perfect and past perfect continuous.

RAGS TO RICHES
Back in 1994, J.K. Rowling, creator of the Harry Potter books, was living in Scotland, and feeling a complete failure. She had just returned from Portugal, where she had been living for two years. She had been teaching English in Porto, and had married a Portuguese man there. But the marriage had only lasted for a few years, and she had moved back to Britain with her baby daughter. She hadn't been feeling well for months and was eventually diagnosed with depression. So, there she was: a jobless, penniless, depressed single mother. She decided that the only thing she wanted to do was write a story that had been going around in her head for a long time. And the rest, as they say, is history.

2 Read the *Learn this!* box. Choose the correct alternatives to complete the rules. Then match an example from the text to each rule.

> **LEARN THIS!**
>
> **Past perfect simple and continuous**
> 1 We use the past perfect **simple** / **continuous** for a completed action that happened before a specific time in the past.
> 2 We use the past perfect **simple** / **continuous** for an action in progress before a specific time in the past. This often shows the cause of something in the past.
> 3 With state verbs (*know*, *be*, *like*, etc.), we use the past perfect **simple** / **continuous** with *for* or *since* to say how long an action had been in progress.
> 4 With action verbs, we use the past perfect **simple** / **continuous** with *for* or *since* to say how long an action had been in progress.

>>> GRAMMAR BUILDER 2.3: PAGE 118 <<<

3 Choose the correct tense.
1 How long had you **had** / **been having** a credit card when you got rid of it?
2 The road was flooded because it had **rained** / **been raining** for hours and showed no sign of stopping.
3 She had **learnt** / **been learning** English for three years before she visited Britain.
4 Had you ever **eaten** / **been eating** Japanese food before you visited Japan?
5 I was thirsty because I'd **run** / **been running** all morning.
6 Martin told me that he hadn't **seen** / **been seeing** the Champions League final on TV.

4 Complete the sentences with the verbs below. Use the past perfect simple or past perfect continuous. Say which use of the tenses in the *Learn this!* box each sentence follows.

go out know learn not have ~~snow~~ wait work

1 The grass was slippery because it <u>had been snowing. Use 2</u>
2 Ed _____ to drive for two years when he took his test.
3 When Jo finally arrived, we _____ for over an hour.
4 They _____ each other for many years when they got engaged, but they _____ only _____ for a year.
5 I was thirsty because I _____ a drink for hours.
6 Sue's hands were muddy. She _____ in the garden.

5 Complete the text with the verbs in brackets. Use the past perfect simple or past perfect continuous.

Now in his 70s, American designer Ralph Lauren is a multi-millionaire, but he wasn't born into fame and fortune. In 1967 Lauren was looking for a job in fashion, but he didn't have any qualifications at all. Earlier that year, he ¹_____ (drop out) of night school. He ²_____ (study) for a business degree in the evenings, but he ³_____ (not finish) it. By day he ⁴_____ (sell) gloves, but he knew he had to make a change. As a child growing up in New York, fashion-conscious Ralph ⁵_____ (not have) much money for nice clothes, so he ⁶_____ always _____ (work) after school in department stores. It was this experience that eventually led to his own huge clothing empire. In 1967 he started working for a tie maker, and by the end of 1968 he ⁷_____ (start) his own tie design company. By the 1970s Lauren ⁸_____ (design) his own ties for several years, and they were very popular. So he started designing suits to match.

6 **SPEAKING** Work in pairs. Think about the last time you were:

delighted embarrassed exhausted irritated relieved
soaking wet starving

Find out why your partner felt that way. Use appropriate past tenses.

> Why were you delighted?

> Because I'd just got my exam results.

> Because I'd been listening to some fantastic music.

1 Work in pairs. Describe the photo. Use the words below to help you.

decoration   dressing gown   lid   surprise

2 Work in pairs. What is the boy thinking and feeling, and why? Make notes about your ideas.

3 🎧 1.14 Now listen to a candidate answering the question in exercise 2. Compare your ideas from exercise 2 with the candidate's ideas. How are they similar and different?

4 Which two extreme adjectives meaning *surprised* and *happy* did the student use?

▷▷▷ VOCABULARY BUILDER 2.3: PAGE 135 ◁◁◁

EXAM TIP

In the picture description task, the examiner can ask you to talk about a personal experience. You will need to use narrative tenses, e.g. past simple, past continuous, past perfect and past perfect continuous, *used to* and *would*.

5 🎧 1.16 Read the Exam tip. Then listen to the candidate answering the examiner's question. Which of the tenses mentioned in the tip does the candidate use?

6 Answer the questions.

1 Why did the girl choose to buy her sister a hoodie?
2 How does she think she came to select the wrong size?
3 Why didn't she see the hoodie herself before giving it to her sister?
4 How did her sister react when she saw the hoodie?
5 How did the girl feel then? Have her feelings changed?

LEARN THIS!

Comment adverbs and adverbial phrases

1 Comment adverbs give the speaker's opinion.
Unfortunately, we can't afford a holiday this year.
To my surprise, he sold his motorbike.

2 Some adverbs can be used as both comment adverbs and as adverbs of manner.
Frankly, I don't believe you.
He spoke frankly about his financial problems.

3 We usually put comment adverbs at the start of the sentence, although they can go with the verb.
Foolishly, I left my wallet at home.
I foolishly left my wallet at home.

7 🎧 1.16 Read the *Learn this!* box. Then complete the sentences with five of the comment adverbs below. Listen again and check.

fortunately   hopefully   ideally   luckily   obviously
stupidly   to be honest

1 I found a great one on a website, but _____ I ordered the wrong size.
2 I _____ didn't realise my mistake until she opened the present on her birthday.
3 _____ , she saw the funny side.
4 _____ , I didn't think it was very funny at the time.
5 _____ , I was able to return it.

▷▷▷ VOCABULARY BUILDER 2.4: PAGE 135 ◁◁◁

8 SPEAKING Describe the photo.

9 SPEAKING Work in pairs. Take turns to ask and answer the examiner's questions. Try to use some comment adverbs.

1 What is the girl thinking and feeling, and why?
2 Do you like spending money on other people? Why?/Why not?
3 Tell me about a really good present that you once received.

1 SPEAKING Work in pairs. Ask and answer. Have you ever lost or found any money? When? Where? What happened?

2 Read the story. Where do you think the money came from?

THE ULTIMATE JIGSAW PUZZLE

It was a day like any other and Graham Hill was doing his normal round as a waste collector. He was putting bags of rubbish onto his handcart, when he noticed something unusual in one of the dustbins. Leaning over the bin, he took a closer look and saw a filthy plastic bag with what looked like money inside. As he pulled it out, he gasped. It was money. Inside the carrier bag were lots of banknotes! But they were all cut into pieces!

As soon as he realised what he'd found, Hill called the police, who quickly arrived on the scene. Having looked in the bag, they calculated that there must be about £10,000 in torn notes. The police thanked Hill and said that the money must have come from a robbery that had gone wrong. As they were leaving, the police told him they would find out what had happened.

Six months later, Hill had forgotten all about the incident. Out of the blue the police phoned with some unexpected and wonderful news. Surprisingly, after investigating for a long time, they had been unable to discover anything about the bag of notes. There was no crime or robbery that they could link the money to. Apparently, under British law, the bag of money now belonged to Hill. What's more, the Bank of England said that for every note that he could put back together, Hill would receive a new one. He had been given the ultimate jigsaw puzzle!

3 Identify the following stages in the story in exercise 2.
- background information that sets the scene
- a first event, often a problem, that triggers the action
- later events that follow from the first event
- the final resolution or outcome

4 Complete the examples in the *Look out!* box. Use the correct tenses. Then find examples of each use in the story in exercise 2.

LOOK OUT! Past simple and past continuous
1 We can use the past continuous to set the scene.
   It _____ (rain) and the wind _____ (blow).
2 We use the past simple for actions that happened one after another.
   She _____ (stand up), _____ (open) the door and _____ (leave).
3 We use the past simple for an action or event that interrupted a background event; we use the past continuous for the background event.
   While I _____ (read) my book, my phone _____ (ring).

>>> GRAMMAR BUILDER 2.4: PAGE 118 <<<

5 Read the *Learn this!* box. Find an example of each type of sequencing clause in the story.

LEARN THIS!

Sequencing clauses
For an action which happens before another action, we can use:
1 *after + -ing*
   After losing his wallet, he called the police.
2 *having + past participle*
   Having found the money, he took it to the police station.
For an action which happens at the same time as another action, we can use:
3 *as + past simple*
   As he put his hand in his pocket he realised his wallet was missing.
4 *the moment/as soon as + past simple*
   The moment I saw his face, I knew he'd been crying.
5 *a present participle*
   Looking up, she saw a police officer approaching.
   The subject of the participle clause and the main clause **must** be the same.
   Crossing the road, she was hit by a car. ✓
   Crossing the road, a car hit her. ✗

6 Combine the pairs of sentences into single sentences. Use the sequencing clauses in the *Learn this!* box. More than one answer is possible.
1 'I've lost my wallet,' said Mary. At the same time, she closed her handbag.
2 I stepped outside. At the same time, it started to snow.
3 He sat down. Then he opened the newspaper.
4 I walked to the shops. At the same time, I thought about what my mum had just said.
5 She had lunch. Then she went out.

1 You are going to do the following exam writing task. First think of some ideas for your story. Use the questions below to help you.

Write a story with a happy ending about a character who loses or finds something valuable. Write 200–250 words.

1 Does the character lose or find something?
2 Where does he/she lose or find it?
3 If the character loses something, does he/she find it again? If the character finds something, does he/she get to keep it?
4 How does the story end?

2 Look again at the stages of a story in exercise 3 on page 22. Think how your ideas will fit into paragraphs. Use your ideas from exercise 1 to make notes under paragraph headings. (You may need more or fewer than four paragraphs.)

Paragraph 1
Paragraph 2
Paragraph 3
Paragraph 4

3 Write the first paragraph of the story. Set the scene briefly with background information, then tell the first event of the story. Remember to use appropriate narrative tenses.

4 Complete the time expressions with the words below. Check the meaning of all the expressions.

after   blue   end   later   same   shortly   time

Time expressions	
eventually	at the ¹_____ time
in the ²_____	³_____ afterwards
⁴_____ a while	meanwhile
two weeks ⁵_____	some ⁶_____ earlier
out of the ⁷_____	

5 Read the Exam tip. Find a sequence of short sentences at a dramatic point in the story in exercise 2 on page 22.

> **EXAM TIP**
>
> In a story, use a mix of long and short sentences. The short ones can make events more dramatic.
> *The moment he arrived home, he made a cup of tea and, sitting down on the sofa, turned on the television to watch the news. Suddenly, he jumped up. Somebody was in the room.*

6 Find the following features which make the writing style interesting in the story on page 22.

1 two extreme adjectives
2 two examples of comment adverbs
3 two examples of reported speech

7 Write the middle paragraphs of the story. Tell the later events in a logical order. Remember to make the language dramatic and varied. Link events together to show time and sequence.

8 Look at the title and the last sentence of the story on page 22. Think of a good sentence to finish your story. Then write a title for your story which links everything together.

9 Write the final paragraph of the story. Give the resolution or final outcome of the story. End with a good sentence.

> **CHECK YOUR WORK**
>
> **Have you:**
> ☐ written 200–250 words?
> ☐ used a variety of narrative tenses?
> ☐ used sequencing clauses and other time expressions?
> ☐ used a mix of short dramatic sentences and longer ones?
> ☐ included some extreme adjectives, comment adverbs, and/or reported speech?
> ☐ included a last sentence that links to the title?

Unit 1

1 Complete the sentences with a suitable adjective. (More than one answer may be possible.)

1 Lucy is very _____ : she only thinks about herself.
2 My dad is so _____ : nothing gets him angry or excited.
3 I'm very _____ : I want to be CEO of a big company.
4 My dad is 42 but acts like he's 12: he's so _____ .
5 Ian is very _____ : he writes songs and paints too.

Mark: _____ /5

2 Complete the sentences with the present perfect simple or continuous of five of the verbs below.

belong do go read remember stay want

1 _____ you _____ where you put the tickets?
2 I _____ *The Hobbit*; I'm about half way through it.
3 My English teacher _____ to England three times.
4 My parents _____ at that hotel every year since it opened.
5 Karen _____ a horse since she was a little girl.

Mark: _____ /5

3 Complete the email. Use the infinitive, the infinitive without *to*, the *-ing* form or the past participle of the verbs given.

✉ **Inbox**

I went into town this afternoon because I needed to get my phone [1]_____ (repair). The man at the shop said it would take an hour. I didn't feel like [2]_____ (stand) around, so I decided [3]_____ (go) to a coffee shop instead. I saw some friends of mine [4]_____ (play) cards, so I sat down with them. They let me [5]_____ (join) in the game and we played for ages. When I got back to the phone shop, it was closed!

Mark: _____ /5

4 Complete the dialogue with the words below.

could like say should though

Boy Have you seen this photo of dad when he was young?
Girl No, I haven't. Let me see! He looks [1]_____ he's feeling sick!
Boy No, he doesn't. I'd [2]_____ he's just trying to look cool.
Girl He looks as [3]_____ he's getting ready to go out.
Boy How old do you think he is?
Girl I [4]_____ think he's about fifteen.
Boy Yes, I agree. He [5]_____ be getting ready to go on a date with Mum!

Mark: _____ /5

Total: _____ /20

Unit 2

5 Choose the best word (a, b or c) to complete each sentence.

1 A broken mirror is _____ .
  a priceless b worthless c mean
2 My grandfather owns three shops, and the rent from those gives him a good _____ .
  a income b budget c allowance
3 The hotel isn't expensive; in fact, it's very _____ .
  a extortionate b pricey c reasonable
4 I wouldn't say I'm rich, but I'm certainly not _____ .
  a comfortably off b affluent c hard up
5 I love that jacket, but I can't buy it – it's too _____ .
  a dear b valuable c precious

Mark: _____ /5

6 Complete the sentences with the verbs below.

'd didn't use to used to would wouldn't

1 My grandmother _____ work, but now she's got a job in a bookshop.
2 I _____ be a football fan, but I prefer basketball now.
3 We had some great parties in those days, but the neighbours _____ always complain about the noise!
4 Every time my uncle went abroad, he _____ buy a painting.
5 She bought a chocolate bar every day after school, but she _____ eat it until she got home.

Mark: _____ /5

7 Choose the best verb forms.

Elena [1]**had looked / had been looking** forward to the day of the garden party for weeks. Now, finally, it [2]**had arrived / had been arriving**. She [3]**had got up / had been getting up** early to give her more time for the preparations. Anxiously, she looked out of the window to check the weather, which [4]**had got / had been getting** worse and worse each day, even though it was June. To her dismay, she saw that the apple tree by the back wall [5]**had fallen / had been falling** down during the night.

Mark: _____ /5

8 Write an extreme adjective which means:

1 very angry: _____
2 very dirty: _____
3 very clean: _____
4 very ugly: _____
5 very funny: _____

Mark: _____ /5

Total: _____ /20

Lead-in

1 Which of these personality traits is the most useful if you're moving abroad to live and work? Give reasons.

adventurous ambitious considerate eccentric energetic friendly loyal outgoing single-minded

Reading

2 Read the email. In which paragraph 1–4 does Libby refer to Anna's (a) brother, (b) new home, (c) ex-boyfriend, (d) new job?

✉ Inbox

Hi Anna,

How are you? I hope you're enjoying your job in Warsaw. How long have you been doing it now? It must be six months or so, I reckon, because you'd been working there for a few days when I got back from my backpacking holiday in Australia. Let me know how it's going and what the people there are like.

Do you ever hear from Mike these days? Maybe you just want to forget about him and your time in Liverpool. He really wasn't right for you. I mean, it's OK to be ambitious, but he was just selfish. And there was something strange about him too. For example, why did he decide to change his name from Jack to Mike? I know we British people are supposed to be eccentric, but that's just ridiculous!

Stefan has been looking for a place to live, and I think he's found one or two possibilities. We've loved having him here, and he's welcome to stay as long as he wants, but he's determined to find his own place. He's very single-minded, your brother, isn't he? I suppose you are too, now I think about it, so maybe it runs in the family! Anyway, I guess he can afford to rent somewhere nice, working in the financial sector – he must be on a good salary. (I've asked him what he earns, but he won't tell me!) I hope he won't get lonely, living on his own. He isn't as outgoing as you are, so I don't think he'll meet people as easily. But still, everybody needs company. He doesn't talk about people from work much, so I guess he hasn't made many friends. I've tried to persuade him to play basketball a few times, but he's refused. He says he's rubbish at ball games, but he might start going swimming when he's got more free time. That's better than nothing, I suppose – OK for keeping fit, but not a great way to meet people!

Anyway, I shouldn't worry about him. I'm sure he can look after himself. Please send me an email with your news – and some pictures of your new flat. You haven't been in touch for ages!
Love,
Libby

3 Choose the correct answers to questions 1–4 below.

1 About six months ago, Libby
   a started a new job in Australia.
   b left her job to visit Australia.
   c went backpacking.
   d arrived home.
2 What is Libby's opinion of Mike's character?
   a Eccentric and selfish.
   b Selfish and strange.
   c Ambitious and eccentric.
   d Ambitious but not selfish.
3 In terms of his personality, Libby thinks that Stefan
   a is very similar to Anna.
   b needs to be more outgoing.
   c is too single-minded.
   d is similar to Anna in some ways but different in others.
4 In Libby's opinion, swimming isn't the ideal hobby for Stefan because
   a it's something he'll do on his own.
   b it requires too much free time.
   c it won't make him as fit as basketball.
   d he'll probably give up soon.

Listening

4 🎧 1.17 Listen. Does Spikey sound more friendly or less friendly towards Stefan by the end of their conversation? What is the reason for this, in your opinion?

5 🎧 1.17 Listen again. Are these sentences true (T) or false (F)?

1 Stefan is planning to buy or rent a flat.
2 The events take place on a Thursday.
3 Stefan started learning English ten years ago.
4 Spikey tells Stefan that he's sharing with seven or eight friends.
5 Spikey describes squatting as a criminal activity.
6 Spikey is not his real name.

Speaking

6 Tell your partner about an occasion when you met somebody for the first time.

Writing

7 Imagine you are Stefan. Write an announcement to be put in a newsagent's window to help you find a flat to rent. Include this information:

- what you are looking for and when you want to move in.
- some personal details about you: job, nationality, etc.
- why you would be a good tenant.
- the best way to contact you.

Reading

1 **Get ready to READ** Talk in pairs about the following questions. Then report your ideas to the class.

1 Do you think you are influenced by advertising? Give reasons for your answer.
2 What different marketing techniques do companies use to make us buy their products?
3 What do you think the term 'neuromarketing' might mean?

2 Do the exam task.

READING exam task

Complete the text with the missing sentences (A–E). There is one extra sentence that is not needed.

Big business has always wanted to see inside our heads. The marketing and advertising departments of the major corporations spend millions every year trying to work out what we want and then find ways to try and sell it to us. The more accurately businesses can predict what we, the consumers, are likely to buy and when and how much for, the more money they can get us to spend.

Understanding consumers has not been particularly easy. Marketing teams have watched what we buy in supermarkets, they have measured how we have responded to their various promotional campaigns, and they have carried out endless surveys asking us why we buy what we do. However, it is not by any means an exact science. [1]_____ And even if they do, they do not always tell the truth.

This is where 'neuro' or brain science steps in. For the first time researchers have begun to wire consumers up to MRI (magnetic resonance imaging) machines to watch what actually happens inside people's brains when they are faced with consumer choices. The researchers followed the areas of activity lighting up inside the shoppers' brains. [2]_____ Something which is definitely of interest to the marketing specialists.

This new area of science is called 'neuromarketing'. Marketing departments of companies say they won't need to watch us shopping or ask us what we'd buy, they'll just 'read our minds'. [3]_____ This is good news for companies, as their massive marketing budgets can be used more effectively, but where's the benefit for us?

If businesses can know more about how we think than we do ourselves, they'll have the power not just to influence us, but also to manipulate us. [4]_____ So far, advertising regulations have merely restricted companies from making unsupported claims for their products. In future, they may have to go one step further and assess whether the marketers are having our behaviour as consumers altered in ways we cannot ourselves detect.

A	Advertising will be cleverly deployed to persuade us more accurately to buy the products on show.
B	They also need to keep in mind that increased activity in the brain doesn't necessarily mean increased preference for a product.
C	This cannot be a good thing for the general public and something will have to be done about it.
D	It seems that people do not always know what they are thinking.
E	Eventually they found that they could predict when a person would make a purchase.

Speaking

3 **Get ready to SPEAK** Work in pairs. Make a list of things you could buy in a jewellery shop. Which pair can write the most in two minutes?

4 Do the exam task.

SPEAKING exam task

Describe the picture. Then answer the questions.

1 Why do you think this couple is buying something in this shop?
2 What are the advantages and disadvantages of having expensive possessions?
3 Tell me about the most expensive thing you have ever bought.

Vocabulary ■ relating to people ■ verbal interaction ■ phrasal verbs
Grammar ■ question forms ■ comparison ■ question tags ■ concession
Speaking ■ role-play
Writing ■ essay: pros and cons

Generations 3

3A VOCABULARY AND LISTENING Relating to people

I can discuss relationships and behaviour.

1 **SPEAKING** Work in pairs. Find out as much information about each other's families as you can in three minutes. Use the ideas below and add your own.

how many in immediate family? extended family?
brothers / sisters / twins? (how many? ages? names?)
oldest / youngest family members?
cousins / aunts / uncles / in-laws, etc.?
relatives living in your home / nearby / far away / abroad?

2 In pairs, put the expressions below into two groups: negative and positive. (In some cases, it is a matter of opinion.)

Relating to people admire adore
be on the same wavelength (as) be (very) close (to)
be wary of despise envy feel sorry for
have a lot in common (with)
have nothing in common (with) look down on
look up to not see eye to eye (with) respect trust

3 🎧 1.18 Listen to six people discussing members of their family. Complete each summary with an expression from exercise 2 and a reason.

1 Brianna **admires / trusts** her mother, because …
2 Ryan **despises / doesn't see eye to eye with** his father, because …
3 Sophia is **very close to / has a lot in common with** her grandfather, because …
4 Isaac **envies / respects** his cousin, because …
5 Ella **looks down on / has nothing in common with** her twin brother, because …
6 David **feels sorry for / is wary of** his uncle, because …

4 **SPEAKING** Find out more about your partner's relationships with family and friends. Ask three questions using expressions from exercise 2. Ask for reasons.

Who do you admire and why?

5 **VOCABULARY** In pairs, check the meaning of the verbs below using a dictionary. Then test each other. Can you remember the translations?

Verbal interaction bicker (with sb) boast (to sb about sth)
confide (in sb about sth) flatter (sb) flirt (with sb)
insult (sb) lecture (sb about sth) nag (sb about sth)
praise (sb for sth) tease (sb about sth)
tell (sb) off (for sth) warn (sb about sth)

What does 'bicker' mean?   It means …

6 Complete the questions with the correct prepositions.

1 Who does Brianna bicker _____ ?
2 Who can Ryan always confide _____ ?
3 What does Sophia's mum nag her _____ ?
4 What does Isaac's cousin boast _____ ?
5 What does Ella's dad tease her _____ ?
6 What does David's aunt praise him _____ ?

7 🎧 1.18 Listen to the extracts again. Answer the questions in exercise 6.

8 🎧 1.19 Listen to six monologues. What is each speaker doing? Choose the best verb from exercise 5.

Speaker 1: praising; Speaker 2: …

9 🎧 1.19 Listen again. Write a one-sentence summary to describe what each speaker is doing.

Speaker 1 is praising somebody for winning a tennis match.

10 Prepare a monologue like the ones in exercise 8. Choose a verb from exercise 5 and invent your own situation.

11 **SPEAKING** Perform your monologue to the class. Can they describe what you are doing?

You're boasting to somebody about your exam results.
Yes, that's right.
No, try again.

▶▶▶ VOCABULARY BUILDER 3.1: PAGE 136 ◀◀◀

Ava Excuse me. I'm doing a survey about families.
¹_____ you could spare a moment?

Tom OK, fine.

Ava Thank you. First, I need a few details about you.
²_____ old you are?

Tom I'm twenty.

Ava ³_____ you do?

Tom I'm a web designer.

Ava ⁴_____ you work for?

Tom I'm self-employed. I work at home.

Ava Great. So, question one. <u>What do you argue about most in your family?</u>

Tom Er … whose turn it is to use the car.

Ava OK. Question two. <u>Who cooks most of the meals in your home?</u>

Tom We don't have family meals. We help ourselves.

Ava And finally, question three. <u>Who do you get on with best in your family?</u>

Tom My sister, definitely. We've got a lot in common.

Ava That's all. Thanks very much for your help.

Tom No problem. ⁵_____ I can ask *you* a question.

Ava Sure. Go ahead.

Tom ⁶_____ you're free this evening.

1 🎧 1.20 Read, listen and complete the dialogue. Does Tom like Ava? How do you know?

2 Read the *Learn this!* box. Then look again at answers 1–6 in exercise 1. Which of these indirect questions include a question word and which include *if* or *whether*?

> **LEARN THIS!**
>
> **Indirect questions**
> Indirect questions are more polite and more formal than direct questions. They use the same word order and verb form as a statement. They begin with a phrase like:
> *Can I ask (you) …?   Can/Could you tell me …*
> *I'd like to know …   I wonder …*
> *Would you mind telling me …?*
> These phrases are followed by a question word (*what, how,* etc.) or, in yes/no questions, by *if* or *whether.*
> *Can I ask where Emma lives? Do you know if she's in?*

3 Rewrite the six indirect questions from the dialogue in exercise 1 as direct questions.

1 *Could you spare a moment?*

>>> GRAMMAR BUILDER 3.1: PAGE 119 <<<

4 Rewrite the questions below as indirect questions. Use a different phrase from the *Learn this!* box for each one.

1 Do you share a bedroom?
2 Who do you bicker with most at home?
3 Are you the only teenager in your home?
4 How often do you all have a meal together at home?
5 Who goes to bed first in your family?
6 Are you often alone in your home?
7 Do you help with the housework?

5 SPEAKING In pairs, ask and answer the indirect questions in exercise 4. Add three indirect questions of your own.

> Can you tell me whether you share a bedroom?

6 Read the *Learn this!* box. Are the underlined questions in the dialogue in exercise 1 subject or object questions?

> **LEARN THIS!**
>
> **Subject and object questions**
> Questions with *Who, What* or *Which* can be **subject** or **object** questions.
> **Object questions** include the normal interrogative form of the verb. The answers are the object of the verb.
> *What did you buy? (I bought a scarf.)*
> *Who did you sit with? (I sat with Jack.)*
> **Subject questions** include the normal affirmative form of the verb. The answers are the subject of the verb.
> *Who bought this DVD? (Darren bought it.)*

>>> GRAMMAR BUILDER 3.2: PAGE 119 <<<

7 Write questions in the present simple using the prompts below. Is each question a subject or object question?

1 Who / live / next door to you?
Who lives next door to you?
2 What / you / have / for breakfast?
3 Which letter / your surname / start with?
4 Which month / have / the fewest days?
5 Which subject / you / have / first on Mondays?
6 Who / buy / your clothes?
7 What / make / you laugh?
8 Who / you / admire most / in the world?
9 Who / have / the most in common with you?

8 SPEAKING In pairs, ask and answer the questions in exercise 7.

1 SPEAKING Work in pairs. Describe the photo opposite. Then agree on a definition of *elderly*. Compare with the class.

2 In pairs, read the facts box and guess the missing numbers.

● **AGEING POPULATION: THE FACTS**

▶ For the first time in history, there are more people in the UK aged over 65 than under [1]_____ .

▶ Average life expectancy for people born today in the UK is about 78 for men and [2]_____ for women.

▶ Forty years ago, life expectancy was [3]_____ for men and 75 for women.

▶ The retirement age for all UK workers will rise to [4]_____ , probably by 2027.

3 🎧 1.21 Listen to the first part of a radio interview and check your answers to exercise 2. What is the most interesting piece of information, in your opinion?

4 🎧 1.22 Listen to the whole interview. Choose the correct answer: a, b, c or d.

1 Professor Clark believes people
  a don't like thinking about getting old.
  b don't mind the idea of getting old.
  c are frightened of the elderly.
  d cannot explain their own view of old age.
2 In Classical times, most people
  a died during infancy or childhood.
  b died around the age of 28.
  c died between 60 and 70.
  d were ill for more than half their life.
3 Life expectancy has increased mainly because people
  a still go jogging when they're in their eighties.
  b spend their state pension on food and exercise.
  c worry less about having poor health.
  d have better healthcare and a healthier lifestyle.
4 Professor Clark's personal opinion is that
  a soon, most people will reach the age of 100.
  b the human lifespan has a natural limit.
  c in the future 100-year-olds will be fitter than 80-year-olds today.
  d people will have to take up keep-fit in their fifties.
5 In Britain and North America, elderly people
  a have to work after the retirement age.
  b are not treated as well as in most other places.
  c are often abandoned by their families.
  d prefer to live in nursing homes.
6 In modern cities in China and India, families are
  a taking better care of the elderly than they used to.
  b allowing elderly people to lead independent lives.
  c asking grandparents to look after children.
  d taking worse care of the elderly than they used to.

5 VOCABULARY Match the two halves of the compound nouns and write them correctly as one word or two. (All the nouns are in exercise 4.)

1 life   a care
2 health   b homes
3 old   c expectancy
4 elderly   d span
5 nursing   e age
6 retirement   f pension
7 state   g age
8 life   h relatives

6 Complete the sentences using the compound nouns from exercise 5.

1 If life expectancy continues to rise, we won't be able to feed everyone.
2 Elderly people should only live in _____ if they have no families to look after them.
3 The average human _____ could be 200 years if scientists continue to make advances in _____ .
4 We won't have enough money to pay retired people the _____ if the number of elderly people increases.
5 You can learn a lot by spending more time with your _____ .
6 Because more people are healthy throughout their _____ , the _____ should be 75 or older.

7 SPEAKING In pairs, ask and answer about the opinions in exercise 6. Do you agree or disagree? Give reasons.

> Do you agree that if life expectancy continues to rise, we won't be able to feed everyone?

> Yes, I do. The world's population is already increasing too fast.

> No, I don't. Scientific advances will mean we can grow enough food for everyone.

8 SPEAKING In pairs, think of three ways to improve the lives of elderly people. Then share your ideas with the class. Try to include nouns from exercise 5.

1 **SPEAKING** Read the quotation below and say if you agree or disagree. At what age do people become adults, in your opinion? Give reasons.

A boy becomes an adult three years before his parents think he does, and about two years after he thinks he does.

2 Read the title and the last sentence of the text opposite. Predict which sentence (a–d) best summarises the opinions of the text's writer.

   a Parents should let their teenage children spend more time alone.
   b Parents should treat their teenage children more like adults.
   c Teenagers should remember that their parents are trying their best.
   d If teenagers want to be treated like adults, they should behave like adults.

3 Read the text, ignoring the gaps, and check your answer to exercise 2. Do you agree with Ellie's view? Why?/Why not?

4 Does the text contain mainly facts or mainly opinions? Find evidence in the text to support your answer.

> **EXAM TIP**
>
> When you do a gapped sentences task, look for connections between the missing sentence and the sentences around the gap. Focus on words that often refer logically to ideas in other sentences:
> - pronouns (*we*, *it*, *this*, etc.) – what do they refer back to?
> - for example – does it exemplify what comes before?
> - comparatives – what is being compared?
> - *more / the same* – what idea is being repeated?
> - *but / however* – what ideas are being contrasted?

5 Read the Exam tip. Match the gaps (1–6) in the text with the sentences below (A–H). There are two extra sentences.

   A Why was it such a big deal?
   B Even more worrying was the fact that my parents weren't talking to each other.
   C A few more rows later and I'd written more than 10,000 words of advice for parents.
   D But part of being a teenager is feeling free to take steps down new paths and learning from our own mistakes.
   E After that, the arguments with my dad just got worse.
   F Just last week, for example, I persuaded Mum to buy me a pair of shoes that she had said I couldn't have.
   G It makes me not want to confide in you.
   H Surprisingly, we all share similar views on what our parents are doing wrong.

HOW TO BE A GOOD PARENT:
a teenager's guide

Sixteen year old Ellie, who lives with her parents, Louise, 38, and Peter, 43, has written a book to tell us what parents of teenagers are doing wrong …

All adults think teenagers are a nightmare. According to them, we're moody, argumentative, rude and disruptive. But have any adults ever stopped to think that perhaps they are responsible for the unpredictable and confusing way we behave?

Take me, for instance. I may be a teenage nightmare, but this is all to do with my parents, not me. With my mother, I stamp my feet, storm out of shops in the middle of arguments and moan until I get my own way. ¹ ☐ But my father, on the other hand, turns me into a shining example of teenage perfection. I do as he asks, I don't answer back and I happily accept that no means no.

My parents have very different parenting styles. While my dad brings out the best in me, by being calm and reasonable and treating me like an adult, my mum, like so many other parents of teenagers, inadvertently makes me want to rebel by being combative and speaking to me as though I'm still a child. Last summer, after yet another row in a shop with my mother, I decided to start writing down the way I felt about things. ² ☐

In December, having contacted various publishers, I signed a book deal. My parenting book, How Teenagers Think, is going to be published next year, the first of its type actually written by a teenager. Much of my book is based on my own experiences, but I've also interviewed my friends about their parents. ³ ☐ And it usually comes down to the fact that our parents care too much about us and don't want to let us grow up. For example, mum drove me crazy a few weeks ago when she kept worrying I'd broken my neck after I fell off my bike. Yes, my neck hurt, but I'd been to the doctor and he'd told me I was fine, so why did she want to take me to hospital?

6 🎧 1.23 Work in pairs. Listen and check your answers to exercise 5 and say which words helped you to work out the answers.

7 **VOCABULARY** Match the phrasal verbs highlighted in the text with the definitions below.

1 change; transform
2 gradually become an adult
3 do something without interruption
4 can be explained by
5 arrive at a situation (often unintentionally)
6 cause a certain type of behaviour in somebody
7 leave quickly and angrily
8 reply impolitely to somebody in authority

8 Explain the meaning of the underlined phrases in these sentences from the text. Rewrite the sentences using different words.

1 All adults think teenagers <u>are a nightmare</u>.
2 I moan until I <u>get my own way</u>.
3 Mum <u>drove me crazy</u> a few weeks ago.
4 Why was it <u>such a big deal</u>?
5 Part of being a teenager is <u>feeling free to take steps down new paths</u>.

9 Match the two parts of the words to make adjectives from the text. Which adjective best describes (a) most teenagers? (b) most adults? (c) you? Compare your ideas in pairs.

1 mood   able
2 argument   able
3 respons   ative
4 unpredict   ible
5 confus   y
6 reason   ive
7 combat   ing

10 **SPEAKING** Work in pairs. How could relationships between teenagers and their parents be improved? Think of three things that (a) parents and (b) teenagers should do. Use the ideas below to help you.

communication   courtesy   friends   holidays
housework   independence   money   privacy
respect   schoolwork   stress   trust   understanding

11 **SPEAKING** Present your ideas to the class. Include as many words and phrases from exercises 7–10 as possible. Use the phrases below to structure your presentation.

> The first thing I think parents/ teenagers should do is …

> Secondly, in my opinion parents/ teenagers should …

> Finally, it would help if parents/ teenagers (+ past tense)

Instead of fussing around their teenagers like we're small children, parents could be using our desire to feel grown-up to their advantage. If we're behaving badly, why not tell us straight out that we don't deserve to be treated like an adult? Then we'll try to earn your respect. And why not reward us when we do behave maturely? Recently, I wanted to take a train to Portsmouth to see a friend – a journey I'd done with Mum before. Dad was fine with the idea of me going alone, but it took weeks of arguments before Mum agreed. ⁴☐

Parents need to learn to trust teenagers. And when parents are worried about us, there is no point becoming angry – that just makes things worse. A few months ago, Mum lost her temper when I told my parents I'd been receiving emails from a stranger I'd met in a chatroom. She instantly banned me from using the Internet and we ended up having a huge row. But I'm not stupid. Most teenagers know talking to strangers online is not a good idea, so I'd told them what was happening – I don't want to get abducted, just as much as they don't want me to. So why be angry with me, Mum? ⁵☐ Surely it's better for me to feel you won't be angry, so I can talk to you?

Many of my friends feel the same way. They end up not telling their parents what they're up to because they'll be cross. Everyone I interviewed for my book loved the idea of being really close to their parents. Despite the way we behave, we all want close relationships with our parents. We also all know deep down that our parents usually do know best. ⁶☐ Our parents have to unwrap the cotton wool they place around us and let us get on with what is just a natural phase of life.

▷▷▷ VOCABULARY BUILDER 3.2: PAGE 136 ◁◁◁

1 SPEAKING How do you and your friends speak compared with people of your parents' generation? Discuss the ideas below in pairs and decide on the biggest difference.

grammar   pronunciation   slang   speed   vocabulary

2 🎧 1.25 Read the text. How many comparative and superlative forms can you find? Are they adjectives or adverbs, regular or irregular?

Although teenagers in the UK generally understand about 40,000 different words, the number of words they actually use is far smaller than you might think – sometimes only 800 words. An inability to distinguish between formal and informal language is almost as worrying. Ever since the 1950s, speaking correct English has been nowhere near as important for teenagers as sounding cool. But experts are worried that today's teenagers are even worse at talking in formal situations than previous generations were.

The language that teenagers use is nothing like as varied as you would imagine, with the twenty commonest words representing about a third of all words spoken. And if you look at younger age groups, the situation is just as worrying: children are developing speech problems more and more frequently. Children watch a lot of TV, as do adults. This creates background noise; and the noisier their surroundings, the harder it is for babies to hear conversations around them.

3 Read the *Learn this!* box. Find at least one example in the text in exercise 2 for each point (1–5) in the box.

> **LEARN THIS!**
>
> **Comparative structures**
> 1 We can qualify comparatives using *far*, *much*, *even*, *a little* or *no*:
>   *She's no better at swimming than her sister.*
> 2 We can qualify comparatives with *as … as* using *just*, *almost/nearly* or *nowhere near/nothing like*:
>   *I'm almost as tall as my dad.*
> 3 Comparatives often have a clause after *than*.
>   *She's less argumentative than she used to be.*
>   *It's much hotter today than I realised.*
> 4 We can use double comparatives for changes:
>   *He's getting taller and taller/more and more handsome.*
> 5 We can use the following structure to say that two things change together because they are connected:
>   *The faster he works, the more mistakes he makes.*

LOOK OUT!

We can use a clause beginning with *as* + an auxiliary or modal verb or the correct form of *be* to show similarity. Pay attention to the word order:
She's a great singer, as is her father.

4 Read the *Look out!* box. Then complete the sentences with a clause to show similarity. Use the words in brackets.

1 I love Lady Gaga, <u>as do my friends</u>. (my friends)
2 We've sold our house, _____ . (our neighbours)
3 She can speak Russian, _____ . (her dad)
4 The school will be closed, _____ . (the pre-school)
5 She loved the film, _____ . (her boyfriend)

5 Match the two halves of the comparative sentences.

1 I speak far more clearly ☐
2 I'm much more intelligent ☐
3 The harder you work, ☐
4 I love sport, ☐
5 I'm nowhere near as moody ☐
6 This dessert is even more delicious ☐
7 She's getting more and more confident, ☐
8 This exercise isn't nearly as difficult ☐

a than everyone thinks I am.
b as do most of my friends.
c as some people I know.
d than I used to.
e than I thought it would be.
f as the next one.
g the more successful you'll be.
h as are most teenagers.

⟫⟫⟫ GRAMMAR BUILDER 3.3: PAGE 120 ⟪⟪⟪

6 Write new beginnings for a–h in exercise 5.

a I'm far more stubborn than everyone thinks I am.

7 Rewrite sentences 1–7 below using a different comparative or superlative form. Include the word in brackets and do not change the meaning. There is more than one possible answer.

1 Nobody in my class is as outgoing as I am. (most)
   I'm the most outgoing person in my class.
2 Jack is far more talkative than Sam. (nowhere)
3 Getting online is becoming easier and easier. (less)
4 My sister drives badly. My dad drives badly too. (as)
5 Everybody in the class sings better than I do. (singer)
6 He plays football much better than he thinks. (badly)
7 The town centre is much emptier than it used to be. (busy)

8 SPEAKING In pairs, think of an appropriate way to finish each sentence. Then compare your ideas with the class.

1 The longer people live, …
2 It's getting more and more difficult to …
3 The hardest thing about being a teenager is …
4 The world is getting more and more …
5 The quickest way to improve your English is …

I can role-play a conversation about a visit.

1 SPEAKING Work in pairs. Describe the hotel in the photo using the words below and your own ideas.

busy / quiet   cheap / expensive   exciting / relaxing
formal / informal   noisy / peaceful   trendy / old-fashioned

2 🎧 1.26 Read the role-play task and listen to a student doing the task with an examiner. What conclusion do they reach for each of the four issues? Complete the chart below.

A teenage foreign friend is coming to visit your town with his/her grandfather. Talk to your friend about the visit, remembering to make plans and arrangements which are suitable for both visitors. Cover these issues:
* where they should stay
* a recommended place to eat out
* a day-trip or excursion that both would enjoy
* the best way to get around

place to stay	
day-trip	
getting around	
eating out	

3 Complete the phrases using the words below. Check you understand the expressions.

1   Suggesting a course of action

could   got   idea   know   other   think

I ¹_____ , why don't we … ?
Here's an ²_____ . Let's …
I've ³_____ it. How about … ?
I ⁴_____ we should …
We ⁵_____ always …
The ⁶_____ thing we should do is …

2   Objecting

alternatively   great   side   sure   that's   why

I'm not ⁷_____/convinced about that.
I don't think that's a ⁸_____ idea.
Let's put that idea to one ⁹_____ for a moment.
I see ¹⁰_____ you're saying that, but …
¹¹_____ not a bad idea but I think …
¹²_____ , we could …

4 🎧 1.26 Listen to the role-play again. Which of the phrases in exercise 3 do they use?

5 🎧 1.27 Read the *Learn this!* box and complete the examples. Then listen and check.

LEARN THIS!

Question tags turn statements into questions. We use affirmative tags after negative verbs and negative tags after affirmative verbs. Tags include a modal verb or auxiliary part of a verb form (*have*, *do*, *did*, etc.).
Your grandfather is coming too, ¹_____ ?
You haven't got a big flat, ²_____ ?
Thai food is spicy, ³_____ ?
Everybody likes Italian food, ⁴_____ ?
I should look online, ⁵_____ ?
Let's decide later, ⁶_____ ?
Don't forget, ⁷_____ ?

>>> GRAMMAR BUILDER 3.4: PAGE 120 <<<

6 🎧 1.27 PRONUNCIATION Listen and repeat the sentences in exercise 5. Does the intonation go up or down at the end of each one? How does that affect the meaning?

7 In pairs, prepare to do the role-play task from exercise 2. Decide which part you will each play and what conclusions you will reach. Make a chart like the one in exercise 2 and write your ideas in it.

8 SPEAKING Do the role-play task in pairs. Make sure you include some question tags.

1 **SPEAKING** Ask and answer these questions in pairs.

1 Do you think you have enough freedom and independence from your family?
2 What are the positive effects of giving teenagers more freedom and independence?
3 What are the negative effects?

2 **SPEAKING** Work in pairs. Read the task below and agree on one advantage and one disadvantage.

Many teenagers spend time looking after themselves at home while the adults are away. Write an essay which presents the advantages and disadvantages of being 'home alone' when you're a teenager.

3 Read the essay. Does the candidate mention your ideas from exercise 2?

Some parents are happy to leave their teenage children alone in the house because they trust them to look after themselves. There can sometimes be drawbacks, but the situation can also bring out the best in teenagers.

Firstly, it's a perfect opportunity to learn how to cook your favourite dishes. Finding good recipes online for, say, lasagne, couldn't be easier. Secondly, it means nobody is there to nag you or tell you what to do, which is great – even though you may forget one or two little things. Thirdly, not having adults around is a chance to prove that you can be independent and even deal with difficult situations occasionally.

On the other hand, there are definitely disadvantages to being at home while your parents are away. Although preparing your own food may be fun, many teenagers will end up eating lots of unhealthy snacks and no proper meals. Secondly, if your parents aren't there to remind you, you may forget something important, like a doctor's appointment. Thirdly, without your parents at home, you need to cope with any domestic emergencies yourself. For example, if the bathroom floods, you need to sort it out!

Overall, I think the advantages for teenagers of spending a little time home alone outweigh the disadvantages. Despite the risk of problems, it's an important part of growing up.

4 Read the Exam tip. Answer the questions in relation to the essay in exercise 3.

1 Does the essay follow the structure in the tip?
2 How many different (a) advantages and (b) disadvantages does the candidate mention?
3 Underline all the places where the candidate gives examples. How are the examples introduced?
4 What phrase does the candidate use to introduce a personal opinion in the conclusion?

5 Read the *Learn this!* box. Underline all the examples of concession in the essay in exercise 3.

6 **USE OF ENGLISH** Rewrite the sentences without changing the meaning. Include the word in brackets.

1 Even though they get on well, they're splitting up. (despite)
   Despite getting on well, they're splitting up.
2 Even though they're friends, they often argue. (despite)
3 Although we tease each other, we're actually very close. (in spite of)
4 In spite of the rain, they walked home together. (although)
5 Many parents watch too much TV, despite lecturing their children about the same thing. (even though)
6 She doesn't respect her dad, even though he's got a well-paid job. (in spite of)

7 **SPEAKING** In pairs, discuss the conclusion of the essay in exercise 3. Do you agree or disagree? Give reasons.

1 SPEAKING **You are going to do the following exam writing task. Read the task and discuss some ideas for advantages and disadvantages with your partner.**

Write an essay which presents the advantages and disadvantages of going on holiday with friends your own age rather than with your family.

2 Plan your essay in pairs.

Student A: Think of as many advantages as you can.
Student B: Think of as many disadvantages as you can.
Make notes using the ideas below to help you.

be on the same wavelength   eat unhealthy food   get ill
get lost   get mugged   make mistakes   make new friends
miss your family   run out of money   stay up all night
stay in hostels

3 SPEAKING **Compare ideas with your partner. Agree on the best two or three advantages and disadvantages, then think of examples where possible. Complete the plan for paragraphs 2 and 3.**

Paragraph 1: introduction
Paragraph 2: advantages

Point 1:	
Point 2:	
Point 3:	

Paragraph 3: disadvantages

Point 1:	
Point 2:	
Point 3:	

Paragraph 4: conclusion

4 In pairs, translate the underlined phrases in the sentences below. Think about how you could use the phrases in your essay. Which section of the essay might they belong to?

1 You might <u>live on junk food</u> for the entire holiday.
2 If you <u>come down with food poisoning</u>, find a doctor.
3 It's important <u>to stick together</u>.
4 Your family <u>are only a phone call away</u>.
5 Holidays can be <u>a bonding experience</u>.
6 Teenagers can be <u>an easy target</u> for criminals.
7 If things go wrong, you may need <u>to grow up overnight</u>.
8 It could be <u>the holiday of a lifetime</u>.

5 In pairs, write the introduction to your essay by completing the outline below.

Some teenagers have the opportunity to go on holiday with friends their own age. Although this can be … it can also …

6 Agree on a conclusion with your partner. Do the advantages outweigh the disadvantages, or vice versa? Make a note of your opinion and the reasons for it.

7 Look back at the essay in exercise 3 on page 34 and complete these three different ways of expressing the idea of being 'home alone'.

1 _____ is a chance to prove you can be independent …
2 … there are definitely disadvantages to being at home _____ .
3 _____ , you need to cope with any domestic emergencies yourself.

8 Do the writing task in exercise 1. Follow the essay plan you made with your partner in exercises 3–6.

CHECK YOUR WORK

Have you:
- [ ] given your essay a clear and logical structure?
- [ ] used at least one concession clause?
- [ ] included some expressions from exercises 2 and 4?
- [ ] rephrased the wording of the task in different ways?
- [ ] written 200–250 words?
- [ ] checked your spelling and grammar?

Listening

1 **Get ready to LISTEN** In pairs, talk about how you prefer to spend your weekends:

alone or with company? with friends or family?
indoors or outdoors?   being active or relaxed?

2 Do the exam task.

LISTENING exam task

🎧 1.28 You will hear five people talking about how they spend the weekend. Match each sentence in the table to the correct speaker(s).

	Which speaker …	A	B	C	D	E
1	loves to expand his/her wardrobe?					
2	spends his/her weekend glued to the screen?					
3	loves to chill out?					
4	has an expensive hobby?					
5	has a hobby which annoys his/her family?					
6	doesn't mind getting dirty?					
7	has a role model?					
8	appreciates nature?					
9	spends weekends with a female family member?					

Use of English

3 Do the exam task.

USE OF ENGLISH exam task

Read the text. Choose the correct answer (A, B, C or D) for each gap to create a logical and grammatically correct text.

UK life expectancy has risen quite dramatically, despite concerns over obesity and its attendant health problems. ¹_____ reports published this month, average life expectancy has risen to 80 years old, eight years higher than in the 1970s. What has made the most difference to the population's health? Has it been increasing the government budget for hospitals, staff and medical equipment? Has it been the ²_____ in medicine with exciting breakthroughs in new treatments for tackling disease? Has it been the fact that we're more conscious of staying healthy these days? These factors have obviously contributed to the health of the nation. But one thing in particular has been an enormous contributing

factor – it was a simple public health campaign about the dangers of smoking.

In 1971, many thousands of men in their early 60s died ³_____ smoking-related heart disease. ⁴_____ 2000 the figure for this age group had halved, while for cancer the number had gone down by a third, and stroke-related deaths had fallen by two-thirds. The dramatic fall in these numbers can be attributed to the first generation of non-smokers arriving at old age.

But what is the likelihood of life expectancy increasing? Health professionals are concerned that this trend ⁵_____ by the time today's youth reach old age. Smoking has been replaced by the equally unhealthy habit of over-eating, and unless a similar public health campaign takes ⁶_____ soon, who knows what the future may bring?

1 A Due to   B According to   C Based on
  D Apart from
2 A growth   B acceleration   C improvement
  D advances
3 A on   B from   C at   D for
4 A Since   B In   C By   D After
5 A is reversing   B has been reversed
  C will be reversed   D reverses
6 A effect   B result   C action   D control

Speaking

4 **Get ready to SPEAK** What things do people generally get better at as they get older? What do they get worse at? In pairs, make two lists.

5 Do the exam task.

SPEAKING exam task

Do you agree or disagree with this statement? Give reasons.

In our society, we do not attach enough value to the wisdom and experience of the old.

THIS UNIT INCLUDES
Vocabulary ▪ politics and protest ▪ elections ▪ suffixes
Grammar ▪ probability: present and future ▪ future continuous, future perfect and future perfect continuous
Speaking ▪ role-play: agreeing and disagreeing
Writing ▪ formal letter: letter of protest

Taking a stand | 4

4A VOCABULARY AND LISTENING Politics and protest

I can talk about politics and political action.

POLITICS HOW MUCH DO YOU KNOW?

1 Look at the four politicians in the photos.
  a What nationality are/were they?
  b Name one thing they are famous for.
2 Name three members of the government in your country.
3 How old do you have to be to vote in your country?
4 How many countries are there in the EU?
5 Who is the current **a** President of the US? **b** British Prime Minister? **c** President of the EU Commission?

1 **SPEAKING** Work in pairs. Do the political awareness quiz. How well-informed are you?

2 🎧 1.29 Complete the text with the correct form of the verbs below. Then listen and check.

call for   change   gauge   influence   join   launch   sign
tackle   take part   write

e-petitions

Most British teenagers aren't very interested in politics. Very few have ¹_____ in a demonstration or ²_____ a letter of protest, let alone ³_____ a political party. But with the advent of the Internet, a new way of ⁴_____ a campaign or ⁵_____ government policy has emerged: e-petitions. Any British citizen can start a petition on the British government website. If more than 100,000 people ⁶_____ the petition, it could be debated in the House of Commons. Recent popular petitions have ⁷_____ a referendum on British membership of the EU, or demanded action to ⁸_____ problems like drug addiction and homelessness. But could a petition ever lead the Government to actually ⁹_____ the law? Or is it just a cynical way for the government to ¹⁰_____ public opinion or, worse, to fool voters into thinking that the Government is actually listening to them? Time will tell.

3 In pairs, check the meaning of all the collocations in red. Then test each other.

launch?   a campaign

>>> **VOCABULARY BUILDER 4.1: PAGE 137** <<<

4 🎧 1.30 Listen to five teenagers being interviewed about their attitude to politics. Match the statements (A–F) with the speakers. There is one statement that you don't need.

A I don't think that politicians ever listen. ☐
B I believe people have a duty to get involved in politics. ☐
C I want to have a say in who governs the country. ☐
D I don't believe that young people care enough to vote. ☐
E I don't think our voting system produces fair results. ☐
F I'll never change my attitude to politics. ☐

5 🎧 1.30 Listen again. Identify one reason that each teenager gives to explain their attitude.

6 **VOCABULARY** What's the meaning of these political terms? How many can you explain?

general public / general election
mainstream politics / single-issue politics
electoral system / political system
left-wing / right-wing
public opinion / public office

7 **SPEAKING** Work in pairs. Say whether you agree or disagree with the opinions in exercise 4. Give reasons.

> I don't agree that politicians never listen. They have to listen in order to get elected.

>>> **VOCABULARY BUILDER 4.2: PAGE 137** <<<

1 🎧 1.31 **Read and listen to the dialogue. Answer the questions.**

1 Who are Sandy and Ryan?
2 What's happening and why?

Ryan	Hey Sandy, move it! Hurry up! Grab a placard and some water. Chances are we'll be out all day.
Sandy	OK. Where are we off to?
Ryan	The university library. Thousands of students will be heading there right now. Hurry!
Sandy	OK, OK. Blimey, there are loads of us! People must be wondering what's going on.
Ryan	That's the idea! Come on!
Sandy	What's the plan then?
Ryan	Well, at least a hundred students are likely to occupy the library. The rest of us could march to the Town Hall, or it might be better to stay in the centre of town to protest there. Either way, people are bound to sit up and take notice.
Crowd	No to student fees! No to student fees!
Ryan	And the TV cameras should be here today as well! The Government can't ignore us any longer. Come on! No to student fees! No to student fees!

2 Read the *Learn this!* box. Underline in the dialogue all the modal verbs and phrases that express probability.

LEARN THIS!

Talking about possibility
1 We use *will* to make predictions about the future.
I don't think the President will be re-elected.
2 We use the future continuous and the future perfect to make assumptions about the present.
It's 8.00. Carolyn will be driving to work.
I think Emily will have left the office by now.
3 We use *must* to conclude that something is certain.
Dad isn't at home. He must be at work.
4 We use *can't* to express impossibility.
He can't be at work. His car's outside.
5 We use *may*, *might* and *could* to talk about the possibility of something happening.
'Where's Max?' 'He could be doing his homework.'
It may rain later, so we might not play tennis.
6 We use *should* to say that something will probably happen, in our opinion.
Spain should beat England.
7 We can use other phrases to express probability.
It's so cold. It's bound to snow tonight. (= certain)
Chances are it'll rain tomorrow. (= very probable)
Are you likely to go to Jeff's party?

>>> GRAMMAR BUILDER 4.1: PAGE 121 <<<

3 Choose the correct answers. Where more than one answer is possible, explain the difference in meaning.

1 This exercise **shouldn't / mustn't / won't** take you too long to complete if you've read the *Learn this!* box.
2 'It's freezing in here. The window **must / could / should** be open.'
3 'Where's Aidan?' 'I'm not sure. He **might / should / will** be playing football.'
4 The plane left London for Paris six hours ago. It will **arrive / have arrived / be arriving** by now.
5 You **shouldn't / mustn't / can't** be listening to the teacher if you are whispering to the student next to you.
6 Emma has revised very hard for her exams so she **should / may / won't** do well.
7 Bring warm clothes to the barbecue next Saturday. The weather **mustn't / can't / might not** be as warm as it's been recently.

4 USE OF ENGLISH **Rewrite the sentences using the words in brackets. Keep the meaning the same.**

1 The phone's ringing. I think it's Tom. (will)
The phone's ringing. It'll be Tom.
2 I'm certain that the Government will be defeated. (bound)
3 I rang Liam at home but there was no answer. There's no way that he's at home. (can't)
4 Do you think that Josh will arrive soon? (likely)
5 I really don't expect Sam will fail his driving test. (shouldn't)
6 Fran is probably lying. (chances)
7 It's one o'clock. I assume she's having lunch. (will)

5 SPEAKING **Work in pairs. Describe the photo. Discuss what is happening now and what might happen. Use language from the *Learn this!* box.**

The protesters must be feeling very …

1 **SPEAKING** What does the map tell us about Ireland? What else do you know about politics and religion in Ireland?

2 **SPEAKING** Describe the photo using the words below.

adjectives (un)armed violent
nouns barricade riot rioter shield weapon
verbs riot protest demonstrate

3 🎧 1.32 Read the text. What is the significance of these dates?

a 1922   c 1969   e 1998
b the 1960s d 1985

4 Read the text again. Answer the questions.

1 What proportion of the population of Northern Ireland is Protestant?
2 Why did the Catholic community feel aggrieved following the partition of Ireland?
3 Why did the British army return to Northern Ireland in 1969?
4 What is the main aim of the IRA?
5 How many people were killed during the 30 years of unrest?

5 **VOCABULARY** Cover the text. Complete the compound nouns with the words below. Find the words in the text to check.

civil group peace rights struggle

1 civil _____   4 _____ initiative
2 _____ unrest   5 armed _____
3 paramilitary _____

6 🎧 1.33 Listen to two teenagers talking about Northern Ireland. Choose the correct answer.

a Neither of them wants a united Ireland.
b One of them wants a united Ireland.
c Both of them want a united Ireland.

7 🎧 1.33 Listen again. Are the sentences true (T) or false (F)?

1 William has some happy childhood memories. ☐
2 Two of William's relatives were killed by terrorists. ☐
3 William can't help thinking of Catholics as enemies. ☐
4 Niamh thinks the IRA made a mistake when it gave up its armed struggle. ☐
5 Approximately 90% of children in Northern Ireland go to faith schools. ☐
6 Niamh will probably send her children to a Catholic school. ☐

8 **SPEAKING** Study the text again for three minutes. Then summarise it in your own words to your partner.

NORTHERN IRELAND

When Ireland gained its independence in 1922, the North, where two thirds of the population were Protestants, remained part of the UK. For decades after, the minority Catholic population in the North felt badly treated. They were less well off and were often excluded from public office. Most of them wanted an end to British rule in Northern Ireland.

In the 1960s some Protestants reacted violently to Catholic demands for equality and civil rights, and police used force to break up Catholic demonstrations. Rioting and civil unrest followed and in 1969 the British Army was sent in to restore law and order. Catholic and Protestant paramilitary groups started planting bombs and murdering people, claiming that they were 'protecting their communities'. One of these groups, the Provisional IRA (Irish Republican Army), wanted Ireland to be united again and started killing British soldiers. The British government acknowledged the Catholics' grievances, but insisted that Northern Ireland would remain part of the UK as long as that was what the majority of its people wanted.

The British government was unable to stop the violence, which lasted for nearly 30 years. This period saw a number of failed peace initiatives, an attempt by the IRA in 1985 to murder Prime Minister Margaret Thatcher, and the deaths of over 3,500 people, including 1,100 British soldiers.

But people in both communities were tiring of the spiral of violence and in 1998 the IRA agreed to give up its armed struggle and seek to achieve its goal by peaceful means. Northern Ireland is still part of the UK, but now has its own government, made up of Catholics and Protestants.

Freedom of speech and information

how much should we have?

SIMON WILSON – libertarian

We libertarians believe that the Government should interfere in people's lives as little as possible. That means that people's right to free speech should not be restricted by law unless what they are saying is certain to incite violence. I believe that extreme right-wing or left-wing views and extreme religious views should all be allowed, even though most people find them abhorrent. This is the essence of a free society. Extreme views should be expressed and challenged. That is the only way to defeat them.

JASON ROMFORD – comedian

It's difficult to be polite in comedy because you are usually making fun of people. So you're bound to offend somebody at some point. But just because somebody is offended doesn't mean they are right. I believe that I have the right to offend you, and if you are offended, that's not a problem. That doesn't mean that I try to be offensive. I don't. I try to be funny, I try to be honest and I try to make people think. If someone feels offended at something I say, that's too bad. That's their problem.

JANE SIMMONS – politician

Governments have the right to censor information and restrict free speech in the interests of national security, for preserving public safety, or for the prevention of disorder or crime. For example, it's a crime to incite people to carry out acts of terrorism. Most people agree that this is sensible. However, there is a danger that governments will use 'the defence of national security' as an excuse to silence legitimate protests and stifle opposition to their policies. It's important therefore that people are able to challenge the limits of free speech in a court of law.

PETER GREENWOOD – civil rights activist

There's a danger that people can use free speech to undermine the human rights of others. Liberalism is a good thing, but we should limit people's rights to express racist, sexist, ageist or homophobic views. There are lessons we must learn from history. If there had been no free speech for the Nazi party in Germany during the early 20s, it is possible that fascism may not have grown in power and influence. The lesson is: be intolerant of intolerance.

SARAH MATTHEWS – online activist

I contribute to a website called Wikileaks, where anonymous volunteers leak confidential government information or hack into government computer files worldwide and put them on the Internet. Governments say our actions are dangerous. I think they just want to conceal their wrongdoings from us. I want to expose the truth. People have the right to know everything that their government is doing. I'm absolutely opposed to censorship of the press.

1 Have you or someone you know ever signed a petition or demonstrated against something? If so, why? If not, would you? Give reasons.

2 🎧 2.02 Read through the texts quickly. Decide who believes that there should be limits to freedom of speech. Which key words/phrases helped you decide?

Simon Wilson –
interfere ... as little as possible
extreme views ... be allowed

BUT: unless ... incite violence

EXAM TIP

Skim read the text before you read the multiple choice questions in order to get the general meaning.
Then read each question and identify the part of the text that contains the information you need.
Reject any options that are clearly wrong and identify the correct answer by looking carefully at the relevant part of the text.
If you are unsure which of two answers is correct, make an intelligent guess.

ANNIE THATCHER – journalist

The press must not invade people's privacy, nor can it say things which hurt a person's reputation without clear evidence that they are true. But is it fair to investigate the private lives of public figures? Journalists tend to justify their intrusion into the lives of famous people by claiming  that certain information is 'in the public interest' (as opposed to something the public is interested in). For example, they argue, if the captain of the England football team is having an affair, then the public should know about it, as he is in a position of authority and respect and a role model for young boys. Ultimately, though, some of the press will print anything that sells newspapers – if they can get away with it.

3 Read the Exam tip on page 40. Then read the texts again and choose the best answer.

1 Simon Wilson says that
  a libertarians don't believe in government.
  b everybody has extreme views.
  c governments cannot ever restrict free speech.
  d we should fight against extreme views.
2 Jason Romford
  a always tries to be polite.
  b thinks that comedians are always offensive.
  c is upset when he thinks he has offended someone.
  d wants to entertain people.
3 Jane Simmons thinks that
  a we need to be able to restrict free speech to guard people's safety.
  b governments are always right to restrict free speech.
  c people are free to carry out terrorist acts.
  d people shouldn't question any government's actions.
4 Peter Greenwood
  a wants restrictions on what people say about others.
  b thinks that we have learned something from history.
  c says that the Nazi party restricted free speech.
  d thinks that people have become more intolerant.
5 Sarah Matthews wants
  a governments to conceal confidential information.
  b to reveal what governments are doing.
  c everyone to hack into government computer documents.
  d everyone to read the Wikileaks website.
6 Annie Thatcher believes that
  a the press isn't allowed the right to freedom of speech.
  b the press always reports information responsibly.
  c journalists have the right to say what they like about celebrities.
  d the press generally argue that they print what the public needs to know.

LEARN THIS!

The suffixes -ism and -ist
1 We often use the suffix -ism for beliefs, ideologies and behaviour (*Buddhism, Marxism*).
2 We often use -ist for people who have those beliefs and ideologies (*a Buddhist, a Marxist*) and for adjectives (*Marxist ideology, a Buddhist temple*).
3 There are exceptions.
  liberalism (n, belief), *a liberal* (n, person), *liberal* (adj)
  criticism (n, behaviour), *a critic* (n, person), *critical* (adj)
4 We also use -ism and -ist for some occupations. (*journalism, a journalist*)

4 **VOCABULARY** Read the *Learn this!* box. Then look through the texts and find the suffixes for these words. Which category does each one belong to?

1 activ_____   5 age_____
2 liberal_____   6 fasc_____
3 rac_____   7 journal_____
4 sex_____   8 terror_____

▶▶▶ VOCABULARY BUILDER 4.3: PAGE 137 ◀◀◀

5 Read statements A–F. On your own, score them from 1 (= disagree strongly) to 5 (= agree strongly). Think of reasons for each opinion.

A We should know everything the Government is doing or plans to do.
B It is right for hackers to try to access government files.
C We have the right to know everything about celebrities' lives.
D Comedians should be careful what they make jokes about.
E People should be allowed to express any opinion, however extreme.
F Racist, sexist, ageist, anti-religious and homophobic views should not be tolerated.

6 **SPEAKING** Work in small groups. Compare your scores for exercise 5. Justify your opinions and give examples to back them up.

7 🎧 2.03 Listen and complete the song.

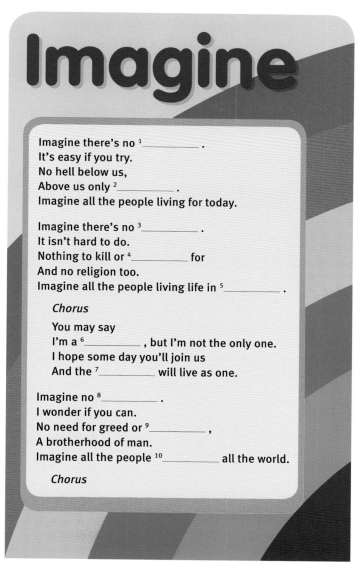

Imagine there's no ¹_____ .
It's easy if you try.
No hell below us,
Above us only ²_____ .
Imagine all the people living for today.

Imagine there's no ³_____ .
It isn't hard to do.
Nothing to kill or ⁴_____ for
And no religion too.
Imagine all the people living life in ⁵_____ .

Chorus
  You may say
  I'm a ⁶_____ , but I'm not the only one.
  I hope some day you'll join us
  And the ⁷_____ will live as one.

Imagine no ⁸_____ .
I wonder if you can.
No need for greed or ⁹_____ ,
A brotherhood of man.
Imagine all the people ¹⁰_____ all the world.

Chorus

8 **SPEAKING** Work in pairs. Discuss these questions. Is John Lennon's vision (a) worth striving for? (b) realistic and achievable? Give reasons for your opinions.

1 Read the flyer. What sort of things do you think the School Council does? Do you have a group like this at your school?

Your School Council NEEDS YOU!

Helping to improve your school

By the end of this week we'll have been running your new School Council for a whole term. We've already had an impact on the way the school is run. We asked to have a say in the new school uniform and the teachers agreed. Next term, we'll all be wearing a uniform designed by you.
And by the end of the year we'll have made our school even better. We'll be meeting more regularly next term. Come along with ideas on how to improve our school.

SEE YOU THERE!

2 Find four examples of the future continuous, future perfect and future perfect continuous in the text. Then match each example with a use in the *Learn this!* box.

Future continuous, future perfect and future perfect continuous
1 We use the **future continuous** to:
 a talk about something we expect will happen.
 b talk about an action in progress in the future.
2 We use the **future perfect** to talk about a completed action in the future.
3 We use the **future perfect continuous**, usually with *for ...* , to say how long an action will have been in progress in the future.

3 Explain the meaning of these sentences. Translate them into your language.
 1 At 4 p.m. we'll watch the film.
 2 At 4 p.m. we'll be watching the film.
 3 By 4 p.m. we'll have watched the film.
 4 By 4 p.m. we'll have been watching the film for an hour.

Future continuous
We can use the future continuous to make enquiries.
Will you be voting in the election?

>>> GRAMMAR BUILDER 4.2: PAGE 122 <<<

4 Read the *Learn this!* box and rephrase the questions using the future continuous to make polite questions.
 1 What time are you leaving school?
 2 What do you plan to do this evening?
 3 Who are you going to see at the weekend?
 4 Where will you go for your next holiday?
 5 What are you intending to wear to school tomorrow?

5 SPEAKING Ask and answer the questions in pairs. Use the future continuous in the questions.

6 🎧 2.04 Listen to the conversation. What will have happened by tomorrow afternoon?

7 🎧 2.04 Complete the sentences with a verb in the correct tense. Then listen again and check.
 1 We'll _____ in Birmingham soon.
 2 By the time I arrive home I'll _____ for eight hours.
 3 Will you _____ something to eat when you arrive?
 4 No, I won't be hungry. I'll _____ .
 5 By five o'clock, we'll _____ down to a lovely meal.

8 Complete the predictions. Use the future continuous or the future perfect of the verbs below.

find   go   live   melt   speak   spread

What will happen in the 21st century?

► By 2030 scientists [1]_____ a cure for cancer.
► By 2040 democracy [2]_____ to every country in the world.
► By 2050 most people [3]_____ English as their first language.
► By 2060 the majority of people [4]_____ beyond 110.
► By 2080 the polar ice-caps [5]_____ completely.
► By 3000 people [6]_____ on holiday to Mars.

9 SPEAKING Work in pairs. Discuss whether you agree or disagree with the predictions in exercise 8. Give reasons.

I don't think scientists will have invented a cure for cancer by 2013 because ...

I agree./I don't agree. I think ...

1 **SPEAKING** Describe the picture. Use the words below to help you.

banner   chant (v)   demonstration   demonstrator   march (v)   megaphone   placard   protest (v)   slogan

2 **SPEAKING** Work in pairs. Imagine there are plans to build a massive car park in the centre of a small town near you. Brainstorm reasons why you might object to this.

3 🎧 2.05 Listen to two teenagers, Ollie and Emma, discussing their objections to the car park. Compare your ideas with theirs.

4 🎧 2.05 Complete the lines from the conversation with the verbs in brackets. Use the present continuous, the present simple, *going to* and *will*. Then listen and check.

1 They _____ (build) a massive car park in the town centre.
2 The council _____ (meet) in a month's time so we need to move quickly.
3 I _____ (go) out this evening. What about tomorrow evening?
4 I _____ (ring) Jane and get her involved.

5 Match the sentences (1–4) in exercise 4 with the descriptions (a–d).

a   an arrangement   c   an intention
b   a timetabled event   d   an instant decision

▶▶▶ **GRAMMAR BUILDER 4.3: PAGE 122** ◀◀◀

6 🎧 2.06 Listen to Ollie, Emma and Jane discussing what form their protest will take. Which of these do they decide to do? Which do they reject, and why?

1 draw up a petition   6 write a letter of protest
2 hand out leaflets   7 put up posters
3 organise a march   8 contact the media
4 make placards   9 hold a rally
5 set up a website

7 🎧 2.06 Complete the phrases with the words below. Check you understand the expressions. Then listen again. Which phrases don't they use?

advantage   don't   it   maybe

Persuading
The big ¹_____ of (my idea) is …
Wouldn't ²_____ be better to … ?
³_____ you think that … ?
⁴_____ , but I still think …

agree   decided   persuaded   right

Compromising or agreeing
I guess you could be ⁵_____ .
OK, you've ⁶_____ me.
OK. Let's ⁷_____ on that.
That's ⁸_____ , then.

8 **PRONUNCIATION** How is the noun *protest* (in exercise 6) pronounced? How would it be pronounced if it were a verb?

▶▶▶ **VOCABULARY BUILDER 4.4: PAGE 137** ◀◀◀

9 **SPEAKING** Work in small groups. You are planning to launch a campaign. Follow the instructions.

• Decide which issue you are going to protest about. Choose from the ideas in the box below or think of your own.
• Discuss what form your protest will take and agree on three types of action. (See exercise 6.)
• Discuss and decide who will be responsible for each.

• the building of a new road through a rural area popular with tourists
• a plan to build a nuclear power station near your town
• the closure of a youth club which you attend
• a global issue such as poverty, disease, endangered species or the arms trade

I can write a letter of protest.

1 How would the beginning and the end of the letter be different if June didn't know the name of the person she was writing to?

42 Mill Lane
Greenford
JK4 9PM

Councillor Mary Jones
Town Hall
Greenford
JK4 7GH

4 April 2013

Dear Mrs Jones,

I am writing to protest against the planned closure of the public library in the centre of Greenford. I understand that it is to close at the end of the year.

I am particularly concerned about the primary and secondary school students who currently use the library to research homework assignments and projects. It is important to recognise that the library is of crucial importance to young people in the town.

In addition, many elderly and less well-off people might not be able to afford to buy many books. The fact is that the closure is bound to adversely affect many such people who rely on the library as their only source of reading matter.

Furthermore, the library serves as a social centre where people drop in to read the papers and meet their friends. The consequences of the closure will be very damaging to people who use the library in this way.

It is for these reasons that I think the council should reconsider its decision and keep the library open for the benefit of all the citizens of Greenford.

I look forward to your response.

Yours sincerely,

June Knight

June Knight

2 Read the letter. Answer the questions.

1 What is the council planning to do, and when?
2 How many objections does June raise in her letter?
3 How do many students currently use the library?
4 How will the closure affect elderly and less affluent people?
5 How else do people use the library, apart from to borrow books?
6 What action does June request?

3 Find and underline in the letter nine phrases from the list below.

Useful phrases for a letter of protest

opening the letter
I am writing to protest against …
I wish to register my opposition to …
I am writing to express my concern about …
1 _____

introducing your reasons for protesting
I am very worried about/that …
I am particularly concerned about …
I fear that (it) will lead to …   It is clearly unfair to/that …
In addition …/Furthermore …
2 _____

making a point forcefully
It is important to recognise that …
The fact is that …   What you don't seem to realise is that …
3 _____

describing ill effects
… will do serious damage to …
… will lead to the collapse/destruction/death etc. of …
… is bound to adversely affect …
The consequences of … will be very damaging …
4 _____

requesting action
It is for these reasons that I think…
Please put a(n immediate) stop to …
Please do everything in your power to …
5 _____

4 Add one of these phrases to each group in exercise 3.

a It is/I find it unacceptable that …
b I would like to point out that …
c I wish to object in the strongest possible terms to …
d I urge you therefore to reconsider your decision/proposal (to …)
e … will have a devastating effect on …

5 Complete the Exam tip. Find the features in the letter. Check you understand the key features of formal letters.

EXAM TIP

- Put [1]_____ at the top on the right, [2]_____ address just below on the left and [3]_____ below that.
- Start and end the letter correctly: Dear [4]_____ or Madam / name … Yours faithfully / [5]_____
- Avoid [6]_____ language and [7]_____ , direct questions and [8]_____ marks.
- At the end, sign your [9]_____ , then print it underneath.

Formal letter: letter of protest

I can write a letter of protest.

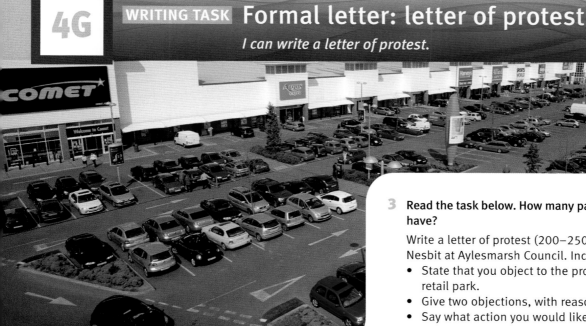

1 Describe the photo. Do you or your family ever shop at out-of-town retail parks? Why?/Why not?

2 Read the newspaper article. Answer the questions.
1 What does the council have to decide?
2 Who is paying for the new retail park?
3 How big will it be and how much will it cost?
4 What two possible advantages of the plans are mentioned in the text?
5 What two possible disadvantages are mentioned?

£20M RETAIL PARK FOR AYLESMARSH

AYLESMARSH COUNCIL are meeting next June to decide whether or not to approve plans for a 200-hectare retail park on the outskirts of the town. The park will include department stores, clothing outlets, media stores, computer and electrical stores.

Harrington plc. the company with plans to develop the greenfield site, say that the project will cost £20 million. A company spokesperson said, 'The park will create over 300 jobs during the construction phase and over 200 permanent jobs once it is open.' The retail park will have parking for 500 cars. A regular bus service will run from the centre of town to the park.

The plans are likely to be controversial. Councillor Mike Nesbit, who is in favour of the development, said it would be a massive boost to the local economy, creating hundreds of jobs and attracting major retailers to the new park. However, local traders are reported to be upset at the effect the retail park will have on town centre shops, and environmentalists say it will destroy fields and ancient woodland. 'We want to consult local people,' said Cllr Nesbit, 'and in the coming months we will be holding a number of public meetings at which people can air their views.'

3 Read the task below. How many paragraphs will your letter have?

Write a letter of protest (200–250 words) to Councillor Nesbit at Aylesmarsh Council. Include the following points:
• State that you object to the proposal to build the new retail park.
• Give two objections, with reasons.
• Say what action you would like the council to take.

4 Plan and write your first paragraph, stating clearly what you are writing about (i.e. that you object to the proposal). Use phrases from exercise 3 on page 44.

5 Work in pairs. Choose two reasons for objecting to the proposed retail park from the list below, or think of your own ideas. Expand the two ideas and make notes.

Possible objections
effect on shops/loss of jobs in the town centre
increased traffic
destruction of a beautiful rural area
effect on wildlife

6 Write the second and third paragraphs of your letter, using the notes you made in exercise 5. Use phrases from exercise 3 on page 44.

7 Work in pairs. Decide what action you would like the council to take. Choose ideas from the list or think of your own. Expand the ideas and write notes.

Possible actions
find an alternative location
abandon the proposal
hold an enquiry and consult local traders
build new shops and a car park in the town centre

8 Write the fourth paragraph of your letter, using the notes you made in exercise 7. Use phrases from exercise 3 on page 44.

CHECK YOUR WORK

Have you:
☐ structured your letter following the task in exercise 3?
☐ included some phrases in each section from page 44?
☐ used a polite, formal style?
☐ used the correct layout and language to start and finish your letter?
☐ written 200–250 words?
☐ checked your spelling and grammar?

Unit 3

1 Read the sentences. Describe what is happening using the verbs below and correct prepositions.

boasting confiding praising telling warning

1 'Rover, sit! Good boy, Rover!' said Joe.
   Joe was _____ his dog _____ obeying him.
2 'I can play football better than any of you,' Brandon said.
   Brandon was _____ _____ his friends.
3 'You can't swim here, there are rocks,' said the lifeguard.
   The lifeguard was _____ them _____ the rocks.
4 'Actually, I'm scared of cats,' Kurt said to his son.
   Kurt was _____ _____ his son _____ his fear of cats.
5 'Tom! Put those crisps away!' said the teacher.
   The teacher was _____ Tom off _____ eating in class.

Mark: _____ /5

2 Write the missing questions.

1 Keira went to Spain with her sister.
   Q: _____ ?   A: Her sister.
2 They stayed in a hotel for two weeks.
   Q: _____ ?   A: Two weeks.
3 They were unhappy about their room.
   Q: _____ ?   A: Their room.
4 They complained to the hotel manager.
   Q: _____ ?   A: The hotel manager.
5 He told the maid off for not cleaning the room.
   Q: _____ ?   A: For not cleaning the room.

Mark: _____ /5

3 Complete the text. Write one or two words in each gap.

Thanks to technology, it's getting harder [1]_____ for teenagers to experience independence. In the past, travelling abroad without your parents was one of [2]_____ effective ways of learning survival skills. But today, going abroad is nowhere [3]_____ liberating as it used to be because teenagers can stay in touch via texts, as [4]_____ their parents. The more connected the world becomes, [5]_____ easy it is for teenagers to find space to grow.

Mark: _____ /5

4 Add question tags to the dialogue.

Boy Let's go out for dinner this weekend, [1]_____ ?
Girl Good idea. We should book somewhere, [2]_____ ?
Boy Yes. I'll do that. How about the new Italian place?
Girl You haven't been there before, [3]_____ ?
Boy No. Nobody said anything bad about it, [4]_____ ?
Girl OK! Don't forget to ask about vegan food, [5]_____ ?

Mark: _____ /5

Total: _____ /20

Unit 4

5 Complete the sentences with the verbs below.

gauge influence launch tackle take part in

1 Did you _____ the demonstration last night?
2 Online surveys are a good way to _____ public opinion.
3 Local politicians have done nothing to _____ vandalism in this city.
4 Can you _____ government policy by donating money to political parties?
5 The Government plans to _____ a new anti-smoking campaign focusing on teenagers.

Mark: _____ /5

6 Complete the dialogue with the words below.

bound chances might must won't

Boy Where's our taxi? It [1]_____ be at least half an hour since I called.
Girl [2]_____ are it's stuck in traffic. It is rush hour.
Boy The gig starts at 7.30. We [3]_____ miss the beginning …
Girl Don't worry. There's [4]_____ to be a support act on first. We [5]_____ miss the main band.

Mark: _____ /5

7 Choose the correct verb forms, a or b.

1 He _____ gone to bed yet, it's only 9 p.m.
   a won't have gone   b won't have been going
2 I can't text you tomorrow afternoon, I _____ an exam.
   a 'll have done   b 'll be doing
3 Sue's on holiday. She _____ a great time, I expect.
   a 'll have had   b 'll be having
4 They _____ together for a year this December.
   a 'll have gone out   b 'll have been going out
5 You need to say it again. He _____ you.
   a won't have heard   b won't have been hearing

Mark: _____ /5

8 Complete the dialogue with suitable words.

Boy Here's an [1]_____ . Why don't we write a letter to the newspaper?
Girl I'm not [2]_____ about that. They probably won't print it. I [3]_____ we should launch a campaign on Facebook. It's easy and effective. We [4]_____ always get our friends to join …
Boy I see [5]_____ you're saying that, but will anyone notice a campaign on Facebook?

Mark: _____ /5

Total: _____ /20

Lead-in

1 Find out if your partner prefers shopping in small, local shops or giant superstores. Agree on two pros and two cons for each type of shop.

Listening

2 🎧 2.08 **Listen. Where does the conversation take place? Choose one, two or three of the places below.**

in a superstore   in the squat   outside a shop

3 🎧 2.08 **Listen again. Choose the correct answers.**

1 Why does Stefan assume Daisy is not English?
   a Her English is worse than his.
   b Her appearance is not typically English.
   c She doesn't seem to know anyone.
2 Daisy lives
   a in the same squat as Spikey.
   b in a flat on Western Avenue.
   c with her Spanish mother.
3 When Spikey tells Stefan he shouldn't buy bananas, Stefan
   a suggests Spikey has got his facts wrong.
   b agrees not to buy any bananas.
   c does not understand how not buying bananas will make a difference.
4 Daisy left home because
   a she didn't like living with a capitalist.
   b she had a big argument with her father.
   c she wanted to live with Spikey.

Reading

4 Read the text. What is it from? Choose from a–d.
   a a newspaper report   c a formal letter
   b a leaflet   d a magazine article

5 Are these sentences true (T) or false (F), according to the text in exercise 4?
   1 Wesley's are planning to build a car park next to an existing row of shops.
   2 An official decision to allow the development has already been made.
   3 Letters of complaint should focus on the fact that local people were not asked to discuss the plans.
   4 The supermarket chain has already bought a playing field from the local council.
   5 There are already traffic problems in the area.

Speaking

6 Imagine you are planning a protest for the campaign against Wesley's. Which of the options below will you choose and why? Why are you rejecting the other options? Take turns to tell your partner.

 a a sit-in    b a stunt    c a march

Writing

7 Imagine you are Stefan. Write a letter, in an appropriate style, to Libby in which you:
   • thank her for letting you stay.
   • describe your new flat.
   • invite her to visit your new flat.
   • describe Spikey and Daisy.

⟫⟫⟫ **CHECK YOUR PROGRESS: PAGE 4** ⟪⟪⟪

S.O.S. SAVE OUR SHOPS!

Supermarket chain Wesley's are planning to demolish a row of shops in Williams Street and build a new, massive superstore and underground car park in the same location. They have already received planning permission for the development from the local council, who own the land, but we believe it is not too late to stop it. Join our campaign – write and complain! We're asking people to write to their local Member of Parliament to complain about the development, and in particular, the lack of consultation with local residents and businesses. We feel the decision to approve the plan was taken without considering its negative impact on the environment and the local community.

Five good reasons to oppose the development:

1 The site for the new superstore includes a 10,000m² playing field which the local government plans to sell off. Our children need green spaces for sports and exercise!
2 Unlike local shops, the profit from a big superstore goes to its shareholders, who do not live locally. The money is not reinvested in the area.
3 Superstores import goods from all around the world, which causes pollution and is unnecessary. Our small, local shops sell local produce whenever possible.
4 Parking and traffic are already a big problem in this part of London. A new superstore will make it worse, especially as the proposed car park is too small for the expected number of customers.
5 Large superstores keep their prices low by exploiting workers in developing countries. Many banana-growers, for example, earn less than £1 a day.

Reading

1 **Get ready to READ** Ask and answer these questions in pairs:

1 What are androids?
2 Will they be part of our lives in the future? Why? / Why not?
3 Do you think the future looks bright or bleak for the human race?

2 Do the exam task.

READING exam task

Read the extract from *Do Androids Dream of Electric Sheep?* by Philip K Dick. Complete the text with the missing sentences (A–E). There is one extra sentence that is not needed.

In a great empty apartment building far from the centre of San Francisco a single television played. ¹_____ There were few people left to miss them.

Nobody really remembered why the war had started or who, if anyone, had won. The radioactive dust that covered the Earth had come from no country and nobody had planned it. ²_____ Under United Nations law each person who left was given an android to work for them. It became very easy to go and difficult to stay. The few thousands who remained moved into areas where they could live together and see each other. There were only a few odd individuals who stayed alone in the suburbs. John Isidore, listening to the television as he shaved, was one of these.

'Let's hear from Mrs Maggie Klugman,' the television presenter was saying. 'She emigrated to Mars a short time ago. MrsKlugman, how does your exciting life in New New York compare with the difficulties of your previous life on Earth?'

There was a pause, and then a tired middle-aged voice said, '³_____ And before we left, my husband and I were always worried that we might become specials. Now our worries have gone for ever.'

For me too, John Isidore thought, and I didn't have to emigrate. He had been a special now for over a year. Since he had failed even a basic intelligence test, the popular name for him and others like him was 'chickenhead' – but he survived. He had a job driving a truck for a false-animal repair company, and Mr Sloat, his boss, accepted him as a human being. There were chickenheads who were much more stupid than Isidore.

Isidore had finished shaving, and turned the television off. Silence. ⁴_____ He experienced the silence with his eyes as well as his ears. It almost felt alive.

A After the war the animals had died, the sun had stopped shining and most people were encouraged to emigrate.

B Before World War Terminus the building had been well looked after, but now the owner of this and other apartments had died or emigrated to other planets.

C It came from the walls, the floor, the ceiling and from all the machines in the apartment that had stopped working years before.

D Life used to be so easy and carefree and leaving Earth behind was such an ordeal.

E Oh, it's wonderful to have an android that you can depend on.

Use of English

3 Do the exam task.

USE OF ENGLISH exam task

Complete each gap in the text with a word formed from the word in brackets.

The number of people without jobs in the UK has risen by 28,000 to 2.67 million during the three months to January, according to the ¹_____ (LATE) figures, which the government says show signs of stabilising. It is the lowest rise in over a year, but 8.4% of the population is still affected. ²_____ (EMPLOY) amongst the female population accounted for most of the rise in the number of ³_____ (JOB) people. They have been most ⁴_____ (SEVERE) hit, making up nearly 80% of the increase. The figures also underlined the extent to which the increase in the number of part-time jobs is masking the problem. They are often ⁵_____ (ADEQUATE) paid and therefore cannot replace the full-time ⁶_____ (EARN) that people generally require. Meanwhile, the government continued to emphasise that despite the latest cuts in public sector jobs, more jobs were being created in the private sector. However, there is some ⁷_____ (COURAGE) data for the UK economy. ⁸_____ (SURPRISE), retail sales rose by an unexpected 0.9% in January, as fears of a recession disappeared.

Vocabulary ▪ computing: phrases and useful verbs ▪ technology components ▪ crime
Grammar ▪ active and passive voices ▪ passive: all forms ▪ participle clauses
▪ future in the past
Speaking ▪ stimulus description
Writing ▪ story

Technology 5

5A **VOCABULARY AND LISTENING** **Computing**

I can talk about everyday technology.

1 SPEAKING Look at the photos. Which of these websites do you visit regularly? What do you do there?

2 Complete the chart using the verbs below. Then in pairs, translate all the phrases. Which words are the same in your own language?

download   join   log on   post   stream   update   upload

Computing: phrases		
edit or 1_____	your profile/status/ personal details/ contact details/ preferences	(on Facebook/ MySpace/Amazon, etc.)
sign in or 2_____	to Facebook/Hotmail/your account, etc.	
3_____	a comment/an entry	(on YouTube/a blog/ an Internet forum)
4_____	a chat/a Wi-fi network, etc.	
5_____	an app/a film/a file, etc.	(from iTunes/the Internet, etc.)
6_____	a video/a photo, etc.	(to YouTube/ Facebook/Flickr, etc.)
7_____	music/video	(to your phone/TV/ computer, etc.)

3 🎧 2.09 Listen to five conversations. Describe what the people are doing using phrases from exercise 2.

4 VOCABULARY Read the verbs below. Then use some of them to complete the sentences from the conversations.

Computing: useful verbs   browse   cancel
click/double-click   delete   enter   highlight
key   press (a key)   scan   scroll up/down   search
swipe   tap   zoom in/out

1 Let's _____ and see what they've written underneath the video.
2 What were we going to _____ for?
3 I don't need to _____ in my card details.
4 _____ on that button.
5 _____ so we can see him more clearly.
6 Just _____ from left to right, then _____ the red button with your finger.
7 Use the cursor to _____ the name of the film and then _____ the return key.
8 We can't wait that long. How do we _____ the download?

5 🎧 2.09 Listen again. Check your answers to exercise 4.

6 Work in pairs. Using the language in exercises 2 and 4 to help you, explain to your partner how to:
1 add a new contact to your phone.
2 download a song from the Internet.
3 find and watch a video clip online.

> First, you need to open the address book app by tapping the icon. Then you tap the plus sign. Next, you key in the name and address …

⟫⟫⟫ **VOCABULARY BUILDER 5.1: PAGE 138** ⟪⟪⟪

1 SPEAKING Choose one or two words from below or your own ideas to complete this sentence. Then compare your opinions in pairs and give reasons.
Trying things on when you go shopping for clothes is ...

a chore embarrassing essential exciting fun
inconvenient off-putting uncomfortable

2 Complete the sentences with the words below.

bought closed done introduced returned tried

1 About 40% of clothes which have been _____ online are _____ , far more than other goods.
2 The advantage of high street clothes stores is that the clothes can be _____ on.
3 New technology is being _____ to stores to make shopping easier.
4 By 2025, most shopping will be _____ online and many high street stores will have been _____ .

3 Study the sentences in exercise 2 and say:

1 which different tenses the passive forms are in.
2 which passive form includes a modal verb.

Passive: all forms
1 We can form the passive of any tense by using that tense of the verb *be* plus the past participle.
   Wi-Fi has been/is being/will be installed at school.
2 We use the past continuous and present continuous forms of the passive, but we don't use other continuous forms because they are very clumsy.
   I'm being watched. ✓
   I've been being watched. ✗
   Someone has been watching me. ✓
3 We can use the passive with present and past forms of modal verbs.
   Shoes must be worn. This puzzle can't be solved.
   I may have been burgled. You would have been told.

>>> GRAMMAR BUILDER 5.1: PAGE 123 <<<

4 Read the *Learn this!* box. Then rewrite the sentences in the passive, unless they contain a tense not used in the passive.

1 A giant asteroid might destroy the earth.
2 They're testing our theories about the universe at CERN.
3 The Chinese may have invented gunpowder.
4 You can join the Wi-Fi network free of charge.
5 They'll have completed the new Metro lines by the time they hold the Olympics.
6 Someone had been reading all my emails, I realised.
7 If they'd received your complaint, they would have notified you.

LOOK OUT!

When we use adverbs with passive verb forms, we often put them immediately before the past participle:
The results will be thoroughly checked.
In compound tenses, adverbs of frequency usually go between the auxiliary and *be* or *been*:
They'll never be told. She's often been warned.
Prepositions which belong with the verb go immediately after the past participle:
Will she be listened to? My laptop is being looked at.

5 Read the *Look out!* box. Then complete the text with the passive forms of the verbs in brackets. Use the correct tense.

Magic mirrors have been a common feature in children's stories ever since the fairytale Snow White [1] was famously made (make / famously) into a film by Disney. But recently, real 'magic mirrors' [2]_____ (install) in several stores in the UK. Thanks to these neat devices, whole outfits [3]_____ (can / try on) without having to undress or even find the items in the store.
The mirror is in fact a computer screen. Stand in front of it and your body [4]_____ (scan / instantly). An image of yourself [5]_____ (display) on the screen and your measurements [6]_____ (calculate / automatically). Once this [7]_____ (do), items of clothing [8]_____ (can / choose) from the on-screen menus. These [9]_____ (superimpose) onto your own image. Shoes and accessories [10]_____ (may / add) to complete the outfit. And because a second opinion [11]_____ (often / need), your new look [12]_____ (can / share / instantly) with your friends: if you click on an icon, it [13]_____ (post) on Facebook a few seconds later.
At the moment, magic mirrors [14]_____ (not find / often) in independent clothes shops, but they [15]_____ (introduce / quickly) in larger stores across the country.

6 SPEAKING In pairs, think of an appropriate way to finish each sentence. Then compare your ideas with the class.

1 Shopping could be made easier by ... (+ *-ing* form)
2 If all shopping was done online, ...
3 Apart from clothes shopping, a magic mirror could be used for ...

5C CULTURE Designer babies

I can recognise and talk about different points of view.

1 In pairs, complete the definition using the words below.

embryo   engineering   fertilisation   genes   implanted

Designer baby: A baby born after IVF (in vitro ¹_____)
whose ²_____ were chosen or altered by genetic ³_____
before the ⁴_____ was ⁵_____ , so that the parents could
choose the baby's sex, hair colour, etc.

Some people see designer babies as a step forward in
technological development. However, many people see it as
a negative step for technology.

2 🎧 2.10 **Listen to five people talking about designer babies.
Is each speaker generally for or against them? Write F (for) or
A (against).**

Speaker	1	2	3	4	5

3 **VOCABULARY** Complete the sentences with six of the words
below. Translate the other four words.

Science   advance (n, v)   diagnosis   DNA
experiment (n, v)   injection   laboratory   laser
patent (n, v)   procedure   side effects   technicians
test tube

1 I don't think a technological _____ is the same as
  progress.
2 The rich will pay _____ to genetically improve their
  babies.
3 I think all babies will be created in a _____ one day.
4 We shouldn't _____ with human embryos.
5 We could accidentally change human _____ forever.
6 I think it's just a medical _____ , like any other.

4 🎧 2.10 **Listen again. Check your answers to exercise 3.**

5 **SPEAKING** Work in pairs. Find out whether your partner
agrees or disagrees with the sentences in exercise 3.

> Do you agree that we shouldn't ... ?

6 🎧 2.11 **USE OF ENGLISH** Choose the correct words (a, b, c
or d) to complete the text then listen and check. Does the text
contain mostly fact or opinion?

1	a make	b ensure	c certify	d convince
2	a keep	b allow	c go on	d continue
3	a warn	b risk	c threaten	d endanger
4	a regard	b think	c imagine	d look
5	a in	b by	c for	d up
6	a already	b just	c yet	d ever
7	a just	b so	c as	d exactly
8	a Better	b Rather	c Sooner	d Instead

We now have the ability to ¹_____ that children are
born free of any one of hundreds of serious genetic
disorders, from cystic fibrosis to early-onset cancers.
But children ²_____ to be born with these diseases.
All would-be parents should be offered screening
to alert them to any genetic disorders they ³_____
passing on to their children. Those at risk should then
be offered IVF with tests to ensure embryos are healthy
before they are implanted. Why isn't it happening?
Because most people still ⁴_____ attempts to
influence which genes our children inherit as taboo.
But fears of 'designer babies' are misplaced. You
cannot select for traits the parents don't have, and the
scope for choosing specific traits is very limited. But
you can make sure children do not end ⁵_____ with
disastrous genetic disorders.
Nearly 150 years after Darwin unveiled his theory* of
evolution, we have ⁶_____ to grasp one of its most
unsettling implications: having diseased children is
⁷_____ natural as having healthy ones. Thanks to
technology, we are no longer entirely at the mercy
of this callous process. ⁸_____ than regarding this
ability with suspicion, we should be celebrating it and
encouraging its use. But instead, we continue to allow
children to be born with terrible diseases because of
our collective ignorance and superstition.

*an opinion or idea that somebody believes is true but that is
not proved

7 Which sentence best sums up the text in exercise 6?

a We shouldn't select traits for babies even though we
  have the technology to do so.
b We should use all the technology we have in order to
  prevent diseases in babies.
c We shouldn't use technology unless we know that a child
  has a serious genetic disorder.

8 **SPEAKING** In pairs, discuss the opinions in exercise 7. Do you
agree or disagree? Give reasons.

5D | READING Jailbreakers

I can talk about jailbreaking and cybercrime.

1 SPEAKING Read the definition below. What would it mean if you said a computer hacker was a 'poacher turned gamekeeper'?

poacher turned gamekeeper (*idiom*) Somebody who uses the skills they learned in an illegal activity to get a legitimate job helping to prevent that activity. For example, a former bank robber who gives advice to banks about security.

2 Read the text, ignoring the gaps. Find and underline:

a a definition of the term *jailbreaker*.
b the online names of two jailbreakers.
c the names of two unauthorised apps.
d three hi-tech companies.

EXAM TIP

When you do a gapped sentences task, check your answers by reading each relevant part of the text with the missing sentence in place. Does it flow? Does it make sense logically and grammatically? Double-check by trying the extra sentences in each gap. They should not fit any of the gaps well.

3 🎧 2.12 Read the Exam tip. Then match the gaps (1–6) in the text with the sentences below (A–H). There are two extra sentences.

A That is easily enough to cover his computer science education so far at the University of Georgia.
B He mowed people's lawns near his home in Peachtree City, Georgia, to earn money to buy the parts for a computer he was building.
C Apple was apparently so impressed with his jailbreaking skills that it persuaded him to join the company instead.
D Without those, it was impossible to develop software for any of these devices.
E His introduction into the world of jailbreaking was accidental.
F However, many other former hackers have taken up positions with software companies.
G That's something you can't do if you are an official developer.
H It was unusual enough that he wrote about it on his blog.

WHO ARE THE JAILBREAKERS?

Computer hackers rarely show their faces in public, allowing the stereotype of the socially awkward loner sitting in the dark in front of a computer screen to flourish. But the reality is rather different – at least when it comes to jailbreaking. Jailbreakers do not commit criminal acts like hacking into government computer systems or writing malicious viruses. Instead, they write code which removes the manufacturers' restrictions on everyday devices like smartphones and games consoles. A 'jailbroken' device can run unofficial software and be used in ways which the manufacturer did not intend. Some of the big technology companies have taken legal action against jailbreakers but with little success.

James Whelton, a smooth-talking twenty-year-old from Cork, started messing around with computers at the age of nine, and began programming soon afterwards. ¹☐ It happened when he won a pink iPod Nano. 'Basically I was on a plane and I was bored, so I just started tinkering with it and found something interesting,' he explained.

He discovered a vulnerability in the iPod's software that could possibly be exploited to jailbreak the device. ²☐ Within a few days he was contacted by another hacker known as DarkMalloc – in reality a sixteen year old from Wales called Joshua Tucker. He introduced Whelton to other hackers – big names in the hacking scene like chronic and ih8sn0w. Chronic – a teenager from the United States called Will Strafach – is the founder of a jailbreaking team called Chronic Dev, while ih8sn0w, a sixteen-year-old called Steven from Canada, is the developer of several well-known jailbreaking tools.

Instead of taking up a place at university earlier this month, Whelton decided to use the exposure that his jailbreaking activities have earned him to help get investors for a software company called Disruptive Developments that he founded in June. 'I did my final exams on a Friday, and became a chief executive on the Monday.'

Aaron Ash is another hacker-turned-entrepreneur. When Mr Ash was fourteen he got his hands on a calculator which he

programmed to do his homework. ³☐ After teaching himself to program it, he worked on video games before getting an Apple iPhone and turning his attention to that.

The young Mr Ash wanted to write apps for his phone, but it turned out that at seventeen he was too young to sign up to Apple's official iPhone development program. That left him with no alternative but to become a hacker and write apps for jailbroken phones. 'This was actually even cooler to my mind, because it let me write programs that change the way the iPhone works,' he said. '⁴☐'

Mr Ash started selling his programs, called Barrel and Multiflow, but at this point he came face to face with the darker side of the jailbreaking scene. 'My Barrel app is being used by three and half million people, but the proportion of people who actually paid for it is now about one in a hundred,' he said.

Despite the rampant piracy Ash has earned over $100,000 from his applications. ⁵☐ The problem he faces now is that he knows more than most of the teachers. 'I'm actually considering leaving uni and starting a software contracting company with a friend I met in the jailbreaking scene.'

'Going straight' at an early age certainly seems to be the pattern in the jailbreaking world, and the scene has lost several of its senior figures to the lure of business. George Hotz, the 22-year-old hacker known as Geohot who was responsible for programs that jailbreak Apple's devices as well as Sony's PS3, left the jailbreaking scene earlier this year to take up a full-time job with Facebook. And Nicholas Allegra – the nineteen-year-old jailbreaking guru better known in the hacking world as Comex – also found an alternative career. ⁶☐ It seems that the old notion of poacher turned gamekeeper still exists, even in our technology-oriented world.

4 Answer the questions.

1 Why are jailbreakers less likely to end up in prison than some other types of hackers?
2 How did jailbreaking help James Whelton to start a business?
3 Why did Aaron Ash start writing apps for jailbroken phones?
4 Why hasn't Aaron Ash earned millions of dollars from his highly successful apps?
5 Why is Aaron Ash thinking of leaving full-time education?
6 In what way has the jailbreaking scene 'lost' many of its senior figures?

5 **VOCABULARY** Complete the chart with words from the text.

verb	noun – the activity	noun – someone who does it
to ¹_____	hacking	a ²_____
to jailbreak	³_____	a ⁴_____
to pirate	⁵_____	a pirate

»» VOCABULARY BUILDER 5.2: PAGE 138 **«««**

6 Work in pairs. Read the descriptions of cybercrime and put them in order from the most to the least serious, in your opinion. Give reasons.

a stealing somebody's identity and using it to buy goods on eBay
b selling pirated copies of films and computer games from a market stall
c leaving racist comments on a Facebook page
d writing 'malware' – software designed to damage people's computers
e sharing all your music, films and TV shows online via an illegal site

7 Compare your ideas from exercise 6 with the class. Can you agree on one order between you?

8 In pairs, choose one of the topics below for a short presentation. Make notes.

a Cybercrime is just as serious as other forms of crime and should be punished.
b Cybercrime often has no victim and should not be compared with other forms of crime.

9 **SPEAKING** Present your ideas to the class.

Use of the passive

I can use the passive in the correct contexts.

1 SPEAKING How much do you know about the company Apple Inc, its co-founder Steve Jobs and its products? Discuss with your partner.

2 Read the facts below. Which column:

1 focuses mainly on the company Apple?
2 focuses mainly on Steve Jobs?
3 contains mainly passive verbs?
4 contains mainly active verbs?

A	B
Apple Computers was founded by Steve Jobs and Steve Wozniak.	Steve Jobs helped design the first Macintosh computer.
In the 1980s, the company was run by John Sculley.	Jobs left Apple in 1985 after a dispute with Sculley.
Sculley was sacked by Apple's directors in 1993 because market share was being lost.	Jobs bought a small computer graphics company and transformed it into Pixar, the company behind *Toy Story*.
The iMac was launched in 1998, after Jobs had been reappointed CEO, and it was an instant success.	Jobs earned only $1 a year as CEO of Apple, although he was already a multi-billionaire.
Will the company's reputation for creativity and innovation be maintained now that Jobs's personal input has been lost?	Millions first learned of Jobs's death in 2011 on a device which had been invented by Jobs himself.

LEARN THIS!

Active and passive voices

1 We use the passive when we want to describe an action but do not know who or what performed it.
Our car window had been smashed.
2 We sometimes choose to use the passive even when we do know who or what performed the action, because it allows us to change the focus of the sentence.
Jonathan Ives designed the iMac when he was 30 years old. (focus on Jonathan Ives)
The iMac was designed by Jonathan Ives and was available in six colours. (focus on the iMac)

3 Read the *Learn this!* box. Use the information to explain your answer to the questions in exercise 2.

⟩⟩⟩ GRAMMAR BUILDER 5.2: PAGE 124 ⟨⟨⟨

4 🎧 2.13 Rewrite the underlined parts of these sentences in the passive to make the focus more clearly on Google. Then listen and check.

1 Google is the world's best-known search engine and about 620 million people use it every day.
2 Google began as a research project, and Larry Page and Sergey Brin created it in 1996.
3 The first Google storage unit was 4GB – less than a modern phone – and they made it from LEGO bricks.
4 Today, more than 450,000 servers around the world store Google's information.
5 People have criticised Google for storing too much information about the public without their consent.
6 In a survey for *Business Excellence* magazine, British adults named Google as the company they would most like to work for.

LOOK OUT!

Verbs like *give, offer, send, award, show*, etc. often have two objects: a person and a thing. The person is usually the indirect object.
They offered Harry a job. (They offered a job to Harry.)
We usually make the indirect object (i.e. the person) into the subject of the passive.
A job was offered to Harry. ✗ *Harry was offered a job.*

5 Read the *Look out!* box. Underline the indirect object in these sentences. Then rewrite them in the passive.

1 My uncle gave me a phone for Christmas.
   I was given a phone for Christmas by my uncle.
2 Her grandfather left her some money in his will.
3 My cousins taught us to ski.
4 Somebody has sent me a really funny video clip.
5 The computer shop has lent my dad a laptop.
6 Somebody had told my neighbours about the party.

6 Make notes about:
• the funniest email you've ever been sent.
• the coolest app you've ever been shown.
• the first phone you were given.
• a gadget you were once lent.

7 SPEAKING Talk to your partner and find out the information in exercise 6. Use the questions below and your own ideas. Include passive forms where appropriate.

What was the ... you've ever been sent/shown?

When/Why were you sent/shown it?

How did you feel when you were given/lent it?

1 Work in pairs. Match the words below with one photo or both. How many more words can you add?

adjectives hi-tech modern precise sterile traditional

nouns components face masks factory instruments production line protection tools

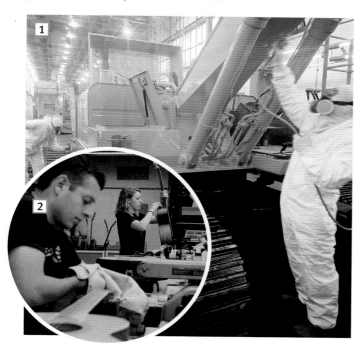

2 SPEAKING In pairs, discuss which of the factories in exercise 1 you would rather work in for a holiday job. Try to think of three different reasons.

3 🎧 2.14 Listen to a student doing the task below in relation to the photos in exercise 1. Does he choose the same factory as you? Are his reasons the same or different?

You're going to apply for a holiday job working in a factory. Which factory will you choose and why? Why are you rejecting the other option?

EXAM TIP

Make sure you say clearly which picture you are choosing and why you are rejecting the other option(s). Use the phrases below to help you:
So, I'd opt for the … , mainly because …
I think the … would be the better/best option because …
So my choice would be the … That's because …
I wouldn't choose the … because …
The reason I wouldn't go for the … is that …
I wouldn't pick the … simply because …

4 Read the Exam tip. Find three verbs which are synonyms for *choose*.

5 🎧 2.14 Listen again. Tick the phrases in the Exam tip which the student uses.

6 🎧 2.15 Listen to a different student doing the task in exercise 3. Which factory does she choose and what is her main reason for rejecting the other one?

7 🎧 2.15 Complete the phrases with the words below. Then listen again and tick the phrases the student uses.

chances imagine likely possible say seems though

Speculating about a photo
There ¹_____ to be …
It looks (to me) as ²_____ / as if …
It's quite ³_____ that …
I should ⁴_____ …
Judging by … , I'd ⁵_____ that …
⁶_____ are (that) …
More ⁷_____ than not …

8 Write five sentences speculating about the photos in exercise 1. Use five different phrases from exercise 7.

9 Work in pairs. Look at the photos and read the task. Choose a language school, then agree on two reasons for your choice and two reasons for rejecting the other one.

You're going to apply for a short course at a language school. Which course will you choose and why? Why are you rejecting the other option?

10 SPEAKING In pairs, take turns to do the task in exercise 9. Include your reasons. Make sure you include phrases from the Exam tip and exercise 7.

1 **SPEAKING** **Ask and answer these questions in pairs.**

1 Where would you use a satnav and what does it do?
2 How might it cause a problem?

2 **Read the task and the story below. Is the main idea in the story the same as your answer to question 2 in exercise 1?**

Write a story in which a piece of technology causes problems for the main character.

A WEEKEND IN THE COUNTRY

'I hate these narrow country roads,' said Zena, trying to make out the landscape in the darkness as her husband Alex drove.

Having worked hard all week, Zena and Alex were looking forward to their weekend away. It was a long drive for a Friday evening, but they would soon arrive at the holiday cottage. Mr Martin, the farmer who owned the cottage, was to meet them there with the key.

'After 50 metres, turn left,' ordered the satnav.

Zena frowned, looking out of the window. 'I'm sure we should go right,' she muttered.

But Alex didn't hear her. Turning the the wheel sharply to the left, he put his foot down. The car bumped loudly on a rock. There was a splash, and the car swerved before coming to a halt.

'I knew the satnav was wrong!' exclaimed Zena.

Alex tried to start the car but the engine was dead. What were they going to do? They couldn't even open the car door because the water would rush in. Zena took her phone out of her pocket and tried to call Mr Martin. There was no signal.

At that moment, there was a loud tap on the window. Zena screamed and dropped her phone. A smiling face appeared at the window.

'Mr and Mrs Henderson? I'm Mr Martin. I've been expecting you. Most visitors from London follow their satnav into the river!'

3 **In pairs, divide the story in exercise 2 into four sections.**

1 setting the scene (characters, background, etc.)
2 the first event: a problem arises
3 efforts to solve the problem
4 how the problem is finally resolved

LEARN THIS!

Future in the past
When we talk about the future from a point of view in the past we can use these verb forms:
*It was Monday. Dad ¹**was coming** home the next day. We were sure he ²**would be** happy with the changes we were making to the house. But ³**were we going to** finish them on time?*
These three verb forms are the past equivalents of (1) present continuous for future arrangements OR present simple for future scheduled events (2) *will* future (3) *going to* future.
In written English, we can also use the expression *was/were to …* to refer to future plans in the past:
*My aunt arrived early on Saturday morning. She **was to spend** the weekend with us.*

4 **Read the *Learn this!* box. How many examples of future in the past can you find in the story in exercise 2?**

▶▶▶ **GRAMMAR BUILDER 5.3: PAGE 124** ◀◀◀

EXAM TIP

There are several good ways to begin a story:
1 **Set the scene:** *It was a warm evening in August and I was on holiday in Thailand with my parents. The sun was going down and the insects were coming out.*
2 **Start with dialogue:** *'Wow! Look at this place!' said my dad as the taxi stopped outside the Grand Palace Hotel in Phuket, Thailand.*
3 **Start by looking back:** *I often think back to the first foreign holiday I went on with my parents and how it changed my relationship with them.*

5 **Read the Exam tip. Which type of beginning (1–3) does the story in exercise 2 contain? Write alternative beginnings for the same story using the other two types.**

6 **Rewrite the story opening below. Change it from dialogue to a paragraph setting the scene. Include some future in the past.**

'The summer holidays start soon!' exclaimed Anna. 'And Jacqui is coming to stay with us for two whole weeks!'
'I know. I'm really excited about that,' said Harry, who always enjoyed having their cousin Jacqui to stay. 'We'll go to the beach every day. We'll teach Jacqui to surf.'
'We'll have a great time,' agreed Anna.

For Anna and Harry, the summer holidays …

7 **SPEAKING** **In pairs, compare your answers to exercise 6 and check each other's work for mistakes. Can you take ideas from your partner's version to improve your own?**

WRITING TASK Story

I can write a story on a given topic.

1 **SPEAKING** You are going to do the writing task in exercise 2, page 56. In pairs, discuss how the items of technology in the photos could cause problems.

2 **SPEAKING** Discuss your ideas from exercise 1 with another pair. Add more details.

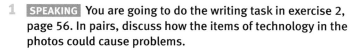

What might happen next?

How would you get out of that situation?

What would your dad/teacher/friend say?

How would X react when that happened?

3 Decide which idea from exercises 1 and 2 you are going to write about. Plan your story by making notes under the headings below.

1 Background: when/where the events happen:
  Main character(s):
2 Item of technology involved:
  What problem it causes and how:
3 What happens as a result:
4 How the story ends:

4 **SPEAKING** In pairs, look at each other's plans and ask three questions about them. Think of answers and add them to your plans.

EXAM TIP

Include a mix of direct speech and ordinary narrative in your stories. To make your writing more vivid, you can use a variety of speech verbs after direct speech: *mutter, shout, joke, sob, moan, insist, urge,* etc.

Direct speech needs inverted commas around the words spoken and a comma, question mark or exclamation mark before the closing inverted commas. Study the examples:

'By that time,' she joked, 'we'll all be dead!'
'Leave now!' she insisted, getting to her feet.

5 Read the Exam tip. How many different speech verbs are in the story on page 56?

6 Match each speech verb in A with a synonym in B.

A admit announce bellow caution complain emphasise promise mutter remark wonder

B acknowledge ask yourself assure comment declare grumble mumble scream stress warn

7 Rewrite these sentences with correct punctuation and an appropriate speech verb in the past simple.

1 You must tell her he _____ before it's too late.
2 What is he doing here she _____, spinning around.
3 Look out Gloria he _____. It's heading straight for us.
4 The worst thing she _____ is not knowing.
5 I hate this film he ___. It's worse than you said it was.

8 Decide how to begin your story. Look back at the three types of beginning in the tip on page 56. Write the opening lines.

9 Write the rest of your story. Follow the plan you made in exercises 3 and 4. Write 200–250 words in total.

CHECK YOUR WORK

Have you:
- [ ] given your story a clear structure and a good opening?
- [ ] written 200–250 words?
- [ ] used a mixture of direct speech and narrative?
- [ ] used a variety of speech verbs?
- [ ] given your story a title?
- [ ] included at least one participle clause?
- [ ] checked your spelling and grammar?

Listening

1 **Get ready to LISTEN** Work in pairs. Match the two halves of the compound nouns.

1	scientific	a	creatures
2	sea	b	sledge
3	marine	c	station
4	research	d	change
5	ice	e	research
6	dog	f	cap
7	climate	g	biology

2 Do the exam task.

LISTENING exam task

🎧 2.16 **Listen to an interview with a scientist. For each sentence, select the correct ending: A, B, C or D.**

1 At the beginning of the programme, the radio presenter says that
  A Elaine comes from a family of scientists.
  B Antarctica is appealing to scientists because it's untouched by civilisation.
  C it's difficult to explore Antarctica because it's so vast.
  D many scientific discoveries have taken place in Antarctica in the last 70 years.

2 At a young age, Dr Glover
  A dreamed of studying insects at university.
  B was never interested in social sciences.
  C collected sea creatures because she lived by the sea.
  D paid little attention to making friends with other kids.

3 Dr Glover says that scientists working in Antarctica have to learn
  A how to use appropriate forms of transport.
  B how to relax when not at work.
  C not to get distracted.
  D to think of the research station as their home.

4 When asked about the future, Dr Glover says that
  A her group needs new maps of the area they're interested in.
  B the ice in Antarctica may sometimes prove too thick to drill for data.
  C more pictures of the whole area are needed for further studies.
  D the studies will involve cooperation with specialists from other fields.

Use of English

3 Do the exam task.

USE OF ENGLISH exam task

Complete the text with an appropriate word in each gap.

In ten years' time, robots will be used in every home, according [1]_____ technology experts and manufacturers. At the Consumer Electronics Show in Las Vegas, all [2]_____ of domestic robots were unveiled. [3]_____ them were robots which are linked into the home's broadband service and which act [4]_____ home organisers. These are capable [5]_____ responding to the family's voice commands in the house and at the [6]_____ time can be operated by mobile phones outside the house. In the future, robots [7]_____ these will be responsible for operating the household's domestic appliances, [8]_____ as washing machines, alarm clocks, heating, lighting, music players and TV sets. [9]_____ effect, they will act as household managers and will even be able to activate smaller cleaning and vacuuming robots. [10]_____ of these types – the managing robot and the cleaning robot – will be able to provide security surveillance. As they travel round the house, an on-board camera will send pictures to your office laptop.

Speaking

4 **Get ready to SPEAK** Work in pairs. Think of three jobs that could be done by a robot and three that could not. Discuss your ideas with the class.

5 Do the exam task.

SPEAKING exam task

Discuss how new kinds of robots might affect everyday life in the future. Talk about:

- robots in the workplace
- robots at home
- robots in leisure and entertainment
- possible dangers of super-intelligent robots

THIS UNIT INCLUDES
Vocabulary ▪ describing food ▪ food and nutrition ▪ food idioms
▪ word formation
Grammar ▪ passive: advanced structures ▪ articles and quantifiers
Speaking ▪ stimulus description
Writing ▪ description of a place

A matter of taste 6

6A VOCABULARY AND LISTENING Describing food
I can describe the taste and texture of food.

1 **SPEAKING** Work in pairs. Discuss this question: *If you could choose any meal in a restaurant, what would it be?* Think of starters, main courses and desserts.

2 **VOCABULARY** Divide the words below into two groups: those that describe taste and those that describe texture.

<u>Describing food</u> bitter bland chewy creamy crispy crunchy crumbly disgusting dry fresh fruity greasy juicy mild mouth-watering peppery raw rich ripe runny salty smoky smooth sour spicy stale sticky stodgy strong sugary sweet tasteless tasty tender tough unpleasant unripe

3 Which adjectives have a negative connotation for you? How many opposites or near opposites can you find?

4 Complete the adjectives in these sentences. Then translate them.
1 Ripe pears are very j_____ .
2 I don't like much milk on my breakfast cereal. I prefer it c_____ .
3 Strong coffee without sugar tastes quite b_____ .
4 These crisps are really s_____ . They make me thirsty.
5 Lean over the plate when you're eating your biscuits. They're rather c_____ .
6 This steak is fantastic. It's really t_____ .
7 This peach is u_____ . It's hard and s_____ .

5 Describe the foods in the photos. Use the adjectives in exercise 2 to help you.

1 take-away lamb curry

2 salad

3 toffee pudding with ice-cream

6 🎧 2.17 Listen to customers complaining in a restaurant. Write the name of the food or dish they are talking about and the adjectives used to describe it.

7 🎧 2.18 Listen to three teenagers talking about food they like and don't like. Write the correct initial: *J* (Jenny), *E* (Ed) or *R* (Rosie).
1 Who completely changed his/her mind about a certain food later in life?
2 Who changed his/her mind about a certain food when he/she tried it in another place?
3 Whose parents made him/her eat something he/she didn't like?
4 Who helped someone else deal with something he/she didn't like eating?
5 Whose parents stopped buying the food he/she really loved?
6 Whose parents used to love the food that he/she couldn't stand?

8 🎧 2.19 Complete the sentences with the verbs below. Then listen and check.

adored bear detested found got had loathed
mind stand

1 I really couldn't _____ the texture.
2 I _____ the smell of it unpleasant, never _____ the taste.
3 I've _____ to like a few types of cheese now.
4 I _____ cauliflower – yuck! – and my brother absolutely _____ Brussels sprouts.
5 He couldn't even _____ the smell of them.
6 As a kid I _____ a passion for baked beans.
7 I _____ the smooth texture of the beans.

9 **SPEAKING** Work in pairs. Tell your partner about two or three foods that you (a) hate or used to hate, (b) love or used to love. Try to give reasons for your answers. Use the sentences in exercise 8 to help you.

▶▶▶ **VOCABULARY BUILDER 6.1: PAGE 139** ◀◀◀

1 🎧 2.20 **Do the food quiz. Then listen and check your answers.**

FOOD QUIZ 🍴

1 It is believed that ice cream was invented in **a** China in about 650 **b** Italy in about 1500 **c** the USA in about 1850.

2 Wheat is first thought to have been cultivated in Turkey in about **a** 1000 BC **b** 4000 BC **c** 9000 BC.

3 The potato is known to have originated in **a** North America **b** South America **c** Africa.

4 **a** Saffron **b** Vanilla **c** Cardamom is considered to be the most expensive spice in the world.

5 Until the 19th century, **a** oranges **b** apples **c** tomatoes were thought by many people to be poisonous.

6 In the 17th century it was thought that bathing in **a** milk **b** sea water **c** wine would cure most ills.

7 There are known to be over 7,500 types of **a** apple **b** banana **c** strawberry.

2 Read the *Learn this!* box. Find examples of each passive structure in the quiz.

> **LEARN THIS!**
>
> **Passive with *know, believe* etc.**
> With verbs like *know, believe, think,* etc., we often use:
> **1** *it* + passive (present or past) + *that …*
> *It is known that too much junk food is bad for you.*
> *It used to be thought that eating honey cured hay fever.*
> **2** *there* + passive (present or past) + *to be/to have been*
> *There are thought to be about 5,200 varieties of potato.*
> **3** subject + passive (present or past) + *to do/to have done something*
> *Until about 1850, bleeding was believed to cure fevers.*
> If we are expressing a present belief about a past event, we use the present simple passive followed by a perfect infinitive (*to have done something*):
> *The Mayans in Central America are thought to have used tobacco.*

3 **Change the examples in the quiz using alternative passive structures from the *Learn this!* box.**

1 Ice cream is believed to have been …

4 USE OF ENGLISH **Complete the second sentence so that it means the same as the first. Start with the words in brackets.**

1 For centuries it was thought that mercury wasn't poisonous. (*For centuries mercury wasn't …*)

2 It is known that the universe is about 13.7 billion years old. (*The universe is …*)

3 It is thought that there are fewer than 500 Siberian tigers living in the wild. (*There are …*)

4 In 16th century England taking a bath was considered to be unhealthy. (*In 16th century England it was …*)

5 The Chinese are thought to have invented tea. (*It is …*)

> **LEARN THIS!**
>
> **Passive modals, gerunds and infinitives**
> **1** We can use passive structures with modal verbs.
> *The sauce should be stirred continuously.*
> **2** Verbs that are followed by an infinitive or gerund can also be followed by a passive infinitive or gerund:
> *My dad hopes to be promoted.* (*hope* + infinitive)
> *I hate being photographed.* (*hate* + *-ing*)

5 **Read the *Learn this!* box. Complete the sentences with the correct passive form. Use the verb in brackets.**

1 If you continue to behave badly at school you'll end up _____ (expel).

2 Everybody wants _____ (love)!

3 The grammar reference for this lesson can _____ (find) on pages 124–5.

4 Put on this cream to avoid _____ (bite) by mosquitos.

5 Tables must _____ (book) in advance.

6 I hope _____ (choose) for the school football team.

7 These books should _____ (handle) with care.

8 Can you imagine _____ (tell) you'd won the lottery?

6 **Work in pairs. Decide if the verbs below take a gerund, an infinitive or both. Then add them to the correct group.**

agree   expect   imagine   remember   can't stand

verb + gerund avoid, be used to, can't face, don't mind, end up, [1]_____ , [2]_____

verb + infinitive arrange, hope, refuse, want, [3]_____ , [4]_____

verb + gerund or infinitive continue, prefer, [5]_____

7 SPEAKING **Work in pairs. Make as many different sentences as you can using verbs from exercise 6 followed by passive gerund or passive infinitive forms of verbs below.**

arrest   call   criticise   film   give   ignore   invite
involve   keep waiting   laugh at   photograph   rob
tease   tell   treat   watch

Most people can't stand being ignored.

⟫⟫ GRAMMAR BUILDER 6.1: PAGE 124 ⟪⟪

1 **SPEAKING** Work in pairs. Look at the photo and title. Discuss what information you might expect to find in the text.

2 🎧 2.21 **USE OF ENGLISH** Complete the text with words formed from the words in brackets.

3 Explain what information is linked to these numbers from the text. Were any pieces of information in your list above?

a 30   c 34   e 147 billion
b 75   d 28

4 Answer the questions.
1 How do people put on weight?
2 How has the American diet changed?
3 What things can prevent people in the US from getting enough exercise?
4 Why is the Government trying to improve the situation?
5 What has caused the obesity epidemic to stabilise in the last decade?

5 🎧 2.22 Listen to three young people talking about whether the Government should be doing more to promote a healthy lifestyle. Which person do you most agree with?

6 🎧 2.22 Listen again. Match the opinions with the speakers: *A* (Anna), *J* (Jonathan) and *K* (Kyle). You can match more than one speaker to each opinion.
1 The Government has a role to play in people's health.
2 Taxing cigarettes has no effect on stopping smoking.
3 It's pointless for the Government to tell people what to do.
4 The Government should take a harder line with food manufacturers.
5 An early education in healthy living is the answer.
6 Healthy food is an important issue.

>>> VOCABULARY BUILDER 6.2: PAGE 139 <<<

7 **SPEAKING** Work in pairs or small groups. Discuss these points in detail and make notes.
1 Do you think your town/country has a problem with an increasingly unhealthy lifestyle?
2 Do you agree or disagree with the opinions in exercise 6? Give reasons.
3 Decide on three initiatives that your government could implement to tackle the problem.

8 **SPEAKING** Present the results of your discussion to the class. Speak for a maximum of two minutes.

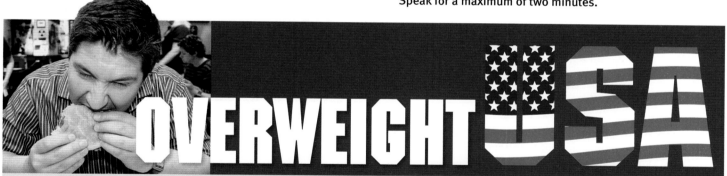

OVERWEIGHT USA

It is common ¹_____ (know) that obesity figures in the USA have risen ²_____ (drama) over the last 30 years. 75% of American adults are now overweight, with 34% classed as obese, meaning they are dangerously overweight. But why is this epidemic occurring?

Weight gain occurs through a straightforward energy imbalance. If you don't use up in energy all the calories that you have consumed, then your body stores the rest in your fat cells. There are several factors in the USA that have contributed to this imbalance.

Firstly, people eat differently now. Too much sugar in the diet makes it harder for the body to burn fat. Snack foods high in sugar, fat and salt are widely ³_____ (advert) and heavily marketed in the USA. Vending machines selling these snacks are found in schools across the country, and calorific 'fast food' is cheap and ⁴_____ (easy) available. Furthermore, portion sizes are famed for being generous. It is therefore easy to eat too much of the wrong food in the USA.

Changes in the way of life have also contributed greatly. Many ⁵_____ (commune) are built in ways that make it difficult to be physically active. Americans can drive everywhere, but find it harder to do anything else, as safe routes for walking or cycling can be non-existent. A sedentary lifestyle has developed at home with the average young American child ⁶_____ (watch) up to 28 hours of TV a week.

In the USA, obesity is therefore considered to be a ⁷_____ (nation) epidemic, with serious consequences for both individual health and medical expenditure. The medical care costs of obesity are staggering – around $147 billion – so the US government has been trying to combat the problem.

The obesity trend does appear to be slowing down owing to government initiatives and greater public ⁸_____ (aware). Over the last ten years obesity levels seem to have levelled off. But Donna Ryan, president of the Obesity Society, says, '… to level off at 34% obesity is no great ⁹_____ (achieve). It's still very, very ¹⁰_____ (alarm).'

1 SPEAKING Work in pairs. Look at the photos of the three drinks: tea, coffee and Coca-Cola. Discuss these questions and make notes.

  1 Where did each drink originate?
  2 What facts do you know about the three drinks?

2 🎧 2.23 Quickly read the three texts. Were you right about where the drinks came from? Were any of your ideas from exercise 1 in the texts? If so, tell the class.

3 Read the texts and choose the correct statement.

  1 All three drinks became popular partly as an alternative to alcohol.
  2 All three drinks became popular through clever advertising.
  3 All three drinks became popular because of royal connections.

EXAM TIP

With a multiple-matching task, read the whole text once and then read the questions. Match any questions that are immediately obvious, and underline the relevant parts of the text. Then carefully read each section of the text again and look for the answers to the remaining questions.

4 Read the Exam tip. For questions 1–9, choose the correct drink.

coffee Coca-Cola tea

Which drink:

  1 doesn't have a legend attached to it?
  2 wasn't immediately popular in Britain?
  3 led to the establishment of special places where it was drunk?
  4 was used by a government as a means of raising money?
  5 wasn't endorsed by someone high up in society?
  6 is the second most popular drink in the world?
  7 was at first unpopular with religious authorities?
  8 is the world's second most important commodity?
  9 became popular following a big advertising campaign?

5 VOCABULARY Write nouns formed from these verbs. The nouns are all in the texts.

  1 discover   5 prohibit   9 operate
  2 know   6 consume   10 argue
  3 approve   7 succeed   11 endorse
  4 converse   8 advertise 12 invent

  ⟫⟫⟫ VOCABULARY BUILDER 6.3: PAGE 139 ⟪⟪⟪

6 SPEAKING Work in pairs. Answer the questions, giving reasons where appropriate.

  1 Which of the three drinks do you like most/least? Put them in order, and explain your reasons to your partner. Now put them in order of unhealthiest first and compare them again.
  2 What do you like to drink, and when?
    What is the healthiest drink you have?
    Is there any drink you think you have too much of?
  3 How much water should we drink and why?
    Do you drink enough water?
  4 If there were one drink you could ban in the world, what would it be? Why?

Drink up!

Coffee

Coffee was first discovered in Ethiopia several centuries ago. There is a legend surrounding its discovery, and there is probably some truth to the tale. It is said that a goat-herd called Kaldi noticed that his goats became very excitable after eating the berries from one particular bush. Kaldi reported this discovery to the Abbot of the local monastery, who made a drink from the berries and found it kept him awake through the long hours of evening prayer. This knowledge of the energising effects of these berries began to spread east towards the Arab world.

The Arabs were the first people to cultivate coffee and also to trade it. Coffee quickly became popular with Muslims who were forbidden by their religion to drink alcohol. By the 16th century, coffee had spread to Persia, Egypt and Turkey. All over

the Middle East, new public coffee houses sprang up as places of social activity.

By the 17th century, coffee had finally found its way into Europe, where religious leaders initially condemned it as the devil's drink. However, the Pope at that time decided to taste the new beverage himself, and liked it so much that he gave it papal approval. By the mid-17th century there were coffee houses in all the major cities of Europe. In London alone there were 300. People gathered in them to engage in stimulating conversation over a cup of the hot, dark, revitalising drink. Coffee has established itself as one of the most valuable crops in the world, and is the world's second biggest commodity, after oil.

Coca-Cola

The world's most popular fizzy drink was invented in Georgia, USA in 1886 as a health drink. Dr John Pemberton, a pharmacist, mixed the secret formula in a big kettle in his backyard. He was prompted by a new prohibition law, which forbade the sale and consumption of alcohol. Pemberton's previous health drink had contained wine, so he came up with a new recipe. His bookkeeper, Frank Robinson, gave the refreshing new drink its name because, until 1905, it contained extracts of cocaine as well as the caffeine-rich cola nut. Mr Robinson also wrote beautifully, and it is his original lettering that we can still see on Coke cans today.

In 1887, businessman Asa Candler bought the formula from Pemberton and very quickly turned it into one of America's most popular soft drinks. At that time people went to ice cream parlours to have a drink. These were often attached to pharmacies and were a popular meeting place. Coke was sold as a health drink, and its success was due not only to its new taste but also to vigorous advertising. Candler bought full-page advertisements with the 'Coca-Cola girls' inviting you to 'pause and refresh'. In 1931, even Father Christmas was used to sell the product, and the resulting picture of a round, jolly, white-bearded man dressed in red has become the iconic image of Father Christmas.

Nowadays, Coca-Cola is one of the most recognised products in the world with more than one billion drinks sold every day.

Tea

The story of tea begins in China in 2737bc. According to legend, the emperor Shen Nung was sitting under some trees while his servant boiled water to drink. Some leaves from the Camellia sinensis tree blew into the water, and the emperor tried the resulting beverage. True or not, tea certainly originated in China many, many centuries ago.

It wasn't until the 16th century that tea arrived in Europe, brought by the Portuguese and Dutch. The British were slow to take to the new drink, but that changed in 1662 when King Charles II married a Portuguese princess, Catherine of Braganca, who was a lover of tea. She made the drink fashionable among the wealthy. Tea was quickly introduced into the cities' coffee houses and British drinking habits were altered forever. The country began to import tea for itself and later started growing it in India.

In the 17th and 18th centuries, the British Government used the popularity of tea to generate revenue and taxed it so highly that a huge smuggling operation sprang up. Soon, more tea was being smuggled into Britain than imported legally, so in 1784 the Government finally abolished high tea taxes.

At the same time there was a great debate about whether tea was good for your health. This argument was finally brought to an end when religious groups decided that tea was much better for people than alcohol. With lower prices and a health endorsement, there was now nothing to stop everybody from drinking tea.

Meanwhile, Britain had introduced tea to America and in the 19th century America introduced the rest of the world to its latest invention – the teabag. This invention has helped tea to become an important commodity in world trade, and the world's second most widely consumed drink, after water.

1 Describe the photo below.

2 🎧 2.24 **SPEAKING** Choose the correct articles to complete the text. Then listen and check.

FOOD FIGHT!

¹**The** / – Food is central to most festivals in ²**the** / – Spain. But it isn't always for eating! Once ³**a** / **the** year in ⁴**a** / **the** small town of La Pobla del Duc, about 100 kilometres from Valencia, up to 90 tonnes of grapes are brought in by lorry from ⁵**the** / – surrounding countryside and dumped in ⁶**the** / – corner of the market square. What happens next is ⁷**a** / **the** massive food-fight as the inhabitants of the town hurl grapes at each other. ⁸**A** / **The** fight, which marks the end of the grape harvest and of summer, can last all day!

3 Complete these rules with *a/an*, *the* or no article (–), and match each answer in exercise 2 with a rule. Check all the rules in the Grammar Builder on page 125.

  a We often use _____ when we mention something for the first time, but _____ when we mention it again.

  b We use _____ when there is only one of something.

  c We use _____ for continents and most countries.

  d We use _____ when we talk about something in general.

  e We sometimes use _____ to mean *per; for each*.

  f We use _____ with some general expressions that refer to the physical environment.

  g We sometimes use _____ when we refer to one of several similar things or people and we don't need to be more definite.

  ⟫⟫ **GRAMMAR BUILDER 6.2: PAGE 125** ⟪⟪

4 Look at the use of articles with other nouns in the text in exercise 2. How many other rules can you identify?

'by lorry' – We don't use an article with 'by' when we are talking about means of transport.

LEARN THIS!

Quantifiers
Examples of quantifiers are: *all, both, many, each, every, several, some, few, no, a lot, a little,* etc.
Most quantifiers can be followed by *of*:
Most of the peaches are ripe. A few of them are unripe.
However, *no* and *every* cannot be followed by *of*; instead, we say *none of* and *every one of*:
I've rung all my friends but none of them are at home.

LOOK OUT!

We use *few/little* instead of *a few/a little* to emphasise the smallness of the number or quantity. Compare:
There are a few good restaurants in town. Let's eat out.
There are few good restaurants in town. Let's eat at home.

5 **USE OF ENGLISH** Read the *Learn this!* and *Look out!* boxes. Then choose the correct words to complete the sentences.

  1 She was so hungry that she ate **each** / **whole** / **most** of the cake within **a few** / **a little** / **some** minutes.

  2 'There's **no** / **any** / **none** use-by date on this yoghurt.' 'Put it back and choose **other** / **another** / **any** one, then.'

  3 I take my tea with **a little** / **much** / **a few** milk.

  4 'Are you **both** / **each** / **either** going to town?' 'No, **both** / **either** / **neither** of us is.'

  5 He finished off **all** / **each** / **whole** of the chips himself! There were **any** / **no** / **none** left for me!

  ⟫⟫ **GRAMMAR BUILDER 6.3: PAGE 125** ⟪⟪

6 Number the expressions of quantity from 1–9: 1 = the least, 9 = the most.

  a a few of / a little of … ☐   **f** none of … ☐
  b all of … ☐   **g** nearly all of … ☐
  c hardly any of … ☐   **h** some of … ☐
  d many (of) … ☐   **i** very few / little of … ☐
  e most of … ☐

7 **SPEAKING** Work in pairs. Find out this information about your partner. Use expressions from exercise 6 in your answers.

  1 how many of his/her friends are on Facebook

  2 how many of his/her friends live within about one kilometre of him/her

  3 how many of his/her classmates he/she sees at weekends

  4 how much of his/her money he/she spends on snacks and drinks

  5 how many of his/her friends he/she would trust with an important secret

  6 how much of his/her time in the evening is spent using a computer

  7 how many of his/her friends share the same taste in music

> How many of your friends are on Facebook?

> Most of them are.

1 SPEAKING Work in pairs. Ask and answer.
1 How often do you eat out?
2 How often do you get a take-away or a home delivery?

2 🎧 2.25 Read the exam task below. Then listen to two students doing the exam task. Which options do they choose and why?

Your cousin, who is the same age as you, is coming to spend the weekend at your house. What kind of meal will you have with him/her on Saturday evening? Choose one of the options in the photos. Justify your choice and say why you rejected the other suggestions.

3 Take turns to do the exam task in exercise 2. Use the phrases below to help you.

So, I'd opt for the ... , mainly because ...
I think the ... would be the better/best option because ...
So my choice would be the ... . That's because ...
I wouldn't choose the ... because ...
The reason I wouldn't go for the ... is that ...
I wouldn't pick the ... simply because ...

4 Complete the useful phrases with the words below.

argued arguing clear feel hand having mind of
opinions sure then time view

Expressing a firm opinion
To my ¹_____ ...
In my ²_____ ...
I'm ³_____ the opinion that ...
I ⁴_____ fairly strongly that ...
It seems ⁵_____ to me that ...

Expressing a tentative opinion
I don't have any strong ⁶_____ about ...
I'm not ⁷_____, really.
It could be ⁸_____ that ...
There might be a case for ⁹_____ that ...

Introducing a counter-argument
On the other ¹⁰_____ , ...
But ¹¹_____ again, ...
¹²_____ said that, ...
At the same ¹³_____ , ...

5 🎧 2.26 Read the Exam tip below. Listen to a candidate answering the examiner's questions. Tick the phrases in exercise 4 that she uses.

EXAM TIP

It's important that you do not give single-sentence answers to the examiner's questions. You should develop your ideas with examples, supporting statements and, if you like, counter-arguments.

6 Do you agree with the candidate? Use phrases from exercise 4 in your answer.

7 SPEAKING Work in pairs. Ask and answer the questions below. Use phrases from exercise 4.
1 Do you think a vegetarian diet is healthier than a diet that includes meat?
2 Do you think that men should do more cooking at home?

8 SPEAKING Work in pairs. Turn to page 144. Do the exam task.

I can write a description of a place.

1 **SPEAKING** Would you like to eat in either of the restaurants in the photos? Give reasons.

2 Read the Exam tip. Then look at the task below and underline the verbs.

EXAM TIP

It's very important to read the exam question very carefully two or three times so that you fully understand the task. It's a good idea to underline the verbs that tell you what you have to do, e.g. *describe a teacher, recommend a film, present advantages and disadvantages, justify your opinion*, etc.

Describe a restaurant which, because of its location, atmosphere and value for money, you would recommend as an ideal place for teenagers to meet and eat.

3 What are the key elements that must be included in the description in exercise 2? Hint: look at the nouns in the instructions.

4 Read the model text below. Put these things in the order that they are described. Which thing is not described?

atmosphere ☐	clientele ☐	decor ☐	food ☐
furniture ☐	location ☐	music ☐	staff ☐
value for money ☐			

5 Which of these plans has the writer followed? Discuss the merits of all four plans. (They are all acceptable.)

1 She described things as you would encounter them if you visited the restaurant for a meal (location, first impressions, decor, etc.).

2 She described what she particularly liked about the restaurant followed by any minor complaints or reservations.

3 She described different aspects of the restaurant, one after the other, with the most important **first**.

4 She described different aspects of the restaurant, one after the other, with the most important **last**.

Description of a restaurant – by Becky

There's a new place in town trying a slightly different approach to serving food, and that's the latest restaurant in Fore Street, conveniently situated for both the town centre and the university. The great thing is that it's very reasonable compared with other restaurants in town that serve similar food. You can get two courses and a drink for under £20. When I went in I was immediately struck by the decor: it's modern, with lots of wood, glass and steel, and it feels bright and trendy. The atmosphere is very lively – there are lots and lots of young people and always plenty of funky background music. The staff struck me as young, friendly and welcoming, and look stylish in their specially-designed T-shirts.

But what I found most appealing is the way they serve the food. It isn't ordered from the waiters; you get it yourself! It's styled like an upmarket cafeteria. The cold section has a wide variety of delicious salads, freshly made and quickly replenished. The middle section offers a varied selection of hot dishes: several meat dishes, one or two spicy fish dishes, and vegetarian options. Finally, they have a mouth-watering selection of cakes and desserts, which are to die for! The sticky toffee pudding was out of this world, and the pear tart had a wonderful crumbly pastry made with almonds, which was truly amazing!

So, I recommend you check this restaurant out next time you're in town, even just for coffee and cake!

1 Use the words below to complete the chart.

attentive central conveniently located lively
mouth-watering old-fashioned pricey reasonable
relaxing trendy varied welcoming

Describing restaurants			
location			
off the beaten track		in a lively/quiet area	
in the Old Town	¹_____	²_____	
value for money			
cheap	expensive	³_____	⁴_____
decor			
bright	dark	traditional	
cheerful	minimalist	⁵_____	
colourful	modern	⁶_____	
atmosphere			
exciting	subdued	noisy	⁷_____
formal/informal	quiet	romantic	⁸_____
staff			
friendly	informal	⁹_____	¹⁰_____
food			
basic	delicious	¹¹_____	¹²_____

2 Find 10 of the words in the chart in exercise 1 in the model text on page 66.

3 Describe the atmosphere and decor of the restaurants in the photos on page 66 using words from the chart in exercise 1.

EXAM TIP

When describing nouns, try to avoid uninteresting or boring adjectives. Think about the particular characteristic you are trying to describe and think of interesting synonyms, e.g.:
big – sizeable, extensive, large, broad.
nice – pleasant, enjoyable, friendly, sympathetic, pretty, attractive, delicious.

---

4 Read the Exam tip. Then replace the underlined adjectives in the text below with more interesting alternatives. There are many possible answers. Use a dictionary to help you.

The restaurant is in a <u>lovely</u> square near the river. It has two <u>nice</u> dining areas, one downstairs and one on the first floor, from where there are <u>great</u> views of the city. It has a <u>good</u> atmosphere and the staff are <u>nice</u>. Most importantly, the food is <u>good</u>. I always have a <u>great</u> time when I go there.

5 Find three of the phrases below in the model text on page 66. Check that you understand all of the phrases.

Recommending
The … impressed me, as did the …
The … struck me as (being) …
I was immediately struck by the …
I immediately noticed the …
What caught my eye was …
What made a big impression on me was …
What I found most (appealing/impressive) was …

6 Put all of the phrases in exercise 5 into sentences.

The lively atmosphere impressed me, as did the excellent service.

7 You are going to do the exam task in exercise 2 on page 66. Decide which plan in exercise 5 on page 66 you are going to follow.

8 SPEAKING Work in pairs. Brainstorm ideas and make notes under these headings.
- Location
- Value for money
- Decor
- Atmosphere
- Staff
- Food
- Other ideas

9 Write the description.

CHECK YOUR WORK

Have you:
- [ ] read the instructions carefully and included everything asked for?
- [ ] included some interesting or more unusual adjectives to make your writing more precise?
- [ ] included some words and phrases from exercises 1 and 5?
- [ ] written 200–250 words?
- [ ] checked your grammar and spelling carefully?

5–6 Language Review

Unit 5

1 Complete the sentences with suitable verbs in the past tense.

1 I didn't buy the CD – I d_____ the tracks I wanted from iTunes.
2 I l_____ on to my account this morning, but there were no new messages.
3 More than a thousand people p_____ comments on our video.
4 We s_____ the film from a website to the TV so everyone could watch it.
5 They u_____ all their holiday photos to a website.

Mark: ___ /5

2 Complete the sentences with the correct passive form of the verbs below.

build damage repair steal tell off

1 Yesterday, the children _____ for being late.
2 The new stadium _____ over the next three years.
3 Oh no! I think my password _____ !
4 I haven't got my phone; it _____ at the moment.
5 We saw houses that _____ by the earthquake.

Mark: ___ /5

3 Rewrite the sentences in the passive.

1 They will send us invitations to the wedding soon.
2 They didn't teach us Latin at school.
3 They may have stolen my credit card.
4 They had warned me about the dangers.
5 They can't offer him the job because he's too young.

Mark: ___ /5

4 Complete the dialogue with the words below.

imagine likely say seem though

Boy Do you fancy going to this holiday camp?
Girl There ¹_____ to be a lot of young children. What's the age range?
Boy It's 10–18. But looking at them, I'd ²_____ most of these kids are under 14.
Girl This other camp looks as ³_____ it's aimed at older kids.
Boy Let's check online. I should ⁴_____ they've got a website.
Girl More ⁵_____ than not, we can find others too.

Mark: ___ /5

Total: ___ /20

Unit 6

5 Write adjectives for describing food which mean the opposite of:

1 mouth-watering
2 tender
3 juicy
4 tasteless
5 sweet

Mark: ___ /5

6 Complete the second sentence to mean the same as the first. Use the passive forms.

1 It is known that some animals sense magnetism.
Some animals _____ magnetism.
2 It is believed that birds evolved from dinosaurs.
Birds _____ from dinosaurs.
3 It was thought that tomatoes were poisonous.
Tomatoes _____ poisonous.
4 It is known that there are many other solar systems in our galaxy.
There _____ many other solar systems in our galaxy.
5 It was believed that snake oil cured various diseases.
Snake oil _____ various diseases.

Mark: ___ /5

7 Choose the best options (a–c) to complete the text.

Although 'Arriba!' calls itself a Mexican restaurant, ¹_____ its dishes are authentic; ²_____ are American variations on Mexican food. Having said that, nearly ³_____ the food we tried was tasty and fresh. The service was fast, but that was ⁴_____ surprise: we arrived early and had ⁵_____ restaurant to ourselves!

1 a many b few c very few of
2 a much b most c many of
3 a much of b most of c all
4 a none b no c a little
5 a the whole b all of c all

Mark: ___ /5

8 Write the missing words to complete the comments.

'To my ¹_____ , French food is more interesting than Italian food. At the same ²_____ , Italian food is very tasty.'
'There might be a ³_____ for arguing that the British prefer ethnic food. But ⁴_____ again, they love their fish and chips!'
'I'm of the ⁵_____ that Scandinavian food is rather bland.'

Mark: ___ /5

Total: ___ /20

Lead-in

1 Work in pairs. Discuss the best place to go on a first date. Choose from the venues below or suggest your own idea.

an art gallery a café a cinema a museum
a shopping centre a restaurant the beach

Speaking

2 Work in pairs. Describe the photo. Then ask and answer the questions below.

1 Do you think the couple are enjoying their food? Why do you say so?
2 What are the advantages and disadvantages of eating outside, in your opinion?
3 Tell me about a recent occasion when you had food outside.

Reading

3 Read the texts. Which restaurant would you (a) most like to, and (b) least like to eat in? Give reasons.

4 Match the restaurants in the text (1–5) with five of the sentences below (A–F). There is one extra sentence.

A The service here is particularly fast.
B The food at this restaurant is European.
C You can get large portions of food here without spending too much money.
D Most of the dishes are very tasty, but rather expensive.
E None of the dishes here contain meat or fish.
F Some of the food on offer here is extremely spicy.

Listening

5 🎧 2.27 Listen. Which restaurant from the text in exercise 3 are Daisy and Stefan at? How do you know?

6 🎧 2.27 Listen again. Are these sentences true (T) or false (F)?

1 Daisy and Stefan are eating out because there wasn't much to eat at the squat.
2 Daisy feels the other people at the squat need to respect her opinions more.
3 Spikey is not particularly easy-going, according to Daisy.
4 Stefan has visited Daisy at the squat only once before.
5 Daisy thinks that seeing Stefan is making Spikey jealous.
6 Spikey and the group are planning to put their propaganda on a supermarket website.

Writing

7 Imagine you have had the worst meal of your life at a restaurant. Write a formal letter of complaint to the manager. Include the following information:

• when you visited the restaurant.
• what you ordered and what was wrong with it.
• what the service was like.
• what you expect the manager to do about the situation.

guide to eating out

▸ HOME ▸ RESTAURANTS ▸ NEWS ▸ REVIEWS ▸ CONTACT   SEARCH

1 CHEZ DIDIER: As the name suggests, this restaurant serves French food in cosy, informal surroundings. It specialises in fish and seafood dishes, and claims to use only the freshest ingredients bought each morning from the nearby London food markets. The dishes can be a little heavy, with plenty of rich, creamy sauces, so if you were looking for a light lunch, this might not be the best place. But if you want a quiet venue for an intimate evening meal, you can't beat it.

2 THE RICE BOX: This canteen-style restaurant offers simple, affordable food in bright, clean surroundings. Meals are ordered at the counter, then brought to the table – usually within five minutes! More a place for quick refuelling than a leisurely feast, making it an ideal choice if time is limited – pre-cinema, for example. The number of regular Chinese customers suggests the food is very authentic. It's certainly very tasty!

3 THE STEAKHOUSE: Although the menu includes one or two vegetarian dishes, this is a place for serious meat-eaters, with eight different types of steak on offer as well as pork ribs and burgers. The American-style dishes are large, tasty and not over-priced. The decor has an American feel too, with sports memorabilia and photos of Hollywood stars on the walls, and the service is friendly and efficient. Finish off your meal with one of the mouth-watering desserts.

4 KO SAMUI: If you love the exotic taste of Thai food as much as we do, this is definitely the place to come. It is believed to be the oldest Thai restaurant in the country. The range of dishes on the menu can be bewildering, especially if you are not an expert on oriental cuisine, but the waiters are happy to advise. When we ate here, we ordered about five dishes and then shared them. All the dishes were very tasty, although a little on the small side. If you have a problem with chilli, some of the dishes should be treated with caution as they are extremely hot!

5 CAFÉ SPICE: This is a vegetarian restaurant which specialises in the cuisine of southern India. Not only is the food delicious, but it's also colourful and attractive – the set meal for four people is a real work of art! Don't worry if you aren't a fan of super-spicy Indian food – nearly all of the dishes are quite mild. Some English dishes, like egg and chips, are also available, but in our humble opinion, you'd be mad to order them!

Reading

1 **Get ready to READ** In pairs, write a definition of *anorexia*. Then compare your ideas with the class.

2 Do the exam task.

READING exam task

Read the text and answer the questions.

Eating disorders are so common in many developed countries that two out of every hundred teenagers will be struggling with one of them in any given year. Anorexia and bulimia are the most recognised disorders. However, there is a newer disorder which is becoming more common – orthorexia. Orthorexia nervosa is an unhealthy obsession with healthy eating. Unlike its relation, anorexia, sufferers are primarily concerned with quality, rather than quantity. It's not about feeling thin, but about feeling 'pure' and healthy. Healthy eating is, of course, seen as a good thing, but when taken to extremes, malnutrition, severe weight loss and even death can occur as a result.

Dr Steven Bratman MD coined the phrase from the Greek 'ortho' meaning 'accurate' and orexis, which means 'appetite'. He feels that the medical profession remains largely unaware of this very modern condition. He himself realised that he was a sufferer after a year of his own extreme dieting. He began to view other people as greedy and animalistic, eating sugar-laden, fatty foods with no restraint or regard for their health. He says, 'Because it requires considerable willpower to adopt a diet that differs radically from the food habits of childhood and the surrounding culture, few accomplish the change gracefully. Most must resort to an iron self-discipline bolstered by a hefty dose of superiority over those who eat junk food.' Two of the questions asked on his website are: 'Does your diet socially isolate you?' and 'Do you care more about the virtue of what you eat than the pleasure you receive from eating it?' If the answer to both of these is yes, then Dr Bratman feels you may have a problem.

Simon Wheeler, a self-confessed mild orthorexic, talks about what it is like to have this particular form of illness. He says, 'I started out small, and then got more and more carried away. First I gave up caffeine, when I read that the plant world uses it as an insecticide. Then I gave up dairy products. After that I stopped eating sugar. And so on. Exaggeration turning into obsession, this is what you need to look out for.' And how has it affected his life? 'Well, none of my friends plan all their meals in advance, and keep a food diary with the calorific breakdown of each meal in it. None of them look at the ingredients of every single packet in the supermarket,

checking for additives, sugar, saturated fats, colourings, and sodium. Only I go to the local markets to buy fresh, local produce in paper bags, and organic wherever possible. And only I suffer from extreme guilt if I so much as consume a single gram of chocolate. It's no wonder that they don't invite me out so much any more. They find it really stressful, but I can't help it.'

1 What is the difference between anorexia and orthorexia?
2 According to Dr Bratman, how does radically changing your diet alter your opinion of other people?
3 How can you tell the difference between orthorexia and a normal desire to have a healthy diet?
4 What was Simon Wheeler's first step on the road to orthorexia?
5 In what way has Simon Wheeler's social life suffered as a result of his orthorexia?

Speaking

3 **Get ready to SPEAK** Work in pairs. Think of two kinds of food which include a lot of:

a fat
b salt
c sugar
d vitamins
e fibre
f protein

4 Do the exam task.

SPEAKING exam task

Describe the photo and answer the questions.

1 How healthy do you think your diet is? Give examples.
2 How could teenagers be encouraged to eat healthier foods?
3 Why do you think teenage girls are particularly at risk from eating disorders?

THIS UNIT INCLUDES

Vocabulary ■ news ■ headline language ■ phrasal verbs
Grammar ■ reported speech ■ reporting verbs ■ indefinite pronouns
Speaking ■ describing a photo
Writing ■ review

Communication 7

7A VOCABULARY AND LISTENING News

I can talk about the news.

1 SPEAKING Describe the photos. What is happening?

2 Can you explain the difference between:
1 a news programme, a news story, a news flash and rolling news?
2 a tabloid newspaper and a broadsheet newspaper?

3 VOCABULARY Complete the texts with the words below. Use a dictionary to help you.

breaking news correspondents live broadcasts
news flashes news programmes rolling news channels
satellite phone

TV news Most people in the UK follow the news on television. TV stations broadcast regular [1]_____ as well as quick [2]_____ to cover important [3]_____ . [4]_____ broadcast news 24 hours a day. With the advent of the 'digital age', news [5]_____ can make [6]_____ from anywhere in the world using just a laptop and a [7]_____ .

articles broadsheet columns editorials front-page
headlines human-interest tabloids

Newspapers There are basically two types of mass-circulation newspaper in Britain: [8]_____ newspapers, that carry 'hard' – meaning serious – news and analysis, with [9]_____ on topics like economics and politics; and popular [10]_____ , that have some news but are more interested in gossip and entertainment and are full of [11]_____ stories. All newspapers have [12]_____ , which give opinions and reflect the paper's political point of view, and regular [13]_____ (written by the same person). They all try to attract readers with exciting or important [14]_____ stories and snappy [15]_____ .

censorship citizen journalism eyewitness accounts
news blogs online editions the press

Online news With the spread of fast broadband, many people now prefer to subscribe to [16]_____ of newspapers or to download the whole newspaper onto an ebook reader. Another recent development is '[17]_____ ', when ordinary people report and spread news. They do this by means of [18]_____ (web pages updated regularly with news), Twitter, and [19]_____ of important events posted online, often with photos and videos. Citizen journalists can play an important role in countries where there is strict [20]_____ of [21]_____ .

⟫⟫ VOCABULARY BUILDER 7.1: PAGE 140 ⟪⟪

4 🎧 2.28 Listen to four teenagers talking about the news. Which person is (a) most interested (b) least interested in the news?

5 🎧 2.28 Listen again. Mark the sentences true (T) or false (F).
1 The programme reports that the majority of American teenagers pay no attention at all to the news.
2 The programme states that young people in America are least likely to get their news from a newspaper.
3 Toby doesn't really pay much attention to the news.
4 Becky needs to keep up with the news daily.
5 Mark likes to follow the news when he can.
6 Sophie reads the headlines in the daily paper.

6 SPEAKING Work in small groups. Answer the questions.
1 How much attention do you pay to the news? Why?
2 How do you find out about the news?
3 Put these news media in the order of most importance for you personally and explain your reasons.
   a newspapers b radio c TV d the Internet e Twitter
4 Do you prefer 'hard' news or 'soft' news? Why?

⟫⟫ VOCABULARY BUILDER 7.2: PAGE 140 ⟪⟪

1 Complete the reported speech. Identify the tense change in each example (if there is one).

1 'My brother's a news correspondent.'
She told me that her brother <u>was</u> a news correspondent.
present simple --> past simple

2 'He works for a newspaper in our home town.'
She says that he _____ for a newspaper in their home town.

3 'He's going to Afghanistan tomorrow to report on the war.'
She said he _____ to Afghanistan the next day to report on the war.

4 'He'd better call me next week.'
She said that he _____ call her next week.

5 'He'll be there for three months.'
She's told me that he _____ there for three months.

2 Read the *Learn this!* box below and find examples in exercise 1 of the two rules.

LEARN THIS!

Tense changes in reported speech
We don't change the tense when:
1 the reporting verb is present or present perfect.
2 we are reporting a past perfect verb, *would*, *could*, *should* or *had better*.

⟫⟫ **GRAMMAR BUILDER 7.1: PAGE 126** ⟪⟪

3 Study the examples in exercise 1. What happens to (a) personal and possessive pronouns? (b) time expressions?

LOOK OUT!
Reported speech with *say* and *tell*
1 If we mention who is spoken to, we usually use *tell*. We don't use *to* before the person spoken to.
2 We use *tell* with the infinitive to report instructions.
3 After *say*, we don't have to mention who is spoken to.
4 After *say*, if we do mention who is spoken to, we put *to* before the person.

4 Read the *Look out!* box. Make up a simple example to illustrate each point.

5 Change the direct speech to reported speech. Use the reporting verb in brackets. (The people are/were speaking to you.)
1 Linda: 'I haven't seen the news.' (says)
2 Kate: 'I'll buy a tabloid tomorrow.' (told)
3 Jo: 'I had never visited a news website before.' (said)
4 Ed: 'You'd better look smart for your interview.' (told)
5 Naomi: 'I'm going to buy a broadsheet.' (says)
6 Marcus: 'I'll be flying to Paris this time tomorrow.' (told)

6 Read a report of a conversation. Match each question with a sentence in the report.

Jake asked me whether I had bought a newspaper that day. I said I had. Then he asked me which one I'd bought. I told him I'd bought *The Daily Mail*. He asked me if he could borrow it. I told him he could. He asked me when I wanted it back. I said I didn't.

1 'When do you want it back?' 'I don't.'
2 'Which one did you buy?' '*The Daily Mail*.'
3 'Can I borrow it?' 'Yes, you can.'
4 'Have you bought a newspaper today?' 'Yes, I have.'

7 Answer the questions about reported questions.
1 Are the tense changes the same as in reported statements?
2 Is the word order in reported questions different from the word order in direct questions?
3 Which word do we add when we report yes/no question? (two answers)
4 What are the rules for reporting short answers?

8 Report the conversation using past simple reporting verbs.
Ben asked Pat if she had seen his MP3 player. Pat said she hadn't.

Ben	Have you seen my MP3 player?
Pat	No, I haven't. Why are you asking me?
Ben	Did you use it yesterday?
Pat	Yes, I did, but I put it back in your room.
Ben	Well, it isn't there anymore.
Pat	Have you looked properly?
Ben	Yes! Will you help me look for it?
Pat	I can't right now. I've got to go out.
Ben	Where are you going?
Pat	Why do you want to know?
Ben	I'm just curious. Is it a secret?
Pat	No, it isn't a secret. But I'd rather not tell you.

9 **USE OF ENGLISH** Complete the second sentence so that it has a similar meaning to the first sentence. Use the words given.
1 a 'Can I borrow your scarf?' Rob asked me. (if)
b Rob asked me <u>if he could borrow my scarf.</u>
2 a 'I'll phone you tonight,' Ann said to Fred. (that night)
b Ann told _____ .
3 a 'Has Sue ever been skiing?' Jo asked me. (whether)
b Jo asked me _____ skiing.
4 a 'Have you had lunch yet?' Dan asked Will. (had)
b Dan asked Will _____ yet.
5 a 'I want to know what you're doing,' Di told Ed. (asked)
b Di _____ was doing.

⟫⟫ **GRAMMAR BUILDER 7.2: PAGE 127** ⟪⟪

Twitter

Twitter can be [1]_____ as part social networking site, part 'micro-blogging' site. It allows users to say what they are doing, or what they are seeing or hearing, by posting messages on the Twitter website that their friends or 'followers' can see. The messages, called 'tweets', cannot exceed 140 characters [2]_____ , which is the defining characteristic of the service. Tweets are displayed on the user's profile page and on the home page of each of his or her followers. At first most people used Twitter to stay [3]_____ touch with their friends and family; like other social networking sites, it was just [4]_____ broadcasting where you are, what you are doing, what you are feeling and thinking. But it has [5]_____ developed into a place where people share information, opinions and advice, and [6]_____ it resembles a blog. [7]_____ purpose it serves, it is incredibly popular and used by a huge number of influential people such as politicians, journalists and celebrities.

1   **SPEAKING**   Work in pairs. What do you know about Twitter?

2   **USE OF ENGLISH**   Read the text. Choose the correct options a–d.

1 a expressed	b reported	c described	d explained
2 a long	b in length	c longer	d in long
3 a on	b to	c at	d in
4 a a way to	b a means of	c in order to	d a process of
5 a since	b formerly	c still	d soon
6 a in respect of	b as regards	c in that respect	d for that matter
7 a However	b What	c Whatever	d Which

3   🎧 2.29   Listen and check your ideas from exercise 1.

4   🎧 2.30   Listen to an interview with a journalist who uses Twitter. Does she think that the advantages of Twitter outweigh the disadvantages?

5   🎧 2.30   Listen again and choose the correct answers.

1 First thing in the morning, Maggie
  a adds breaking news stories to Twitter.
  b looks for new stories on Twitter.
  c contacts about 1,000 other journalists via Twitter.

2 Maggie uses Twitter
  a to spread news and to ask about news.
  b just to find interesting news stories.
  c just to request information from other journalists.

3 Twitter has helped Maggie
  a to use lots of very short words.
  b to include lots of important information in every tweet.
  c to write more economically and accurately.

4 In order to gauge the truth of a story on Twitter, Maggie
  a tweets the same message to lots of other people.
  b checks the writer's background.
  c asks the writer if he or she is a journalist.

5 One disadvantage of Twitter is that
  a it can't be used by serious journalists.
  b important events can't be described in few words.
  c anybody can use it so there are too many different opinions.

6   **VOCABULARY**   Complete the collocations from the interview.

context   events   impact   misinformation   news   picture

1 build up a _____ (of)
2 have an _____ (on)
3 give the _____
4 democratise the _____
5 spread _____
6 analyse _____

7   **SPEAKING**   Work in pairs.

Student A: summarise two advantages of Twitter.
Student B: summarise two disadvantages.

8   **SPEAKING**   Work in pairs. Ask and answer the questions.

1 Do you have a Twitter account? If so, what do you use it for?
2 If not, would you like one? Why, and what would you use it for?/Why not?
3 Do you or does anyone you know have (a) a blog? (b) a Facebook (or other social networking) account? What do you/they use if for?

9   **PROJECT**   Visit an English-language news website (e.g. BBC News, CNN, Yahoo News). Choose an interesting news story and write a summary of it in no more than 150 words.

1 SPEAKING **Look at the pictures. Ask and answer the questions.**

1 What is happening in the painting? How do you think the girls are feeling?
2 What are the people doing in the photo?

2 🎧 2.31 **Read the text. Which sentence (a–d) best summarises the main idea?**

a A postman's job has changed greatly over the past 200 years.
b The postal service was revolutionised in the mid-nineteenth century and has brought many benefits to the average British citizen.
c Roland Hill persuaded the Government to allow him to change the Royal Mail.
d The average working person in Britain could no longer afford to pay to receive a letter so stamps were invented.

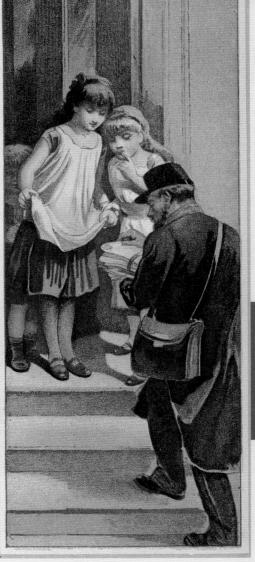

With instant messaging and social networking, sending a message by post may not be something that you would automatically think of. However, until very recently the post was the main means of communication and many people today still look forward to the postman's arrival every morning.

By contrast, in the 1800s the knock of the postman was something to dread. At that time, the person receiving a letter had to pay for it. The cost was dependent upon the distance the letter had travelled and the number of pages it consisted of. Most ordinary people couldn't afford to receive a letter. So how had this situation come about?

In 1516 King Henry VIII set up the Royal Mail for royal communications and reasons of national security. From there a demand arose for a public postal service due to an increase in literacy amongst the general population and for business requirements. By the mid-nineteenth century the British had to put up with a very complex, expensive postal service.

Roland Hill, a young enthusiastic Victorian man, wanted to reform it. His intention was to make postage accessible to all citizens by introducing much cheaper

charges. Hill's new idea was to charge a universal single rate of postage. This would reduce at one stroke the complicated calculations necessary to organise payment of a letter, and make the post office efficient. He argued that his reforms would result in more people sending more letters, which in turn would lead to wider social benefits and increased profits.

Hill bombarded the Government with his ideas. At first they were not well received by anyone in a position of power, but eventually the Government agreed to set up an enquiry. During this enquiry ministers from all over the country reported what their constituents had told them. They said that ordinary people felt terribly burdened by high postage costs and told stories of poor people having to sell furniture to receive a letter from their loved ones. Ministers reported that post office fees had placed an intolerable burden on the working classes. People had to go away to find work, but could not afford to stay in touch with their families.

The debate dragged on for months but finally Hill was given two years to reform the British Post Office. First, he needed to come up with a way of showing that the letter was pre-paid. He experimented with various kinds of envelopes, but settled on a type of 'stamp'. But what could he put on it that was instantly recognisable and difficult to forge? The answer was staring out at him from the coins in his hand – the head of the Queen, Victoria. On 1 May 1840, the world's first postage stamp was put on sale. At first no one wanted to lick a stamp – and the idea of licking the Queen seemed quite impolite! – but the idea eventually caught on. To this day British stamps are the only ones that do not bear the name of the country. Shortly after, another invention became necessary, as people now needed a letterbox at home. At first, many people objected to having a hole cut in their front door, but again this new idea soon became commonplace.

Overnight the post office was revolutionised. People started writing more and more letters to each other, and the postman was no longer feared, but became a local hero. For the first time, Britain had a fair, cheap and efficient postal service and this had a profound impact on ordinary people's lives. Businesses flourished. Children wrote to parents, families to relatives across the world, lovers to each other. Valentine, Christmas and birthday cards were invented. Nowadays, we write far fewer letters than we used to, but the post office is still very busy – delivering goods ordered online!

3 Mark the sentences true (T) or false (F).

1 In the nineteenth century, the postal service was essentially for the use of royalty and government.
2 At the beginning of the 1800s, the post office had a simple method of calculating the cost of a letter.
3 Roland Hill didn't find it easy to convince the government and post office of the value of his ideas.
4 The British public had no problem at all in adapting to Roland Hill's new ideas.
5 Hill's argument that cheaper postage would improve people's lives was proved to be true.
6 With the new postal service the British public quickly found more reasons for writing letters.

4 VOCABULARY Match the highlighted phrasal verbs in the text with the definitions.

1 continue for a very long time
2 establish
3 think of an idea for
4 make a decision on something
5 become popular
6 endure or tolerate

>>> VOCABULARY BUILDER 7.3: PAGE 140 <<<

5 Explain the meaning of the underlined phrases in these sentences from the text.

1 ... in the 1800s the knock of the postman was something to dread.
2 Hill bombarded the Government with his ideas ...
3 ... post office fees had placed an intolerable burden on the working classes.
4 The debate dragged on for months.
5 ... again this new idea soon became commonplace.
6 Britain had a fair, cheap and efficient postal service and this had a profound impact on ordinary people's lives.

6 Find three indefinite pronouns in the text, one beginning with any-, one with no- and one with some-.

>>> GRAMMAR BUILDER 7.3: PAGE 127 <<<

7 SPEAKING Work in pairs. Ask and answer the questions.

1 Do you like writing or receiving letters? If so, how often? And who to/from?
2 What was the last thing that you sent or received in the post?
3 What is the most common way that you and your friends communicate? How often?
4 In what circumstances would you write a letter rather than use some other form of communication?

I can report what people have said in a variety of ways.

1 🎧 2.32 Listen to the interview. Who does the politician blame for the state of the economy? What specific measures does she promise to carry out?

2 🎧 2.32 Complete what the minister said in her interview. Use the reporting verbs below. Listen again and check.

agreed   announced   denied   reminded   warned

1 The minister _____ that the economy had not been performing well.
2 She _____ that it was the Government's fault.
3 She _____ the interviewer that the previous government left the nation's finances in a mess.
4 She _____ that increasing public spending would be very dangerous.
5 She _____ that the Government was going to cut taxes and create jobs.

> **LEARN THIS!**
>
> **Reporting verbs**
> We can use other verbs instead of say and tell when we report statements, e.g. *explain, deny, insist, agree, persuade, convince, repeat, beg, assure, etc.*
> *'I stole a TV,' he said. 'I also stole a DVD player.'*
> *He admitted that he had stolen a TV. He added that he had also stolen a DVD player.*
> *He convinced me that he was telling the truth.*

3 Read the *Learn this!* box. Then report the sentences using one of the verbs in brackets. More than one answer is possible.

1 Matt said to Sue, 'The film starts in ten minutes.' (remind / admit / warn)
2 Jessica said, 'I've already done my homework.' (point out / announce / warn)
3 Ross said, 'I was tired because I hadn't slept well.' (promise / explain / assure)
4 Jim said, 'I wouldn't have crashed if there hadn't been ice on the road.' (argue / explain / persuade)
5 Mandy said, 'Sally lost my gloves!' (deny / complain / announce)
6 Beth said to Emma, 'You're wearing my scarf!' (claim / insist / assure)

4 🎧 2.33 Listen and match the speakers (1–6) with the reported speech (a–f).

a She admitted that she'd stayed out late.
b She begged her parents to allow her to stay out late.
c She assured her parents that she wouldn't stay out late.
d She insisted that she was staying out late.
e She repeated that she would be staying out late.
f She denied that she'd got home late.

5 Read the sentences. Then complete the *Learn this!* box with the base form of the reporting verbs in blue.

1 Freddie denied hitting the police officer.
2 Martha insisted on going out without a coat.
3 The minister refused to give an interview.
4 My teacher suggested that I should study law at university.
5 Jonty reminded me to post the letter.
6 Dad congratulated me on passing my driving test.
7 She insisted that he wear a tie.

> **LEARN THIS!**
>
> **Other reporting structures**
> We can use other structures when we report offers, promises, requests, commands, suggestions, etc.
> 1 **verb + infinitive with *to***
>   agree, offer, promise, [1]_____ , threaten
> 2 **verb + object + infinitive with *to***
>   advise, ask, beg, encourage, forbid, instruct, invite, order, [2]_____ , tell, warn
> 3 **verb + gerund**
>   admit, [3]_____ , recommend, suggest
> 4 **verb + preposition + gerund**
>   apologise for, boast of, confess to, [4]_____
> 5 **verb + object + preposition + gerund**
>   accuse sb of, [5]_____ , warn sb against
> 6 **verb + *that* + *should* clause / verb + *that* + subjunctive clause**
>   demand, propose, recommend, request, [6]_____
>   [7]_____

▶▶▶ GRAMMAR BUILDER 7.4: PAGE 127 ◀◀◀

6 Complete the sentences with a preposition if necessary and the correct form of the verbs below.

buy   copy   go   ground   lose   show   sit   stay out

1 My parents threatened _____ me for the weekend if I didn't keep my bedroom tidy.
2 Our teacher warned us _____ essays from the Internet.
3 My dad forbade me _____ after midnight.
4 Tim insisted _____ me lunch, even though I tried to pay.
5 The police officer requested that I _____ her my ID.
6 Sally ordered her dog _____ .
7 I recommend _____ to see the new Johnny Depp film.
8 Jo apologised _____ her temper.

7 SPEAKING Work in pairs. Using reported speech, tell each other about something:

1 that your parents ask you do.
2 that your parents forbid you to do.
3 that you were accused of doing.
4 that you promised to do.

I can describe a photo and answer questions about it.

1 SPEAKING Work in pairs. Which of these things do teenagers most often argue about with their parents? Choose the top five or add your own ideas. Compare your opinions with the class.

alcohol and drugs
being untidy
clothes
computers and TV
homework and schoolwork
parents treating siblings differently
parents treating teenagers like young children
staying out late
wasting money

2 SPEAKING Work in pairs. Describe the photo.

3 Work in pairs. Decide if these sentences about the photo are certainly true (CT), possibly true (PT) or certainly untrue (CU).

1 The boy has just arrived home.
2 It's late at night.
3 He stayed out too late.
4 He's been to a party.
5 He told his mum he'd be home earlier.
6 He's feeling sorry for his behaviour.
7 His mum is telling him off.
8 She's been staying up to wait for him to get home.
9 She's happy with his behaviour.
10 She expected him to arrive home late.

LEARN THIS!

must/might/can't (have)
You can use *must/might/can't (have)* to speculate about events in the present and the past.
He's smiling so he must be happy.
It's wet outside. It must have been raining.
His hands are all muddy. He might have been working in the garden.
She can't have left yet. Her car's still in the drive.

4 Read the *Learn this!* box and make sentences using *must/ might/can't (have)* and the sentences in exercise 3. Add a reason for your opinion.

The boy must have just arrived home because the front door is open and he's still wearing his jacket.

5 Complete the useful phrases with the words below.

explain   kind   know   mean   moment   question   say
see   something   thought   what   words

Asking for clarification
I'm not sure what you ¹_____ .
Could you ²_____ what you mean, please?

Paraphrasing
I'm not sure how to ³_____ it in English.
I don't ⁴_____ what it's called in English.
In other ⁵_____ , ...
⁶_____ I mean is, ...
It's ⁷_____ you (use for ...)
It's a ⁸_____ of ...

Gaining thinking time
Let me think about that for a ⁹_____ .
I haven't given that a great deal of ¹⁰_____ before.
Let me ¹¹_____ , ...
That's an interesting ¹²_____ .

EXAM TIP

- If you can't remember how to say something in English, try to paraphrase.
- When you need time to work out what to say next, use phrases for gaining time.

6 🎧 3.03 Read the Exam tip. Listen to a candidate answering the examiner's second question. Tick the phrases in exercise 5 that he uses.

7 SPEAKING Work in pairs. What's your opinion? Do you think young people should be allowed to stay out late? Why?/Why not?

8 SPEAKING Work in pairs. Do the picture description exam task on page 144.

1 SPEAKING Work in pairs. Ask and answer.

1 Do you enjoy going to the cinema? Why?/Why not?
2 When was the last time you went to the cinema? What did you see?
3 Think of your favourite film.
  • What kind of film is it?
  • Who stars in it?
  • Why do you like it?

2 What kinds of information would you expect to find in a film review?

3 Read the Exam tip and questions below. Identify the particular angle or point of view that you need to adopt in each question.

> **EXAM TIP**
>
> In the exam you will not be asked simply to write a straightforward review of a film, book, magazine, etc. that you liked or disliked. You will have to approach the task from the particular angle or point of view specified in the task.
> 1 Write a review of a film that got rave reviews but which you were disappointed by.
> 2 Write a review of a film that you didn't think you would like, but which you really enjoyed.
> 3 Write a review of a film that you really liked but which your friends didn't enjoy.

4 Read the introduction to the film review. Which of the questions in exercise 3 is it answering?

5 Read the whole review.

1 Underline phrases and sentences in the review where the writer reports other people's opinions of the film.
2 Find where the writer contrasts these opinions with his/her own views.

6 In which paragraph does the writer mainly talk about (a) the characters? (b) the plot?

7 Which tense does the writer use in the review to describe the characters and what happens in the story?

8 Find eight of the following adjectives in the review.

Adjectives to describe a plot or story entertaining exhilarating far-fetched fast-moving hilarious gripping intricate light-hearted moving predictable scary serious thought-provoking upsetting

Adjectives to describe characters clichéd complex convincing familiar fascinating two-dimensional uninteresting unconvincing well-rounded

A I recently saw the comedy *Bruce Almighty*. Made in 2003, it was directed by Tom Shadyac and stars Jim Carrey, one of my favourite actors. However, it received mixed reviews from the critics, and my friends weren't impressed by it, so I wasn't sure if I'd enjoy it. Despite my initial doubts, however, I have to say I was pleasantly surprised.

B The protagonist is Bruce Nolan, a TV reporter who covers local interest stories. My friends maintain that Carrey gives an unconvincing performance in the leading role, but I couldn't disagree more. He comes across to me as very well-rounded and extremely funny. The other main character is God, played by Morgan Freeman. Freeman is a fine actor and the perfect complement to Carrey.

C The story is set in a TV station and begins when Bruce complains to God that He is making his life miserable. In response, God gives Bruce all His powers for a week and tells him to do a better job! There are some hilarious moments and very witty lines. Some critics were of the opinion that the story was far-fetched and silly, but I think they are missing the point. By becoming God, Nolan learns the importance of helping other people. That's the serious message of this entertaining comedy.

D To sum up, *Bruce Almighty* isn't just a light-hearted comedy; it's also thought-provoking. And in spite of the views of my friends and the critics, I thoroughly enjoyed the film and would recommend anyone to see it.

9 Think of films and film characters you know that could be described using adjectives from exercise 8.

10 SPEAKING Work in pairs. Talk about the characters and what happens in one of the films that you mentioned in exercise 1. Use the present simple.

1 **You are going to do the exam task below.**

Write a review of a film that both critics and friends of yours recommended, but which you found disappointing when you went to see it.

2 **Find out some background information about the film. Make notes on some of these things:**

1 Title? Type of film? Main theme? Part of a series? Made when? Based on a book or a true story? Famous around the world?
2 Director: Nationality? Has he/she won any prizes? Any other interesting information about him/her?
3 Main actors: Nationality? Have they won any prizes? Any other interesting information about them?

3 **Make notes about what happens in the film. Use some of the phrases below and the adjectives in exercise 8 on page 78 to help you.**

Talking about the plot

The film is set in (where/when?)   At the start of the film, ...
The story begins when ...   In the course of the film ...
It's the story of ...   By the end of the film ...
The plot revolves around ...   There's a twist at the end.

4 **Make notes about the characters in the film. Use the nouns below and the adjectives in exercise 8 on page 78 to help you.**

Types of character/role

action hero   anti-hero   comic actor   extra
hero/heroine   leading role   protagonist   romantic lead
side-kick   star   supporting actor   supporting cast
villain

5 **SPEAKING** **Work in pairs. Present the film to your partner. Give background information, then talk about the characters and the plot. Start with:**

I'm going to talk about (name of film). It's a (type of film). It's directed by (name) and it stars (names).

6 **Complete the sentences, which all express conflicting opinions about films. Which ones might be useful in your review?**

expectations   expected   made out   pleasantly   praise
raved   reservations   reviews

1 In spite of my _____ , I'm glad I made the effort to see it.
2 Despite the _____ heaped on the film by the critics, it wasn't as good as I had anticipated.
3 Although I didn't expect to enjoy it, I was _____ surprised by both the story and the quality of the acting.
4 In spite of the glowing _____ , I was very disappointed with many aspects of the film.
5 Despite what others said, the film wasn't as bad as had been _____ .
6 Notwithstanding my low _____ , I was thoroughly entertained.
7 Although I had _____ to enjoy it, I was bored from start to finish.
8 Even though my friends _____ about the film, I found it dull and predictable.

7 **Make notes for a concluding paragraph. Summarise what you think of the film, contrasting other people's opinions with your own. Use some of the phrases in exercise 6 and those below to help you.**

Summing up a review

All in all, ...
In conclusion, ...
To sum up, ...

8 **Now write your review using the notes you made.**

CHECK YOUR WORK

Have you:

☐ approached the task from the particular angle or point of view specified in the task?

☐ explained other people's opinions and contrasted them with your own?

☐ used the present simple to describe the plot and characters?

☐ written 200–250 words?

☐ used some of the useful phrases to describe character and plot?

☐ checked your spelling and grammar?

Listening

1 `Get ready to LISTEN` In pairs, discuss which of these types of show you would like to see most, and why.

a musical   a classic drama   stand-up comedy
a mime show   a piano recital

2 Do the exam task.

LISTENING exam task

🎧 3.04 **Listen to descriptions of five performances. Match each event (1–5) with the appropriate summary sentence (A–F). There is one extra sentence that is not needed.**

Event 1	Event 3	Event 5
Event 2	Event 4	

A Get in line to be dazzled by a legend.
B Sing along and be part of this amazing show.
C You won't get a second chance for such a laugh!
D Act quickly to see a great dance show free of charge.
E Stand up for this unusual performance where actors don't speak.
F It's literature on stage but, unlike the book, it's never the same thing twice.

Use of English

3 Do the exam task.

USE OF ENGLISH exam task

Read the text. Choose the correct answer (A, B, C or D) for each gap to create a logical and grammatically correct text.

For a generation brought up on reality TV shows, ¹_____ their accompanying public humiliation of fame-hungry volunteers, the film *The Hunger Games* will not appear too far-fetched. This futuristic fantasy thriller explores the theme which has violent and fatal results. Directed by Gary Ross, it is based on the 2008 bestselling teen novel by Suzanne Collins.

The action is ²_____ in a future North America with a population suffering chronic food shortages under a totalitarian government. The outlying districts of the evil Capitol once attempted to rebel against this government, but were cruelly suppressed. ³_____ punishment, all twelve rebellious provinces have to provide 24 young people every year, one girl and one boy each, to take part in a televised gameshow in which they must fight to the death. As in the times of Roman gladiator fights, only one survivor is allowed.

The main protagonists are tough, practical Katniss (actress Jennifer Lawrence) and softer Peeta (Josh Hutcherson). When Peeta ⁴_____ his feelings for Katniss, the TV ratings shoot up. Now the bloodthirsty audience tunes in eagerly to watch the two lovers ⁵_____ fight each other to the death.

The Hunger Games is at ⁶_____ a clever satire on today's reality TV shows and an exciting thriller. It is highly effective entertainment and well worth seeing on the big screen.

1 A for   **B** having   **C** with   **D** including
2 A placed   **B** set   **C** located   **D** put
3 A In   **B** Like   **C** To   **D** As
4 A confesses **B** tells   **C** confides **D** owns up
5 A having to **B** had to   **C** must   **D** to have to
6 A time   **B** once   **C** first   **D** utmost

Speaking

4 `Get ready to SPEAK` In pairs, discuss what you would do if you had to audition for a talent show.

5 Do the exam task.

SPEAKING exam task

Describe the picture. Answer the questions below.

1 What kind of show do you think this woman is auditioning for?
2 Would you like to audition for a TV talent show? Why / Why not?
3 Do you enjoy watching TV talent shows? Why / Why not?

THIS UNIT INCLUDES
Vocabulary ▪ energy and the environment ▪ space vocabulary ▪ wildlife and endangered species ▪ prefixes
Grammar ▪ talking about ability ▪ relative clauses ▪ *do* and *did* for emphasis
Speaking ▪ stimulus description
Writing ▪ opinion essay

Our planet | 8

8A   VOCABULARY AND LISTENING   Global warming

I can talk about energy and global warming.

1 SPEAKING **Work in pairs. What do these terms mean? What do you know about them?**

1 global warming   2 renewable energy   3 fossil fuels

2 VOCABULARY **Complete the word sets with the words below. Use a dictionary to help you.**

biofuel   coal   oil   solar   tidal   wave

Sources of power		
1 _____ power	2 _____ power	3 _____ power
natural gas	shale gas	4 _____
5 _____	renewable energy	6 _____
hydroelectric power	nuclear power	wind power

mine   panel   power   pylon   rig   turbine

Generation and distribution			
7 _____ station	8 _____		wind farm
wind 9 _____	oil 10 _____	coal 11 _____	solar 12 _____

change   CO$_2$ footprint   greenhouse

Global warming	
carbon 13 _____	climate 14 _____
15 _____ emissions	exhaust fumes
16 _____ gases	methane pollution

3 🎧 3.05 **Listen to three people talking about global warming. Match each person (1–3) with three opinions.**

a Rich countries have no right to tell developing countries to reduce carbon emissions.
b Unusual and extreme weather is evidence of climate change.
c Global warming is a natural as well as a man-made phenomenon.
d Governments should spend more money on renewable energy technology.
e As individuals we can all find ways to help prevent global warming.
f It's impossible to persuade people to live 'greener' lives.
g We should rely more on nuclear power.
h If we are serious about stopping climate change, we should stop eating meat.
i We should adapt to climate change, not try to prevent it.

4 🎧 3.05 **Complete the collocations used by the speakers. Listen again and check.**

nuclear waste   your carbon footprint   renewable energy
energy   wind turbines or solar panels
the atmosphere and oceans   natural resources
carbon emissions   fossil fuels

1 invest in _____   4 conserve _____   7 cut _____
2 dispose of _____   5 pollute _____   8 rely on _____
3 reduce _____   6 install _____   9 use up _____

5 SPEAKING **Describe the photos. Discuss these questions.**

1 How is electricity generated in your country?
2 What are the advantages and disadvantages of
  a fossil fuel energy?   c renewable energy?
  b nuclear energy?

6 SPEAKING **Work in pairs. Do you agree or disagree with the statements in exercise 3? Give reasons for your opinions.**

> I agree/disagree that … That's because …

⟫⟫ **VOCABULARY BUILDER 8.1: PAGE 141** ⟪⟪

Unit 8 ▪ Our planet | **81**

GRAMMAR Talking about ability

I can talk about ability in the past, present and future.

1 Read the sentences. Underline the expressions which refer to ability.

1 If developing countries don't cut carbon emissions, we won't be able to prevent climate change.
2 New York's first power station, built in 1882, could supply electricity to only 59 customers.
3 The biggest wind turbines can generate enough electricity to power more than 2,000 households.
4 We managed to cut our fuel bill by insulating the loft.
5 I can't help you take the bottles to the bottle bank this evening as I'm going out. But I'll be able to help you tomorrow.
6 George W. Bush bought an oil company in Texas, but they couldn't find any oil and it went bust.
7 As we approached the factory, we could smell the fumes from the chimneys.
8 The Government isn't able to cut carbon emissions.

2 Match each sentence in exercise 1 with a rule in the *Learn this!* box.

1 Present ability
- We normally use *can* to talk about ability in the present.
- However, it's also correct to use the present tense of *be able to*, but it's less natural.

2 Ability in the past
- We only use *could* for general ability in the past.
- When we're talking about one occasion, we use a different expression, such as *managed to do* or *succeeded in doing*.
- However, we use the negative *couldn't* whether we are talking about general ability or one occasion.
- We use *could* with verbs of perception, like *see, smell, hear, taste, feel*, even if it's one occasion.

3 Ability in the future
- We normally use *will be able to* to talk about ability in the future.
- We can use *can* or *will be able to* to talk about future arrangements.

3 Choose the best answers. Sometimes both answers are acceptable.

1 I **couldn't hear / didn't hear** the radio so I turned it up.
2 **Can you / Are you able to** play the piano?
3 I **don't manage to / can't** type very fast.
4 I was short of money so I **couldn't / wasn't able to** go to the cinema with my friends.
5 I'm having a party on Saturday. **Can you / Will you be able to** come?
6 After three attempts I **managed to / could** pass my driving test.

4 **USE OF ENGLISH** Complete the second sentence so that it has a similar meaning to the first. Use the word in brackets.

1 Jo was able to find a job when she left school. (managed)
Jo _____ when she left school.
2 Perhaps I can ring you after work. (might)
I _____ after work.
3 It annoys me that I can't drive. (able)
I don't like _____ drive.
4 Susan was able to get a place at Oxford. (succeeded)
Susan _____ at Oxford.
5 I was ill so I wasn't able to go to school. (couldn't)
I _____ because I was ill.
6 The house was visible through the trees. (see)
I _____ through the trees.

⟫⟫⟫ **GRAMMAR BUILDER 8.1: PAGE 128** ⟪⟪⟪

5 Describe the photo. What is the person doing, and why? Then read the text in exercise 6 and check your ideas.

6 Complete the text with the correct tense and form of *can, could, be able to, manage* or *succeed*. Sometimes there is more than one possible answer.

Jason Edwards has been involved in eco-protests for as long as he [1]_____ remember. 'One of the most memorable was in 2010,' says Jason. 'We were trying to prevent them from building a bypass through some ancient woodland. We [2]_____ dig tunnels under the route of the road and we hid in them. For two months the police [3]_____ find us. But despite our best efforts we [4]_____ . In the end, the police [5]_____ to evict us and the bypass went ahead as planned. Some friends of mine are going to take direct action to stop them building a new airport near London. I hope I'll [6]_____ get involved in that too. This time we might [7]_____ prevent the project from going ahead.'

7 **SPEAKING** Work in pairs. Tell each other about:

1 two things you could do when you were three years old.
2 two difficult things that you managed to do (or succeeded in doing) last year.
3 two things that you have tried to do in the past but couldn't.
4 something that you don't like not being able to do.

Solving the
FOOD CRISIS

Every night, almost one billion people go to bed hungry. How can we feed all these undernourished people? Farmers all over the world have to contend with weather, insects, and natural disasters, which are capable of destroying crops and ruining years of hard work. And the population is set to rise to nine billion by 2050. Here are four possible solutions.

GM crops

Proponents of genetically modified crops (GM crops) claim that they will hugely increase food production. Scientists have developed drought-resistant and disease-resistant crops, more productive crops, and crops with increased vitamins. Anti-GM protesters worry about health risks and damage to other plants that grow near the GM crops.

Vertical farming

Another answer could be to grow food in buildings. Advocates of vertical farming are suggesting we construct multi-storey, climate-controlled farm buildings in the heart of our cities. One indoor hectare of land would be equivalent to about five hectares outdoors, so we could grow year-round crops that would easily feed whole cities. Opponents point to the cost, the increased energy use and the effect on farmers.

Eat less meat

Others say the solution lies not in new technologies, but in eating less meat. It takes about seven kilos of corn to produce one kilo of beef. That quantity of corn will keep more people alive than that quantity of beef. But this is a message the world doesn't want to hear. Meat consumption is rising steeply.

Increase aid

Rich countries have far more food than they need and waste vast amounts of it – 6.7 million tonnes a year in the UK alone. We can afford to send surplus food to people who desperately need it. We could also simply give more money to developing countries, so they can buy food. Critics say that this makes people dependent on rich countries and is only a short-term solution.

---

1 🎧 3.06   **SPEAKING**   Work in pairs. Discuss these questions. Read the text and check your ideas.

  1 What causes food shortages?
  2 What are some of the arguments against GM crops?
  3 Are people generally eating more or less meat?

2 What do these refer to, according to the text?

  1 one billion   4 seven kilos/one kilo
  2 the year 2050   5 6.7 million tonnes
  3 5 hectares/1 hectare

3 **VOCABULARY** Read the *Learn this!* box. Find examples of the three prefixes in the text.

> **LEARN THIS!**
>
> **Prefixes**
> Some prefixes give adjectives, nouns and verbs a particular meaning.
> *anti = against   anticapitalism*
> *under = not enough   underpaid*
> *multi = many   multimillionaire*

  ▶▶▶ **VOCABULARY BUILDER 8.2: PAGE 141** ◀◀◀

4 🎧 3.07   Listen to Dr Samuel Friedman talking about the advantages of vertical farming. Which countries does he mention and why?

5 🎧 3.07   Listen again. Are the sentences true (T) or false (F)?

  1 The idea of vertical farming is definitely more than 50 years old
  2 At the moment there's a shortage of farmland.
  3 Food would not have to be transported long distances.
  4 Vertical farming would encourage other industries to develop and increase employment.
  5 The climate in the vertical farm buildings would match the climate outside.

6 **SPEAKING** Work in pairs. Develop these possible arguments against vertical farming:

  cost   energy use   variety of food   effect on farmers
  effect on shops and supermarkets   effect on world trade
  vulnerability in a war

7 **SPEAKING** Work in pairs.

  Student A: Argue for vertical farming.
  Student B: Argue against it. Use the phrases below.

  I see your point, but I still think …
  I agree with you up to a point, but in my opinion …
  You have to admit that …
  There may be some truth in that, but …

1 **SPEAKING** Work in groups. Look at the photos and the title. What do you understand by the term *space junk* and why might it be a problem?

2 🎧 3.08 Read the text quickly, ignoring the gaps. Check your ideas from exercise 1.

3 Read the text again and match the sentences (A–G) with the gaps (1–6). There is one sentence that you do not need.

   A The other 90% is a jungle of junk – leftovers from half a century of human activity in space.

   B Fortunately, most of them landed in the sea.

   C Because of the extra CO_2 in our atmosphere now, space junk is staying up longer.

   D They were forced to get to their escape capsules and prepare for an emergency journey back to the Earth.

   E These satellites then attach a device to the debris which pushes it into the Earth's atmosphere, where it burns up.

   F And in the next ten years, the number of satellites will grow by around 50%.

   G On average, one object a day survives re-entry.

SPACE JUNK

A dangerous mission

A piece of rubbish in outer space has threatened the lives of six astronauts, prompting calls for something to be done about the mess we have created around our planet. The six astronauts - three Russians, two Americans and one Japanese - form the crew of the International Space Station (ISS). [1] ☐ The piece of debris came very near to the station but fortunately passed by without causing any damage.

What a load of rubbish

A Russian official said that only a tenth of all objects in space are working pieces of equipment. [2] ☐ There are not only 22,000 large pieces of rocket, shuttle, satellite and sputnik, but also over 500,000 smaller bits, which are only a few centimetres in size. Surrounding all of these are also millions of tiny particles, for example, flakes of paint that have come off space vehicles. The problem is that all of this stuff is travelling at several kilometres per second. Even the tiniest, almost invisible speck could create a centimetre-deep hole in the side of a rocket or space station, potentially causing a leak. And a larger chunk could possibly destroy it – and any human life on board.

A growing problem

Unfortunately, the situation can only get worse. The number of satellites being sent into space is increasing rapidly. In the past ten years, an average of 76 satellites per year have been launched. [3] ☐ The latest analysis of the situation suggests that 1,145 new satellites could be launched during that time, mostly for broadband and satellite phone systems. When satellites become defunct, they stay in low-Earth orbit, eventually falling and burning up when they re-enter the Earth's atmosphere, as meteorites do. New satellites will have to be built to new standards, so that when they reach the end of their useful life, they will have enough energy left to travel back immediately into our atmosphere to burn up. At the moment, 80% of all space junk is around 1,200 miles above the Earth, which is called low-Earth orbit. Spacecraft have to orbit lower than this to avoid all the debris, and satellite companies have to navigate a way through the junk to place their equipment.

And we're not safe down here, either

Unfortunately, not all space junk burns up while re-entering the Earth's atmosphere. [4] ☐ An American woman in Oklahoma was knocked down in January 1997 when she was struck by a lump of metal. Fortunately, she wasn't injured. 'The weight was comparable to an empty soda can,' the woman said. It was identified as debris from a rocket. Other parts of the rocket, including a steel tank and a titanium sphere, fortunately landed without causing any harm.

4 Are the sentences true (T) or false (F)?

1 The crew of the ISS had to leave the space station and return to the Earth.
2 Flakes of rocket paint hitting working space equipment could damage it.
3 Space junk eventually burns up in the sun's atmosphere.
4 Space junk caused a serious injury in Oklahoma in 1997.
5 The Mir space station caused large pieces of space junk to fall to the Earth.
6 We can't use low-Earth orbit because of a chain reaction of fragmenting debris.

5 VOCABULARY Complete these words that have a similar meaning to *piece*. They are all in the text. Can you explain any differences in meaning?

1 b_____ (paragraph 2)   5 c_____ (paragraph 2)
2 p_____ (paragraph 2)   6 l_____ (paragraph 4)
3 f_____ (paragraph 2)   7 f_____ (paragraph 5)
4 s_____ (paragraph 2)

>>> VOCABULARY BUILDER 8.3: PAGE 141 <<<

6 VOCABULARY Put these things in order of size, from the smallest to the largest (as you'd reasonably expect them to be). Find three of them in the text (in paragraphs 1, 3 and 5).

asteroid constellation galaxy meteorite moon planet solar system star universe

SMALLEST >> _____ >> _____ >> _____ >> _____ >>
>> _____ >> _____ >> _____ >> _____ >> LARGEST

7 SPEAKING Work in small groups. What extra-terrestrial events are we in potential danger from? Look at the list below and put it in order from least dangerous to most dangerous. Think about the probability of the event occurring and the likely consequences.

• space junk falling from the sky
• aliens visiting from outer space
• a meteorite hitting the Earth
• the sun dying
• the Earth colliding with the Moon or another planet

8 SPEAKING Present your ideas to the class, giving reasons for your decisions.

The biggest bit of rubbish to date

However, in the world of space litter, the biggest piece of junk would have to be Mir, the Russian space station, which is the heaviest object ever to orbit the Earth, apart from the Moon. The fifteen-year-old station began heading downwards on 23rd March 2001, and a month later, re-entered the Earth's atmosphere over the Pacific Ocean near Fiji. Though most of the station, weighing 130,000 kilogrammes, burned up in the atmosphere, about 1,500 fragments reached the Earth's surface. Holidaymakers on beaches in Fiji took photos of little bits of burning debris as they whizzed noisily through the sky above them. 5☐

Time to clean up the sky

Occasionally debris collides with other debris, creating thousands more tiny pieces of space junk. So far, it is thought that there have been few such collisions, but what is feared is a kind of chain reaction, with debris fragmenting and going on to collide with other debris, creating a cloud of rubbish that would make it impossible for us to use the low-Earth orbit around our planet at all.

Some scientists think they might have come up with a solution to the problem of space junk. They want to put big 'cleaning robots' into the sky, in effect satellites which are able to locate and manoeuvre alongside large pieces of space junk. 6☐ The scientists say that each robot could safely remove up to ten objects a year. This would go some way to improving the situation, as long as collisions between debris do not increase in the meantime. Whatever the solution to the problem, experts all agree that something needs to be done to tidy up space sooner rather than later.

1 Read the quotes. Which of these causes would you support? Which other charities do you know about?

'I support a charity called Anti-Bags, which encourages people to stop using plastic bags.'

'I'm raising money for people whose homes were destroyed in last year's floods.'

'The charity which I support raises money for children who are seriously ill.'

'I donate to charities dedicated to helping poor people in drought-affected areas, who are at risk from starvation and disease.'

LEARN THIS!

Defining relative clauses
1 A defining relative clause adds essential information. The sentence often doesn't make sense without it.
This is the coal mine where my grandad worked.
2 We do not put a comma before the clause.
Non-defining relative clauses
1 A non-defining relative clause adds extra information. The sentence still makes sense without it.
Global warming is caused by greenhouse gases, which include carbon dioxide and methane.
2 We put a comma before the clause, and also after it if the sentence continues.
Fossil fuels, which include coal and oil, are running out.
Relative pronouns
1 In informal contexts, we can replace *who* or *which* with *that* in defining relative clauses, but not in non-defining relative clauses.
2 In defining relative clauses *which* or *who* can be omitted if it is the object of the clause.
I welcome the measures the Government is taking to combat climate change.
3 We can replace *who* with *whom* if it is the object of the clause, but it is formal.

2 Read the *Learn this!* box. Then look again at the quotes in exercise 1 and:
1 decide which are defining relative clauses and which are non-defining relative clauses.
2 identify the relative clause in which the relative pronoun can be replaced with *that*.
3 identify the relative clause in which the relative pronoun can be omitted.

3 All these sentences contain mistakes in grammar, punctuation or style. Correct them.
1 The man, who's wearing a tie, is my uncle.
2 Space junk is a problem, which is getting worse.
3 I've got a friend what lives in Japan.
4 Solar energy is an idea which time has come.
5 Whom did you dance with at the night club?

>>> GRAMMAR BUILDER 8.2: PAGE 129 <<<

4 Rewrite each pair of sentences as one sentence. Use defining or non-defining relative clauses and appropriate punctuation.
1 Here's the money. I owe it to you.
2 I run three times a week. It keeps me healthy.
3 I made Joe a sandwich. He ate it at once.
4 I live in a village called South Milton. It has a population of 600.
5 We look after stray dogs. Their owners can't be traced.

5 Read the *Learn this!* box below. Find one participle clause in the quotes in exercise 1.

LEARN THIS!

Shortened relative clauses
1 Shortened relative clauses contain either a present participle, which replaces an active verb:
The charity protects animals facing extinction.
or they contain a past participle, which replaces a passive verb:
Global warming is mostly caused by CO_2 emitted by power stations.
2 The verb they replace can be in any tense.
The dodo was a bird hunted to extinction within a century of its discovery

6 Rewrite the sentences using shortened relative clauses.
1 People who work for private companies usually get paid more than those in the public sector.
2 Is that your dog that's making a mess on the lawn?
3 This self-portrait, which was painted by Van Gogh in 1889, is one of his finest.
4 I saw a young girl who was stealing a CD.
5 We visited a castle that was built in the sixteenth century.
6 I only eat food which is made with fresh ingredients.

>>> GRAMMAR BUILDER 8.3: PAGE 129 <<<

7 SPEAKING Work in pairs. How many sentences can you make in one minute by adding different relative clauses and other words and phrases?
1 Last week I met someone …
2 … is the place …
3 What did you think of the film …
4 I've got a friend …
5 I was born in 19___ …
6 A good student is one …

I can discuss recycling.

1. Look at the posters. What are they encouraging people to do? Which is the most visually appealing? Why?

2. 🎧 3.09 Read the task and the Exam tip below. Then listen to a student saying which poster she'd choose and why. To what extent did the student follow the advice in the tip?

   Your school wants to encourage the students to recycle more. Which one of these posters would work best? Justify your choice and say why you rejected the other posters.

   EXAM TIP

   When you are justifying your choice, try to give at least two reasons. When you are saying why you rejected the other options, try again to give at least two reasons, and don't simply give the opposite reasons. Vary your arguments.

3. Use the words below to complete the phrases.

   another   believe   main   reason   thing   top

   Justifying your opinion
   The reason I ¹_____ that is because …
   The ²_____ reason is that …
   Why do I think that? Well, for one ³_____ , …
   ⁴_____ thing is that …   Another ⁵_____ is …
   On ⁶_____ of that, …

4. **SPEAKING** Work in pairs. Do you agree with the student's opinions in exercise 2? Give reasons. Think about the design (colour and images), the message, the amount of information and how appealing it is to teenagers. Use phrases from exercise 3 in your answer.

5. 🎧 3.10 Listen to a student answering this question: *What can be done to improve the environment where you live?* Answer the questions below.

   1. Which phrases from exercise 3 did the student use?
   2. What specific examples did the student give to support her arguments?

Help make our school greener! 2

RECYCLE!

3 **THINK!**
What can I recycle at school?
YES!
plastic, steel and aluminium, glass, paper
NO!
food, cardboard, sweet wrappers and crisp packets, styrofoam

REMEMBER!
Separate metal, plastic and paper and place them in the correct bins. Ensure that cans and bottles are completely empty.

6. 🎧 3.10 Read the *Learn this!* box below. Then listen again and identify two examples of *do/did* for emphasis.

   LEARN THIS!

   do and *did* for emphasis
   We can use *do* and *did* to make statements stronger and to show a contrast. We stress *do* and *did* when they're used in this way.
   I *do* think we need to do something about global warming.
   I *did* enjoy the concert.
   The first poster is attractive but I *do* find it a bit depressing.

7. Do you agree with the student's opinions? Give reasons. Use phrases from exercise 3 in your answer.

8. 🎧 3.11 **PRONUNCIATION** Make these statements more emphatic using *do* or *did*. Then listen and repeat.

   1. We've got bins for recycling paper but we need to recycle glass too.
   2. I'm all for cutting our carbon footprint but I think the Government should come up with some better ideas.
   3. We didn't install double glazing, but we insulate the loft.
   4. It isn't easy to save energy, but we have to try.
   5. The Government didn't cut carbon emissions, but it promised to invest in renewable energy.

   ⟫⟫ GRAMMAR BUILDER 8.4: PAGE 130 ⟪⟪

9. **SPEAKING** Work in pairs. Choose one question each and take two minutes to prepare your answer. Then speak for one minute.

   1. Does your local council encourage you to recycle, and make it easy for you to do so?
   2. Do you think that plastic bags should be banned?

10. **SPEAKING** Work in pairs. Turn to page 144. Do the exam task.

I can write an opinion essay.

1 Read exam questions a–d. Then look quickly at the essay below and say which question it is answering.

  a Global warming is the most significant environmental problem facing us today. Do you agree?

  b Who bears the greatest responsibility for pollution: businesses, individual people or the government?

  c It is impossible to improve people's standard of living and at the same time avoid damaging the environment. Do you agree?

  d It's not worth combatting global warming. We should learn to live with it. Do you agree?

It's worth acknowledging from the start that while we have made ourselves richer, we have done enormous damage to the environment. The question we need to ask is whether one is an inevitable consequence of the other. My view is that it is possible to care for our world and at the same time improve our standard of living. Firstly, it's important to recognise that in the past we relied exclusively on fossil fuels to generate energy, and we couldn't avoid pouring millions of tonnes of CO_2 into the atmosphere. We should also remember that we had little alternative but to dispose of factory waste in rivers and the sea. Nowadays, we have sources of renewable energy, such as solar and wind power, and the technology to dispose safely of most hazardous waste. Secondly, we must bear in mind that we used to be simply unaware of the damage we were causing. We now understand the consequences of our actions and can therefore act more wisely. Some people argue that you cannot make cars and televisions without using up natural resources. That said, scientists are continually developing new materials which reduce our reliance on natural resources. Moreover, nowadays we are able to recycle many non-renewable materials. All things considered, I really do think that we can make our lives better and more comfortable without seriously harming the environment. While a little damage may be inevitable, we now have the knowledge and technology to avoid the mistakes of the past.

2 Look at the plan for the essay in exercise 1. Then mark where the paragraph divisions should be. Which words helped you decide?

  • **Paragraph 1** Introduction: explaining the title and giving your initial opinion.

  • **Paragraph 2** 1st argument in support of your opinion.

  • **Paragraph 3** 2nd argument in support of your opinion.

  • **Paragraph 4** Argument(s) in support of the opposite opinion, and counter-argument(s)

  • **Paragraph 5** Summary, re-stating opinion.

3 Look at these expressions. Which of these expressions are in the essay in exercise 1?

Introducing additional points
Furthermore, …   Moreover, …   What is more, …
Similarly, …   We should also remember that …

Introducing contrasting points
On the other hand, …   However, …   Having said that, …
And yet, …   That said, …   Even though …

4 Link these sentences together using an appropriate phrase from exercise 3 to start the second sentence.

  1 In the past, hunting elephants and tigers was considered acceptable. Most people had no regard whatsoever for the welfare of wild animals.

  2 Today we are much more aware of environmental problems. Governments often ignore warnings given by environmental scientists.

  3 There are lots of ways individuals can reduce their carbon footprint. To make a really big difference we need government action.

  4 You can't deny that global warming is taking place. Not everyone believes it is caused by human activity.

  5 We should use renewable sources of energy. We can use nuclear power, which does not produce greenhouse gases.

5 Read the Exam tip below. Then read the final paragraph of the essay and identify all the elements listed in the tip.

EXAM TIP

A good way to finish an opinion essay is to:
1 start with a concluding phrase and state your opinion
2 concede an opposing opinion, then repeat your strongest argument in favour.

6 Rewrite the last paragraph of the essay to express the opposite opinion. Use the same structure. Choose a different concluding phrase from the list below.

Concluding phrases
In conclusion, …   All things considered, …   To sum up, …
On balance, …   All in all, …   In the final analysis, …

(concluding phrase), (state opinion). While …
(concede an opposing point), (repeat strongest point in favour).

1 Work in pairs. Choose one of the other tasks from exercise 1 on page 88. Decide on the key question that needs to be answered. Then agree on your opinion.

The key question we need to answer is: …
Our opinion is: …

> **EXAM TIP**
>
> Make sure that you provide good points on both sides of the argument, even if you strongly agree with one side only.

2 Read the Exam tip. Then make notes for and against the opinion you expressed in exercise 2. Write down as many ideas as you can in the chart below.

Points supporting your opinion

Points supporting the opposite opinion, and counter-argument

3 Choose ideas from your chart in exercise 2 to complete the plan for paragraphs 2–4. Use the chart in exercise 2 on page 88.

4 Complete these useful phrases with an infinitive with *to* or with an *-ing* form. Use the verbs in brackets. Which two are in the essay in exercise 1 on page 88?

1 It's no use/good _____ that … (argue)
2 It's fair _____ that … (say)
3 It's important _____ that … (recognise)
4 It's worth _____ … (acknowledge)
5 It's hard _____ that … (deny)
6 It's impossible _____ whether … (say)
7 It's easy _____ … (point to)
8 It's worth _____ that … (point out)

5 Use some of the phrases in exercise 3 on page 88 to introduce the points you listed in exercise 2.

6 Write paragraph 1 (the introduction) of your essay using your answer to exercise 1. Begin by explaining the key question in your own words, then state your initial opinion.

It's worth acknowledging from the start that …
The question we need to answer is …
My own opinion is …

7 Use your notes from exercise 3 to write paragraphs 2–4 of your essay. Use the phrases in exercise 4 to help you and the ones in exercise 3 on page 88.

8 Now write the final paragraph, summing up your own opinion. Use the plan in the Exam tip and the phrases in exercise 6 on page 88 to help you.

9 Count the total number of words in all five paragraphs. If there are fewer than 200, do one or more of these things:

1 Add more arguments to paragraphs 2 and/or 3.
2 Give more examples to support the arguments in paragraphs 2 and 3.
3 Expand the introduction or conclusion.

If you have written more than 250 words, do one or more of these things:

1 Look for unnecessary repetition.
2 Look for words or sentences that you can cut without spoiling the 'flow' of the arguments.
3 Cut one or more examples that support arguments.

10 Check your work using the following checklist.

> **CHECK YOUR WORK**
>
> **Have you:**
> ☐ followed the paragraph plan?
> ☐ used some of the useful phrases from exercise 3 on page 88 and exercise 4 on page 88?
> ☐ included strong points on both sides of the argument?
> ☐ checked your spelling and grammar?

11 Now write the final version of your essay.

Unit 7

1 **Match the two halves of the compound nouns.**

1	breaking	a	broadcasts
2	live	b	journalism
3	human-interest	c	news
4	citizen	d	accounts
5	eye-witness	e	stories

Mark: ____ /5

2 **Read the quotations, then complete the reported speech.**

'I'm not going on holiday this year.'

'I'd better go home.'

'Why did you get so angry?'

'Put your clothes away!'

'When will my car be ready?'

1 My mum _____ my clothes away.
2 Mary _____ go home.
3 Dad asked the mechanic _____ ready.
4 My aunt has told me _____ holiday this year.
5 The policeman asked me _____ so angry.

Mark: ____ /5

3 **Complete the sentences with the verbs below. Use the past simple.**

claim convince insist offer warn

1 They _____ that I tell the whole story again.
2 He _____ me against talking to the police.
3 The check-out assistant _____ to help me pack.
4 My sister _____ me to apply for the job.
5 My brother _____ not to know why my laptop was broken.

Mark: ____ /5

4 **Complete the sentences with *must*, *might* or *can't*.**

1 She _____ like JLS. She's got all their albums.
2 They _____ have been swimming. The pool is closed.
3 I'm not sure where Brandon is. He _____ be in town.
4 You _____ have seen this film last month. It was only released today.
5 Elsie knew about my accident. Somebody _____ have told her.

Mark: ____ /5

Total: ____ /20

Unit 8

5 **Complete the missing words.**

1 We should all try to reduce our c_____ footprints.
2 The Government is planning to build twenty new wind t_____ off the coast of Devon.
3 In the past, we all relied on f_____ fuels for our energy.
4 They have s_____ panels on the roof to generate electricity.
5 They built a dam across the river in order to generate h_____ power.

Mark: ____ /5

6 **Complete the text with the words below.**

be able   could   couldn't   managed to   succeeded in

Jason noticed the crowd in the street, but he [1]_____ see what they were all looking at. He tried to push his way through, but only [2]_____ annoying a large man in a leather jacket. Then he had an idea: if he returned to the café and went upstairs, he would [3]_____ to look down onto the street. He raced through the door, up the stairs and [4]_____ find a table by the window. Finally, he [5]_____ see what the crowd were looking at. He turned away.

Mark: ____ /5

7 **Complete these sentences with a relative clause. Your sentences must be true as well as correct.**

1 A vandal is a person _____ .
2 Barack Obama, _____ , was born in 1961.
3 A device _____ is called a satnav.
4 Mount Everest is in the Himalayas, _____ .
5 A stadium is a place _____ .

Mark: ____ /5

8 **Write the missing words to complete the monologue.**

'The Government should ban plastic bags completely. Why? Well, for one [1]_____ , they cause litter because people drop them. On [2]_____ of that, they harm the environment because they aren't biodegradable. Cloth bags are much better. The main [3]_____ is, you can re-use them lots of times. [4]_____ thing is that they're very strong. Paper bags aren't as strong, but they [5]_____ biodegrade, at least.'

Mark: ____ /5

Total: ____ /20

Lead-in

1 Look at the headlines. In pairs, decide what a 'hacktivist' is. Where do you think the word comes from?

Hacktivists attack UK Home Office

60% of IT professionals fear hacktivists

HACKTIVISTS HIT BACK AT FBI

Reading

2 Read the text. Use it to improve your definition of 'hacktivist'.

Anonymous is the name of a group of computer hackers who take part in cyber attacks on companies, organisations and even governments. They are often referred to as 'hacktivists' (a mixture of the words 'hackers' and 'activists') because, unlike many hackers, they use cyber-attacks as a form of protest. [1] [ ] Generally speaking, they oppose any form of Internet censorship and support total freedom of expression online. They are considered by some to be courageous activists, and by others to be irresponsible cyber-criminals. As an organisation, Anonymous does not have a clear structure or leadership. It is thought that most of the people involved are aged between 18 and 24. A small, inner circle of members is believed to make the final decisions about when and where the specific cyber-attacks take place.

The group rose to prominence in 2008, when it launched a campaign against the Church of Scientology. The campaign targeted the organisation's website, bombarding it with web traffic from thousands of different PCs. [2] [ ] In 2010, Anonymous launched a campaign to support the anti-secrecy site WikiLeaks. Any organisation which was believed to be hostile to WikiLeaks was likely to be targeted for cyber-attacks. These included the United States Department of Justice, who had begun an investigation into possible criminal charges against the founder of WikiLeaks. [3] [ ]

Anonymous has also supported websites which offer free file-sharing services. When the Megaupload file-sharing site was shut down by authorities in the USA in 2012, Anonymous responded with what was described as 'the single largest Internet attack in its history'. The targets were the Justice Department, the FBI, Universal Music Group and the Motion Picture Association of America. But while Anonymous continues to campaign for a completely free and open Internet, other groups insist that laws are needed to prevent online piracy. Defending the right to swap files online, they claim, risks fatally damaging the music and film industries. [4] [ ] That is a debate which will be held not only in cyberspace but in courts of law around the world.

3 Match the gaps (1–4) in the text with four of the sentences (A–E) below. There is one extra sentence.

A When it comes to Internet freedom, where should the line be drawn?

B By doing this, they managed to make the website crash repeatedly over a period of several days.

C However, the group's activities are only considered illegal in countries where hacking is against the law.

D They also targeted Mastercard and PayPal, who had stopped accepting donations to WikiLeaks.

E Their attacks are not vandalism but part of a wider campaign with a moral and political dimension.

Listening

4 🎧 3.12 Listen. List all the different locations.

5 🎧 3.12 Listen again. Choose the correct answers.

1 Stefan doesn't chat with Daisy because
   a she isn't at home. **c** he doesn't know what to say.
   b Spikey won't allow it. **d** Daisy is angry with him.
2 Spikey blames Stefan for the failed cyber-attack because
   a he's the only other person who knew about it.
   b he knows about Internet security.
   c he admits that he mentioned it to somebody.
   d he told a friend he was going to stop the attack.
3 On the phone, what reason does Daisy give Stefan for being at the charity event?
   a She wants to support the charity.
   b She wants to discuss something with him.
   c She doesn't give a reason.
   d Spikey convinced her to go.
4 Why is Daisy meeting her father?
   a Spikey asked her to talk to him.
   b She wants to find out more about Wesley's.
   c She wants to see him, but not at his house.
   d She wants to discuss moving back to his house.
5 When Daisy talks about her group's next big protest, she
   a tells Stefan which day it will take place.
   b explains what kind of protest it will be.
   c says where the protest will take place.
   d gives away none of the information above.

Speaking

6 Discuss the following statement, saying if you agree or disagree and giving reasons.

It should be possible and legal to exchange whatever files you want to online.

Writing

7 Write an opinion essay discussing the statement in exercise 6. Remember to include some points supporting the opposite opinion from your own.

Reading

1 Get ready to READ Tell your partner about a childhood memory. Why has it stuck in your mind?

2 Do the exam task.

READING exam task

Read the text. For each question, select the correct option: A, B, C or D.

I am on the boat, looking out blindly, counting on my frozen fingers the people I love. Sandeep, my daughters, my mother, my brother. It is a pitifully short list, and does not cheer me up at all. My mother is dying – perhaps she is already dead. How much of my husband's fondness for me is simply daily habit? In how many ways will my daughters and I disappoint each other as they grow up? And my brother? Is he as anxious for me to go as I am to leave?

Don't cry, I order myself. Make yourself smile. You did your best. You're going home tomorrow.

'Look!' Tarun is pointing to something white on a nearby piece of floating ice. I hope my eyes haven't turned red, and try to show some interest. Will this miserable boat trip never end? 'Look!' It's some sort of large bird, with thin red legs. As the boat gets closer, it spreads its white wings and looks calmly at us. I've seen a bird like this somewhere before.

'Didi, doesn't it look like a sharash?'

Yes, indeed it does. But I am more surprised by the Bengali name for the bird, so unexpected in my brother's mouth. And the childhood name for me, which he hasn't used for years. Didi. A small word of love, like a magic jewel from one of my mother's stories.

I remember when we last saw sharash. It is soon after my father's death. I am eight, my brother three. My mother has sent us to stay at Third Uncle's house, out in the country. We are homesick and miserable, and do not get on with our cousins, who know how to milk cows and swim across the river. We hurt ourselves trying to climb trees with them, and they laugh at us when we cry.

But one day, after a morning filled with rain, the sun comes out, and Tarun and I run across the fields. We get muddy from head to toe, but we don't care. Perhaps we can reach the railway, jump on a passing train, and make our way back to our mother in Calcutta? Then suddenly we see them, fifteen or twenty sharash feeding in the flooded rice fields. My brother lifts his delighted hands, Look, Didi! as the birds fly up, a speeding cloud of silver light. For a moment the sky is full of wings. Whiteness and possibility. We stand with our arms around each other until they disappear.

The ferry is closer now, and everyone is looking at the bird. Even the noisy young men are quiet. The bird's eyes shine. It looks back at us, at me. I am sure of this. It has flown all the way from Bengal, to bring me a message that will save us – if only I can hear it.

The intelligence of wild things by Chitra Banerjee Divakaruni

1 The narrator of this story
 A has her whole family come and see her off.
 B is unsure of her spouse's affection.
 C is disappointed with her family.
 D has a brother who wants to go with her.
2 When they see the bird
 A it looks scared by the boat.
 B she learns that it has a name in Bengali.
 C she recognises it as a bird from her mother's stories.
 D her brother surprises her with his tenderness.
3 When the children were at Third Uncle's house
 A some of their relatives were unkind to them.
 B they ran away back to their mother.
 C they found out their father had died.
 D they had to learn how to milk cows.
4 How do the children react to the flock of sharash?
 A They wave their arms in the air.
 B They follow them across a flooded field.
 C They lose them in the sun and clouds.
 D They keep still and watch them fly away.
5 Seeing the sharash makes the narrator feel
 A bitter. **B** hopeful. **C** irrititated. **D** nervous.

Use of English

3 Do the exam task.

USE OF ENGLISH exam task

Complete the text with a suitable word in each gap.

A narrow rock that stands ¹_____ than the Empire State Building does not look like the ²_____ welcoming place to set up home. But that did not stop an insect which was ³_____ to be extinct for 80 years from building its last known colony on the 562-metre ⁴_____ Ball's Pyramid in the South Pacific Ocean. Scientists have discovered 24 of the creatures living around a plant on the rock. The 'tree lobster' insect, ⁵_____ is as large as a human hand, had somehow made its camp ⁶_____ the lack of food.

In 2001 Australian scientists decided to investigate claims by climbers who tackled Ball's Pyramid that they had seen fresh droppings there. They too saw the droppings and upon returning ⁷_____ dark with flashlights were stunned ⁸_____ discover the insect colony around the only plant on the rock. Mr Carlile said: 'It felt like stepping back into the Jurassic age, ⁹_____ insects ruled the world.'

THIS UNIT INCLUDES

Vocabulary ▪ describing behaviour ▪ adverbs ▪ adjective prefixes and suffixes
Grammar ▪ *should/could/might/needn't have* ▪ third conditional ▪ mixed
conditionals ▪ wishes and regrets ▪ purpose and result clauses
Speaking ▪ role-play
Writing ▪ story

Mistakes | 9

9A | VOCABULARY AND LISTENING Behaviour

I can discuss behaviour.

1 **SPEAKING** Look at the photos. What are the people doing? How do you think they are feeling?

2 **VOCABULARY** Work in pairs. Check the meaning of the adjectives below. Then choose one or two adjectives to describe the behaviour in each photo.

<u>Describing behaviour</u> altruistic careless clumsy considerate courageous cowardly cunning cynical deceitful disloyal eager foolish forgetful heroic hospitable hysterical over-sensitive pushy pretentious reckless romantic ruthless short-sighted spiteful thoughtless

3 🎧 3.13 Listen to six monologues. How would you describe the speakers' actions? Choose the best adjective from exercise 2 for each person.

Speaker 1: altruistic.

> **LEARN THIS!**
>
> We often use these structures to describe somebody's behaviour:
> 1 *It + be + adjective + of somebody to do something*
>   *It was kind of you to help.*
>   *It would be short-sighted of Eva to leave school.*
> 2 *It/That + be + adjective + of somebody*
>   *It/That was thoughtless of him.*

4 🎧 3.13 Read the *Learn this!* box. Then listen again and make notes about the speakers' actions. Describe the actions using the structure in the *Learn this!* box.

l *It was altruistic of him to give his cousin his ticket.*

5 Complete these sentences with your own ideas. Then compare your ideas in pairs.

1 It was deceitful of the police officer to …
2 It was forgetful of the doctor to …
3 It was cunning of the teacher to …
4 It was over-sensitive of the student to …
5 It was pushy of her mother to …
6 It was cynical of the government to …

> **LEARN THIS!**
>
> We usually form regular adverbs by adding *-ly* to the adjective (*loud → loudly*). But remember:
> • if the adjective ends *-ic*, we usually add *-ally*: *erratic → erratically (exception: public → publicly)*.
> • if the adjective ends *-y*, we replace it with *-ily*: *happy → happily, angry → angrily*.
> • if the adjective ends *-ly*, we either use the same form for the adverb (*early, daily, yearly*) or we use an adverbial phrase instead of an adverb: *friendly → in a friendly way*.
> • Some adverbs are the same as the adjective (*fast, better*, etc.) Some others (*high, deep, late*, etc.) have two forms with different meanings, one with *-ly* and one without.

6 Read the *Learn this!* box. Then form adverbs or adverbial phrases from the adjectives in exercise 2.

7 **SPEAKING** Choose three adverbs from exercise 6. Ask your partner about a time when he or she behaved in that way.

> Tell me about a time when you behaved recklessly.

> Well, about a year ago, I …

▶▶▶ **VOCABULARY BUILDER 9.1: PAGE 142** ◀◀◀

I can talk hypothetically about the past.

1 🎧 3.14 **Listen and complete the dialogue with the words below. Is Archie right to be annoyed? Why?/Why not?**

could   might   needn't   should   shouldn't

Archie You ¹_____ have invited Ava to your party. I only split up with her two weeks ago. I didn't want to see her again so soon.

Libby But you know she's a close friend of mine. I didn't want to take sides. I had to invite both of you.

Archie But you ²_____ have told me she was coming!

Libby She asked me not to. Maybe it was a mistake, but I promised her that I wouldn't tell you.

Archie Well, you ³_____ have given me a hint. If you'd warned me, I'd have stayed at home.

Libby But it was nice to see her, wasn't it? I mean, you got on fine. You ⁴_____ have been so worried about seeing her!

Archie True. But still … you ⁵_____ have warned me.

LEARN THIS!

should/could/might/needn't have + **past participle**

1 We can use *shouldn't have* to express disapproval of past actions.
She shouldn't have laughed at her brother.
2 We use *should have*, *might have* or *could have* to say what the right way to behave was, in our opinion.
She should/could/might have been kinder!
3 We use *needn't have* to say an action was unnecessary.
You needn't have shouted, I was right beside you.

2 **Read the *Learn this!* box. Then join the sentences using *should have*, *shouldn't have* or *needn't have*, and *because*.**

1 She told me Sam's address. I already knew it.
She needn't have told me Sam's address because I already knew it.
2 You didn't go to the doctor's. You were feeling very ill.
3 She didn't give her dad a card. It was his birthday.
4 Mark took his camera to the match. He took no photos.
5 We took sun cream on holiday. It rained every day.
6 You spent all your money. You needed some for the bus.

>>> GRAMMAR BUILDER 9.1: PAGE 130 <<<

LEARN THIS!

Third conditional

1 We use the third conditional to talk about how a situation in the past could have been avoided.
If we hadn't stayed out so late, I wouldn't have overslept. (But we did stay out late so I did oversleep.)
2 The *if* clause can come before or after the main clause. We use the past perfect in the *if* clause and *would/wouldn't have* in the main clause. Be careful: *had* and *would* both have the same short form *'d*.
I'd have come if you'd invited me. (But you didn't invite me, so I didn't come.)

3 **Read the *Learn this!* box. Find an example of the third conditional in the dialogue in exercise 1 and write an explanation like the ones in brackets in the box.**

>>> GRAMMAR BUILDER 9.2: PAGE 130 <<<

4 USE OF ENGLISH **Complete the second sentence so it means the same as the first. Include the word in brackets.**

1 We only arrived on time because we ran. (wouldn't)
If we _____ arrived on time.
2 I wish you'd taken some photos! (might)
You _____ photos!
3 It was a bad idea to eat at the hotel. (shouldn't)
We _____ at the hotel.
4 He panicked – that's the only reason he got lost. (if)
He wouldn't have _____ panicked.
5 We'd never have won without your help. (helped)
If _____ we wouldn't have won.
6 You didn't have to buy me a present. (needn't)
You _____ a present.

5 **Make notes about what you would have done if you had found yourself in these situations:**

1 a pet was sick on your school bag
2 you overslept by an hour
3 all your school clothes were dirty
4 you saw a house on fire
5 you couldn't find your keys/phone

6 SPEAKING **In pairs, take turns to ask and answer questions about the situations in exercise 5.**

> What would you have done if a pet had been sick on your school bag?

> I would have …

I can talk about the risks of using social networking sites.

1 SPEAKING **In pairs, ask and answer these questions.**

1 Have you got an account on Facebook or any other social networking site? If so, how often do you use it and what do you use it for?

2 Which family members, if any, are Facebook friends of yours? Do you like the idea of a parent being your Facebook friend? Why?/Why not?

2 🎧 3.15 **Read the text. In your own words, say why Dr Wright thinks parents should be Facebook friends with their teenage children. Do you agree? Why?/Why not?**

Parents of boys at a Sydney private school have been urged to monitor their sons' use of Facebook, with a warning that any mistakes made in teenage years could be permanently recorded on the Internet and catch up with them later in life.

The headmaster, Timothy Wright, wrote to parents on Thursday, explaining that younger boys were too immature to fully gauge the possible consequences of disclosing private information on social networking sites. 'We now know that those parts of the brain that deal with decision-making are still developing in a man in his 20s,' he said. 'But mistakes made at fifteen may be still retrievable by an employer ten years later.

'Modern technology means that a careless word, a slanderous comment or an inappropriate photograph, are on permanent record and freely available to anyone who has access. Stupidities that were once forgotten now last, spread and damage in ways unknown before this decade.'

Dr Wright said that harsh words spoken in the playground could be more easily forgotten, but those captured on the Internet or on mobile phone text messages could have far more lasting and more hurtful consequences. He said there was widespread use of Facebook by students, including those of primary school age, which was against the site's guidelines for use.

He urged parents to set ground rules for use of mobile phones and the Internet and in particular to set boundaries on taking and sending images that may be used to bully others. 'Parents who are paying for the Internet service have an unquestionable right to insist they are a friend on Facebook. I would certainly insist on this until at least the end of year 10* if not later,' he wrote.

* Students are usually sixteen at the end of year 10.

3 **Answer the questions about the text.**

1 Why does it matter if a fifteen-year-old makes a mistake on Facebook?

2 Why might it be difficult for fifteen-year-olds to think about the consequences of their online activity?

3 Why can online arguments often be more damaging than playground arguments?

4 What kinds of rules does Dr Wright want parents to make?

4 VOCABULARY **Work in pairs. Explain the meaning of the highlighted adjectives in the text. Then list the words with a prefix and those with a suffix in the chart below. Which adjective has a suffix and a prefix?**

prefixes	suffixes

⟫⟫ **VOCABULARY BUILDER 9.2: PAGE 142** ⟪⟪

5 🎧 3.16 **Listen to a radio journalist talking about Rebecca Black. Does he think it was a mistake for Rebecca to post the song on YouTube? Why?/ Why not? Do you agree?**

6 🎧 3.16 **Listen again. Are these sentences true (T) or false (F)?**

1 Ark Music Factory charge $4,000 for recording a song and video, and extra for writing it.

2 Rebecca Black's mother paid for Rebecca to record a song with Ark Music Factory.

3 Only 167 people watched Rebecca's video the first month it was on YouTube.

4 Most of the people who watched the video on YouTube clicked 'dislike'.

5 Rebecca was not particularly surprised by the reaction.

6 The song, *Friday*, was removed from YouTube but posted again later.

7 Rebecca travelled to Australia to publicise her new music video.

7 **Look at the online activities below. Do you think they might turn out to be mistakes? Why?/Why not?**

You're fifteen years old and you:

• post a love poem to a girl/boy you like on his/her Facebook page.

• post a funny clip of your friend falling over on YouTube.

• put an invitation to your birthday party on your public Facebook page.

• leave a negative comment about a photo on your friend's Facebook page, for a joke.

8 SPEAKING **In pairs, discuss your ideas from exercise 7. Do you agree or disagree? Give reasons.**

1 SPEAKING If you had been brought up by a different family, what things about you might be the same or different? Discuss the ideas below in pairs.

appearance education food friends language
money religion sport

2 🎧 3.17 Read the text below about two girls brought up by the wrong families. Which sentence (a–d) is true?

a The parents and children all get on well with each other.
b The children get on better than the parents.
c The parents get on better than the children.
d None of the people involved get on well.

EXAM TIP

When you read a complex text, it's often helpful to make simple notes to remind you of key details. These might even be in the form of a diagram – do whatever is most useful. For example, your notes could show:
* relationships between characters
* a basic sequence of events
* the layout of a place being described.

HOSPITAL MIX-UP

TWO RUSSIAN FAMILIES are united by a terrible event that took place more than a decade ago. Their newborn daughters were accidentally mixed up in the maternity hospital and grew up with the 'wrong' parents.

In a tiny flat in the Ural Mountains, Yulia Belyaeva and her twelve-year-old daughter Irina are looking through family photos.

One of the pictures shows Irina as a newborn baby wrapped in a blanket. It was taken the day mother and daughter left hospital. But twelve years on, Yulia Belyaeva has discovered that the baby she'd taken home – the daughter she'd thought she'd given birth to – is not her child.

'I found this out when my ex-husband refused to pay maintenance,' says Yulia. 'I took him to court to prove that he was Irina's father. We did all the DNA tests. But the results were a total surprise. Not only does my ex-husband have no biological link to Irina – neither do I.'

Police believe that on 17 December 1998, there was a terrible mix-up at the local maternity hospital. Two babies were given the wrong name tags – and the wrong parents.

'At first I thought it was a joke,' recalls Yulia. 'Then I couldn't stop crying. My whole world had turned upside down. I kept worrying what Irina would say. And I kept thinking about my real daughter. Maybe she'd been abandoned or put in an orphanage. Or perhaps she was begging on the streets.'

Desperate to find her, Yulia went to the police and they launched a search for her biological daughter. Within weeks they had found her.

In a village half an hour's drive from Yulia Belyaeva's flat lives twelve-year-old Anya Iskanderova. In a meadow opposite her house, she shows me her favourite cow, April. Anya is the girl Yulia had given birth to. She is the spitting image of her biological mother.

3 Read the Exam tip. Then complete the diagram below with the correct names from the text.

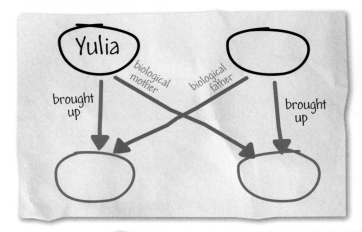

In the house is Naimat Iskanderov – the man Anya thought was her father. Naimat is from Tajikistan. He had married a Russian woman, but they had divorced. It was Naimat who brought up Anya and his other children as devout Muslims. When police told him about the mistake at the maternity hospital and that Anya was not his daughter, to begin with he refused to believe it.

'Then the detective showed me a photo of the other girl, Irina, the one they said was my real daughter,' Naimat tells me. 'When I saw her face, it was like seeing myself. My arms and legs began shaking. It was awful to think that my child had grown up with another family and that I had brought up someone else's daughter.'

The two families meet regularly now. But the parents admit there is tension between them.

'It is difficult,' concedes Naimat. 'One family is Christian, the other is Muslim. We have different traditions. What I fear most is that the daughter I've raised will start going drinking in bars, that she will stop praying and working. I'm worried she will lose her religion.'

'There is tension between the adults,' says Yulia. 'Naimat doesn't like some things that go on in our family, I don't like some things in their home. Both of us are used to life as it has been. Not as it is now. Now it is a nightmare.'

More than anything Yulia fears that both children will desert her. She can see that the daughter she brought up is keen to spend time now with her biological father. And the child she actually gave birth to is like a stranger.

'I try to show Anya motherly love,' Yulia says, 'But she doesn't accept it. She's been brought up differently. She's not used to tenderness. We don't really understand each other. When your own daughter looks at you like a stranger, that's so painful.'

Both families are suing the Kopeysk Maternity Hospital for more than $300,000 in damages. Its chief doctor went on Russian TV to apologise for the mistake, but argued the hospital could not afford to settle such a claim. Prosecutors are considering bringing criminal charges against the hospital staff responsible for the mix-up – although that seems unlikely, considering so many years have passed.

For now the two girls say they do not want to swap parents. They are just glad to have found each other.

'To begin with we were a bit shy,' Irina tells me, 'but now we've become the best of friends.'

'What I'd like,' says Anya, 'is for all of us to live in one big house.'

Irina and Anya were born fifteen minutes apart. Now the truth about what happened in hospital has brought them together.

4 Choose the best answers. How did your diagram from exercise 3 help you do this task?

1 Yulia only found out that Irina was not her biological daughter
  a when they looked at some family photos.
  b when they got home from hospital.
  c after twelve years.
  d after ten years.

2 Yulia's family had DNA tests in order to confirm
  a who Irina's father was.
  b whether Yulia was Irina's mother.
  c whether there had been a mix-up at the hospital.
  d whether a family member had committed a crime.

3 When Yulia found out about the mistake, she
  a felt very upset and worried.
  b thought it was funny at first.
  c tried not to think about it too much.
  d was not very surprised.

4 Anya, Yulia's biological daughter, lives with
  a her biological mother's ex-husband.
  b her biological father.
  c Irina's biological father.
  d her biological parents.

5 Naimat is worried that
  a Anya will reject her Muslim traditions.
  b Anya will want to live with her biological mother.
  c Irina will want to come and live with him.
  d Irina won't want to become a Muslim.

6 Yulia is particularly worried that
  a Irina will convert to Islam.
  b Irina will have terrible nightmares.
  c Naimat won't approve of her family.
  d neither Anya nor Irina will want to live with her.

7 What Anya would like best is
  a to go and live with Irina and Naimat.
  b to get money from the hospital.
  c to prove that the hospital is guilty of a crime.
  d to live with Yulia, Anya and Naimat.

5 **VOCABULARY** Work in pairs. Take turns to explain the meaning of the underlined phrases below to your partner.

1 Two Russian families are united by a terrible event …
2 My ex-husband refused to pay maintenance.
3 I took him to court to prove that he was Irina's father.
4 My whole world had turned upside down.
5 She is the spitting image of her biological mother.
6 But the parents admit there is tension between them.
7 Now it is a nightmare.
8 She's not used to tenderness.
9 Both families are suing the Kopeysk Maternity Hospital for more than $300,000 in damages.
10 The hospital could not afford to settle such a claim.

6 **VOCABULARY** Underline the phrasal verb below in the text. Then underline the noun formed from it.

drop out   get away   hold up   mix up   sell out   turn out

7 Form nouns from the other five phrasal verbs in exercise 6. Then write an example sentence for each one.

8 🎧 3.18 Read and listen to the song. Choose the two best adjectives to describe the singer's feelings. Find evidence in the lyrics for your choices.

conceited   courageous   determined   heroic   optimistic
pessimistic   regretful   ruthless

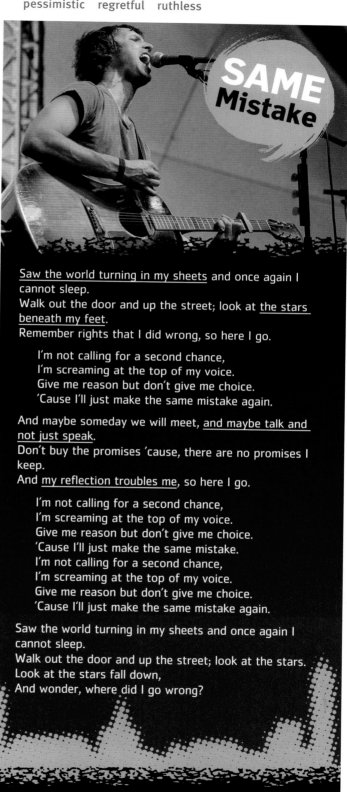

SAME Mistake

Saw the world turning in my sheets and once again I cannot sleep.
Walk out the door and up the street; look at the stars beneath my feet.
Remember rights that I did wrong, so here I go.

  I'm not calling for a second chance,
  I'm screaming at the top of my voice.
  Give me reason but don't give me choice.
  'Cause I'll just make the same mistake again.

And maybe someday we will meet, and maybe talk and not just speak.
Don't buy the promises 'cause, there are no promises I keep.
And my reflection troubles me, so here I go.

  I'm not calling for a second chance,
  I'm screaming at the top of my voice.
  Give me reason but don't give me choice.
  'Cause I'll just make the same mistake.
  I'm not calling for a second chance,
  I'm screaming at the top of my voice.
  Give me reason but don't give me choice.
  'Cause I'll just make the same mistake again.

Saw the world turning in my sheets and once again I cannot sleep.
Walk out the door and up the street; look at the stars.
Look at the stars fall down,
And wonder, where did I go wrong?

9 **SPEAKING** In pairs, discuss what the four underlined phrases in the song might mean. Then share your ideas with the class.

1 **SPEAKING** Look at a product that was invented by mistake. What do you think the inventor was trying to make? Choose from the ideas below.

a cleaning product
food for animals
glue
a weapon

2 🎧 3.19 Complete the text with the words below. Then listen and check.

could   didn't   hadn't   were   would   wouldn't

'Mistakes are the portals for discovery,' wrote the Irish novelist James Joyce, and it's true that certain mistakes in history have turned out to be lucky for the people who made them. Many familiar items ¹_____ not exist if their inventors ²_____ made lucky mistakes. In 1886, a pharmacist's assistant used fizzy water by mistake to mix a new medicine. The result? Coca-Cola.

Around 1940, a scientist called Dr Percy Spencer was doing military research with microwaves when he discovered that a chocolate bar in his pocket had melted. As a result, he realised that microwave radiation ³_____ be used for cooking. If he hadn't had that candy bar, microwave ovens probably ⁴_____ exist today!

Perhaps the most important accidental discovery was penicillin. If today's doctors ⁵_____ have penicillin and other antibiotics, many of the students in your class wouldn't have survived childhood. We have Alexander Fleming to thank for its discovery. Back in 1928, he noticed the drug when it grew by accident in his messy laboratory. This proves another interesting fact: If scientists ⁶_____ always tidy and well organised, they wouldn't have made some of the most important discoveries in history!

LEARN THIS!

Mixed conditionals
A mixed conditional is a mixture of the 2nd and 3rd conditionals. It tells us about an imaginary situation which mixes past and present. There are two types.
A When the *if* clause is about the past, we use the past perfect. We use *would* + base form for the main clause.
(past) *If I had worked harder at school,* (present) *I would be rich now.*
B When the *if* clause is about the present, we use the past simple. We use *would have* + past participle for the main clause.
(present) *If I were really tall,* (past) *I would have joined the basketball team.*

3 Read the *Learn this!* box. Underline all the examples of mixed conditionals in the text in exercise 2. Is each one type A or type B?

4 Match the two halves of the mixed conditional sentences. Then say if each one is type A or type B.

1 If you'd accepted that job at the bank,   [e] [A]
2 If she weren't so romantic,   [ ] [ ]
3 If we were Australian,   [ ] [ ]
4 If you hadn't forgotten the map,   [ ] [ ]
5 If it hadn't rained so much,   [ ] [ ]
6 If your grandparents were alive,   [ ] [ ]

a she wouldn't have got married after three months.
b we wouldn't be lost.
c they would have been proud of your results.
d we'd have grown up speaking English.
e you'd be on a high salary by now.
f the garden wouldn't look so beautiful.

>>> **GRAMMAR BUILDER 9.3: PAGE 131** <<<

LOOK OUT!
We often use *were* instead of *was* in the *if* clause of a second or mixed conditional sentence.
If she were older, they would have let her into the nightclub.
We use *could* to mean *would be able to (would + can)*.
If you hadn't used all the milk, we could have coffee now.

5 Read the *Look out!* box. Then write mixed conditional sentences which express the same information as each pair of sentences below.

1 It's summer. That's why I went out without my coat.
   If it weren't summer, I wouldn't have gone out without my coat.
2 I can't speak Portuguese. That's why I didn't visit Brazil.
3 I left my phone at home. That's why I can't call for a taxi.
4 We got on the wrong train. That's why we aren't at Heathrow Airport now.
5 I don't eat meat. That's why I didn't go to the barbecue last weekend.
6 It didn't snow again after the burglary. That's why the burglar's footprints are still visible.

6 **SPEAKING** Work in pairs. Complete the sentences with your own ideas. Then discuss them with another pair.

1 If mobile phones hadn't been invented, people today would/wouldn't …
2 If my family were billionaires, I would/wouldn't have …
3 If I had studied harder since the age of six, I would/wouldn't …

1 SPEAKING Describe the photo in pairs. What do you think might happen next? Use the words below to help you.

accuse   alarm   item of clothing   security guard
shoplift   shoplifter   thief

2 🎧 3.20 Work in pairs. Listen to three candidates doing the task below. Which candidate performs best, in your opinion? Discuss your reasons.

After you and a friend have been shopping in London, you realise that you have an item of clothing in your bag which you didn't pay for. You're discussing the situation. Address the following issues:
- what the item is.
- the reason for the mistake.
- how you feel about the situation.
- what you'll do next.

EXAM TIP

Make sure you clearly say something about all four issues in the task. You will lose marks if you don't. Look carefully at the four issues before the conversation starts and think of one or two key words for each issue. Then tick them off in your mind as you mention them during the conversation.

3 🎧 3.20 Read the Exam tip. Then listen again, and in pairs try to write the key words for each candidate.

candidate:	1	2	3
what the item is			
the reason for the mistake			
how you feel about it			
what you'll do next			

LEARN THIS!

Expressing regret
We can use these phrases for expressing regret about the past:
I (really) wish I had/hadn't (seen it).
If only I had/hadn't (spoken to her).
I'd rather I had/hadn't (been there).
When the verb is can, we normally use could have or had been able to:
I wish I could have helped/had been able to help.

4 Read the *Learn this!* box. Then imagine you are one of the candidates from exercises 2 and 3. Use two different structures to express two regrets about the situation.

5 USE OF ENGLISH Rewrite sentences 1–5 using the words in brackets. Don't change the meaning.

1 If only I'd put the T-shirt on the floor. (wish)
2 I wish I hadn't answered the phone. (if)
3 I wish the alarm had gone off. (rather)
4 If only I'd looked in my bag earlier. (wish)
5 I wish I hadn't gone into that shop. (if)
6 If only I'd done my shopping online. (rather)

≫ GRAMMAR BUILDER 9.4: PAGE 131 ≪

6 Look at the speaking task below. Then write down one key word for each of the four issues.

During a day in town, you picked up somebody else's phone by mistake. You're discussing the situation with a friend. Address the following issues:
- the reason for your mistake.
- the best way to find the phone's owner.
- how you feel about the situation.
- what you'll do next.

7 Think of two regrets you can include in your answer to the task in exercise 6. Make a note of them using two different structures from the *Learn this!* box.

8 SPEAKING Do the task in pairs, taking turns to be the candidate and the examiner.

Candidate: Use your notes from exercises 6 and 7.
Examiner: Check that the candidate addresses all four issues in the task.

It was a Saturday night in January and I was on my way to a sleepover at Nathan's house. I'd never been to his house before, but I'd been sent the address by text: 39 Western Avenue.

As I turned the corner into Western Avenue, a cloud went in front of the moon. Was this next house Nathan's? It was so dark now that I couldn't see the numbers clearly, but I walked up the driveway anyway, rang the bell and waited. Nobody came to open the door so I rang again. Then I saw I had gone to number 37 by mistake.

Then the door opened abruptly. There were no lights on in the house so I couldn't see much. There was a shout and a man pushed past me and ran towards the street. Another man followed. They were in such a hurry to leave that they dropped most of the things they were carrying. I picked one of them up so I could look at it more closely. It was a brooch. Suddenly, I understood what had been happening and phoned the police.

After waiting for five or ten minutes on the doorstep, an unmarked police car arrived and two detectives got out. One of them went into the house so that he could look for clues while the other asked me for a description of the men. 'You did well,' he said. 'It really was heroic of you to interrupt those burglars and chase them away.'

1 **SPEAKING** Read the task below and the story above in pairs. Explain in your own words what mistake the main character makes and why it turns out to be a good thing.

Write a story in which the main character makes a mistake which turns out to be a good thing.

2 **Put the events of the story in the order they happened.**

a The narrator arrived in Western Avenue. ☐
b The narrator called the police. ☐
c The front door opened and two men ran out. ☐
d The narrator was sent Nathan's address. ☐
e Two detectives arrived at the scene of the crime. ☐
f The narrator rang the bell of 37 Western Avenue. ☐
g The narrator picked up a brooch. ☐

Talking about mistakes

1 We can use these phrases for talking about mistakes:
to make a mistake (doing something)
to do something by mistake/by accident
to get something wrong (e.g. I got her name wrong.)
the wrong + noun (e.g. I phoned the wrong person.)
mistakenly (e.g. I mistakenly paid twice for the tickets.)
2 We add the prefix *mis-* to some verbs to show error:
I misread/misheard/misspelt/mistyped his address.
They misjudged/misunderstood/misquoted me.

3 **USE OF ENGLISH** Read the *Learn this!* box. Then complete the second sentence so it means the same as the first. Include a word or phrase from the *Learn this!* box.

1 I didn't put the correct address on the envelope.
I _____ the envelope.
2 She didn't mean to mention her party on Facebook.
She _____ on Facebook.
3 They didn't spell my name correctly on the poster.
They _____ on the poster.
4 We didn't mean to get on that train.
We _____ train.
5 He didn't understand the instructions properly.
He _____ the instructions.

EXAM TIP

It's important to find a good ending for your story. You could finish with:
• a surprise or a revelation
It turned out our cleaner was really a spy!
• something which links back to the beginning of the story
So finally, I found the book I'd been searching for.
• something which links the story to the present
And now, years later, I still think about her every day.
• something mysterious, chilling or open-ended
As he was leaving, he turned and gave me an evil look: 'This isn't over,' he snarled.

4 Read the Exam tip. Then choose the best ending for the story in exercise 1 from a–d below. Think about why you prefer it. There is no correct answer.

a 'Oh, I don't need a reward,' I replied, putting my hand in my pocket to feel the diamond brooch.
b The detectives put everything the burglars had dropped in a bag, got into their car and drove away. As they left, a police officer arrived on a motorbike. 'Did you call the police?' he asked me.
c I still think about that night often and wonder if it was heroic of me or just foolish!
d There was the noise of an engine starting, and I turned round just in time to see the burglars drive off in the police car, laughing and waving out of the window.

5 **SPEAKING** Discuss the ending in pairs. Do you agree which ending is best? Can you think of a better one?

WRITING TASK Story

I can write a story on a given topic.

1 SPEAKING You are going to do the writing task on page 100. Read the Exam tip below, then work in pairs and think of some more ideas for types of mistakes. Make notes.

EXAM TIP

Brainstorming is the first stage of writing a story. You need to think of several different ideas and write them down. You can then choose the best and use them in your story.

Mistakes

wrong bus / train / plane

late for school / exam

send text/email to wrong person   fall over

spelling mistake   mistake with recipe when cooking

2 SPEAKING Discuss your ideas from exercise 1 and try to think how each of the mistakes could end up being a good thing. Reject the idea if you can't think of anything.

3 Match the two halves of these story ideas. Which do you think is the best? Are any of your ideas from exercise 2 better, in your opinion?

1 You miss your train because you're late. ☐
2 You mean to send a message to your friend about X, a girl/boy you fancy, but you send it to Y by mistake. ☐
3 At the theatre, you can't find your friends because you're sitting in the wrong seat. ☐
4 You fall over while demonstrating your snowboarding skills to a friend. ☐
5 While making a birthday cake for a friend, you get the ingredients completely wrong. ☐

a The funny video clip makes you a YouTube star.
b You get a reply which makes it clear he or she feels the same way.
c You accidentally invent a new and delicious kind of cookie.
d You see a brilliant flashmob dance at the station.
e You get on really well with the people next to you and you become good friends.

4 Choose one idea from exercise 2 or 3 for your story. Make notes using the headings below or a similar writing plan. Remember the advice in the Exam tip on page 100 about endings.

- Setting the scene (where? when?):
- The mistake (what? why?):
- The result (why was it good?):
- The ending:

Expressing purpose and result

1 We can express purpose with a simple infinitive or the phrase *in order (not) to* or *so as (not) to*.
I went into town to buy/in order to buy a coat.

2 The phrases *with a view to* and *with the intention of* express purpose and are followed by an *-ing* form.
I went to the police station with the intention of complaining about my noisy neighbours.

3 We can also express purpose with *in order that, so that* or *so* followed by a clause.
He stood on a chair in order that / so / so that we could all see him.

4 We can express a result with *so* (but not *so that*)
The café was closed so I went home.

5 We can also express a result using *so* + adjective or *such* (+ adjective) + noun followed by *that* and a clause.
She was so tired that she fell asleep immediately.
It was such a small bed that I fell out.

5 Read the *Learn this!* box. How many purpose and result clauses can you find in the story in exercise 1 on page 100?

>>> GRAMMAR BUILDER 9.5: PAGE 132 <<<

6 Combine each pair of sentences into a single sentence that includes a result or purpose clause. Include the word in brackets.

1 It was a cold night. I didn't want to go out. (such)
It was such a cold night that I didn't want to go out.
2 Tia wanted to see us. We went into London. (order)
3 We left the cinema. We weren't enjoying the film. (so)
4 They wanted to make me angry. They put an unkind comment about me on Facebook. (view)
5 He's very self-centred. That's why he hasn't got any friends. (so)
6 She was talking very quickly. I couldn't understand her. (that)

7 Write your story. Follow the plan you made in exercise 4. Write 200–250 words in total.

CHECK YOUR WORK

Have you:

☐ followed your writing plan?
☐ written 200–250 words?
☐ included an effective ending?
☐ included at least one of the expressions for talking about mistakes in the *Learn this!* box on page 100?
☐ included at least one purpose or result clause?
☐ checked your spelling and grammar?

Listening

1 **Get ready to LISTEN** Work in pairs. Make a list of things that could go wrong when going on holiday by plane.

2 Do the exam task.

LISTENING exam task

🎧 3.21 Listen to an account of a holiday full of problems. For each sentence select the appropriate option: A, B, C or D.

1 The first problem with their trip was that
   A the tickets were very expensive.
   B the family went to the wrong airport.
   C they had to change airlines.
   D the time of their flight was changed.

2 In St Maarten
   A the family had to phone all the airlines one by one.
   B the airport officials were not very eager to help.
   C they realised they had left some luggage on the plane.
   D they were relieved to have the basic necessities.

3 Which sentence is true about the cruise?
   A It was delayed so the family had to wait a few days.
   B Although everyone was a little upset, it was wonderful.
   C They had to buy new equipment before joining it.
   D They had to wear dirty clothes.

4 When the cruise was over,
   A they felt the airlines should give them some money.
   B the airport staff said some new baggage had arrived.
   C all their luggage was waiting for them in the storage room.
   D the family had to sit in the airport for a long time again.

Use of English

3 Do the exam task.

USE OF ENGLISH exam task

Complete each gap in the text with a word formed from the word in brackets.

Technically, an outtake is any part of a film or a TV programme that is removed in the final cut. However, outtakes have now come to represent the humorous mistakes made in the process of filming. The ¹_____ (INCLUDE) of outtakes in a film started with the action-comedy film *Hooper* in 1978. The director wanted to show various angles of the film's ²_____ (IMPRESS) stunts in the end credits. He also included funny mistakes by the actors, which proved so popular with audiences that subsequent films copied this. Now there are TV shows dedicated to these outtakes.

Why are we so enamoured with these 'bloopers'? Actors are often not keen to be seen making mistakes. Obviously, it's embarrassing for them to seem silly and ³_____ (PROFESSION), which is probably why we, the audience, love seeing famous people getting it wrong. It makes them seem more human and a lot less ⁴_____ (GLAMOUR)! Everyone can identify with saying the wrong thing at the wrong time, or having to do something ⁵_____ (REPEAT) because it just won't go right. And someone knocking into things or falling over ⁶_____ (INTENTION)? That has always made us laugh. Professional circus clowns have taken this one step further. Their whole performance is comprised of these classic 'bloopers'.

Speaking

4 **Get ready to SPEAK** Read the phrases below. Put them into two groups: (1) making a complaint and (2) responding to a complaint.

   a I'm afraid I'm not at all happy about …
   b Leave it with me and I'll see what I can do.
   c I'm afraid there's nothing I can do about that.
   d I'll do what I can, but I can't make any promises.
   e I'm sorry, but this really isn't acceptable.
   f I'm afraid that just isn't good enough.

5 Do the exam task.

SPEAKING exam task

You and two relatives are staying at a hotel that has made several mistakes with your reservation. Speak to the manager about these problems:

- Your two hotel rooms are too far apart.
- You have been given two double rooms instead of one double and one single.
- You asked for quiet rooms but they overlook the street.
- You booked for five nights but have been told the rooms are only available for three nights.

THIS UNIT INCLUDES

Vocabulary ▪ sports equipment ▪ sports venues ▪ sports disciplines ▪ noun suffixes
Grammar ▪ emphasis and inversion ▪ unreal past ▪ *had better* ▪ *might as well*
▪ adverbial phrases
Speaking ▪ photo description
Writing ▪ description of an event

Game on! 10

10A VOCABULARY AND LISTENING Sports

I can discuss sport.

1 SPEAKING Describe the photos. Use some of the words below to help you.

<u>Sports equipment</u> ball bat board cap club cue flag goal gloves goggles helmet hoop net pads puck racket shuttlecock skates strip stick wetsuit

2 SPEAKING In pairs, underline the words in exercise 1 that you didn't use. In what sports might you use these things?

bat – baseball, table tennis, ...

3 VOCABULARY Complete the list of sports venues using the words below. Can you also add the person who does each sport?

circuit course court pitch pool ring rink slope table track

Sports venues		
in		
a boxing ¹_____	a swimming ²_____	a skating ³_____
boxer	⁴_____	⁵_____

on	
an athletics ⁶_____	⁷_____
a golf ⁸_____	⁹_____
a tennis ¹⁰_____	¹¹_____ _____
a football ¹²_____	¹³_____
a ski ¹⁴_____	¹⁵_____
a pool ¹⁶_____	¹⁷_____ _____
a Formula 1 ¹⁸_____	¹⁹_____

4 SPEAKING Work in pairs. How many more sports can you think of which take place (a) in a ring? (b) on a court? or (c) on a pitch?

5 🎧 3.22 Listen to five descriptions of an event. For each description, identify the venue and two pieces of sports equipment mentioned.

> **EXAM TIP**
>
> When you answer a true / false question, don't mark the sentence as true just because you recognise some of the details. Remember that the answer is only true if the whole of the sentence is true. If it contains any false details, the answer is false.

6 🎧 3.22 Read the Exam tip. Then listen again and mark the sentences true (T) or false (F). Which sentences contain one or two true details but are still false?

1 A dog ran on during the match and one of the linesmen caught it.
2 A golfer sneezed at the same time as playing a shot and ended up playing a bad one.
3 The winner of the race was angry with another competitor.
4 A young boy played a few points because the professional was angry with himself.
5 When the fight started, the other players didn't try to stop it.

7 SPEAKING Work in pairs. Imagine you are setting up a sports summer camp for teenagers. You can buy six different items of sports equipment. Which will you choose?

8 SPEAKING Compare your ideas with other pairs. Give reasons for your choices. Explain why you are rejecting other items.

⫸⫸⫸ VOCABULARY BUILDER 10.1: PAGE 143 ⫷⫷⫷

I can use sentence structure to create emphasis.

message board ⊠

The person I'm looking forward to watching is Torah Bright. It's her technique that I really admire. Australians are just natural sportspeople. She'll win gold, I'm sure. **SHREDDER**

Not sure I agree about Torah, Shredder. It's Aimee Fuller who has shown the best form in the first half of the season. All she needs is a bit of luck. **ROXY**

I'm a big Aimee fan too. What's amazing is that she's from Northern Ireland, a country with no mountains! How she learned to snowboard in the first place I really don't know! **DREAMER**

It's no mystery, Dreamer. What happened was that she went to live in the USA for a few years as a teenager. That's where she learnt to snowboard. **ROXY**

Aimee Fuller? No way will she win. The person with the best chance, in my opinion, is Cilka Sadar. She's from Slovenia. What gives her a big advantage is that she used to be a gymnast. She has lots of strength and stamina. **GOOFY**

1 Read the snowboarding message board. What are the names and nationalities of the different snowboarders it mentions? Have you heard of any of them?

2 Read the *Learn this!* box. Underline all the examples of these structures in the message board.

LEARN THIS!

Emphasis and inversion

1 We can make a sentence more emphatic by adding an extra clause to highlight key information.
It was John who broke your bat. (John broke your bat.)
The person I feel sorry for is Eva. (I feel sorry for Eva.)
All we need to do is (to) ask. (We just need to ask.)
What happened was (that) it began to rain. (It began to rain.)

2 We can also make a sentence more emphatic by putting important words at the start. After a negative adverb or phrase, the subject-verb word order changes.
*Never **had I seen** such an exciting game.*
*Under no circumstances **was I going to** leave early.*

---

3 Rewrite the sentences you underlined in the message board without emphasis.

1 I'm looking forward to watching Torah Bright.

LOOK OUT!

After *All* or *What (I) did was …* we use an infinitive with or without *to*.
What she did was (to) finish the course on one ski.
However, after *All that / What happened was …* we need a subject and a verb. We can put *that* before the subject:
All that happened was (that) they deducted five points.

---

4 Read the *Look out!* box. Then rewrite the sentences with *What …* or *All (that) …* at the beginning.

1 They had to postpone the snowboarding final because of the weather. (What …)
2 They just held the final the next morning. (All …)
3 There was a snow storm. (What …)
4 Nobody could see the snowboarders in action. (What …)
5 So they just turned the floodlights on. (All …)

>>> GRAMMAR BUILDER 10.1: PAGE 132 <<<

5 Rewrite the sentences below starting with the words in brackets. Use structures from the *Learn this!* box in exercise 2 and the *Look out!* box.

1 The spectators were most excited about seeing the young Czech snowboarder. (The person …)
2 The Czech girl had the best chance of winning the event. (It was …)
3 She just needed to finish the course without falling. (All …)
4 She lost her board within ten seconds of starting the course. (What …)
5 A crowd has rarely looked so disappointed. (Rarely …)

6 **SPEAKING** Ask and answer the questions in pairs. Begin your answers with the words in brackets and use structures from the *Learn this!* and *Look out!* boxes.

1 Which sports star do you most admire and why? (The sports star I …)
2 How can sports stars be good role models for young people? (What they need …)
3 What should sports stars never do, in your opinion? (Under no circumstances …)
4 Can you describe the last time you watched or played sport? (What I did … / What happened …)
5 Which sport is the easiest to start playing/doing? Why? (I think … is the easiest because all you need …)

1 SPEAKING List the following people in order of income, from the highest earning (1) to the lowest (4). Then list them in the order you think they should be. Are your lists different?

a P.E. teacher ☐   a top footballer ☐
a TV sports commentator ☐   a top triathlete ☐

2 SPEAKING Compare your second list from exercise 1 in pairs. Justify your ideas.

3 🎧 3.23 USE OF ENGLISH Complete the text with appropriate words.

The top ten sports stars ¹_____ the world, from disciplines as diverse ²_____ tennis, golf, racing and football, all earn more than $30 million a year. Much ³_____ this is from endorsements rather than prize money or salary, with the result that the biggest names can continue earning huge sums even after their retirement ⁴_____ the sport.

A previous England football manager, Fabio Capello, believed that the players' high earnings ⁵_____ a negative effect on discipline. 'They are young players, young boys, rich boys and this is the problem,' he said. Basically, it was impossible for young players to have the right work ethic and attitude when they were already rich beyond their childhood dreams. And one of the most famous footballers of recent years, David Beckham, agrees ⁶_____ him. In his view, young sportspeople need to be hungry for achievement – and too ⁷_____ money kills that hunger. 'You want that hunger there, you want the hunger to be rewarded. Unfortunately, that's not the case these days. They can all afford to buy ⁸_____ own cars.' Mind you, if it's taken you five minutes ⁹_____ read this article, Beckham himself has earned more than $1,000 ¹⁰_____ you began it!

It isn't only the players who are affected by commercialism; the top few clubs in all the most popular sports are now big businesses, with multi-million dollar sponsorship and TV deals. Since this allows them to buy and keep the best players, their position ¹¹_____ the top becomes unassailable. But ¹²_____ long can a sport survive when there is no real competition?

4 Look back at the Exam tip in Lesson A. Then decide if these sentences are true or false, according to the text.

1 Most top sportspeople earn over $30 million a year from endorsements.
2 Fabio Capello believes his players were too young to be well-disciplined.
3 David Beckham believes rich players have less desire to win.
4 David Beckham earns more than $200 a minute.
5 There is less competition in sport these days because there are fewer clubs.

5 VOCABULARY Complete these nouns from the text with the correct suffixes.

1 achieve_____   3 earn_____   5 commercial_____
2 retire_____   4 child_____   6 sponsor_____

▶▶▶ **VOCABULARY BUILDER 10.2: PAGE 143** ◀◀◀

6 🎧 3.24 Listen to five people giving their opinions of the role of money in sport. Which speakers think in general that some sportspeople are paid too much?

7 🎧 3.24 Listen again. Match the sentences (A–G) with the speakers (1–5). There are two extra sentences.

A It's OK for sports stars to earn a lot of money provided they give to charity and help less fortunate people.
B Sports stars' massive earnings may not be deserved, but they're inevitable since sport generates so much money.
C People who complain that sports stars are overpaid are basically just jealous of their wealth.
D Other people earn even more than sportspeople, who often cannot work for more than a few years.
E There are other jobs which deserve far greater financial rewards than playing professional sport.
F Today's sports stars have lost touch with the general public and are more interested in money than sport.
G It's unfair for some people to earn so much money when others in our societies have nothing.

Speaker	1	2	3	4	5

8 Complete the phrases used by the speakers to introduce statements and opinions.

ask   doubt   face   fact   line   look   see   thinking

Introducing statements and opinions

The ¹_____ is ...
So, basically ...
Personally, I think ...
If you ²_____ me, ...
The way I ³_____ at it, ...

To my way of ⁴_____ , ...
There's no ⁵_____ about it, ...
The way I ⁶_____ it, ...
Let's ⁷_____ it, ...
The bottom ⁸_____ is, ...

9 SPEAKING In pairs, discuss all the ideas in exercise 7. Do you agree or disagree? Give reasons. Use at least three phrases from exercise 8 in your answers.

I can understand a text about ways to boost performance.

1 SPEAKING **Ask and answer the questions in pairs.**

1 Do you ever drink energy drinks or eat energy bars? Do you think they work?

2 Do you wear anything (bracelets, crystals, etc.) which has been designed to improve your health?

3 If you hurt your leg running or playing sport, which of the following would you be most likely to do?
a rest it   **c** take painkillers
b put ice on it   **d** nothing

2 🎧 3.25 **Look quickly through the text opposite. Is each section (1–5) about something you (a) wear? (b) eat? or (c) lie in?**

3 **For each paragraph (1–5) choose the best summary (A–F). There is one extra summary.**

A This can definitely increase the speed of recovery from minor injuries by increasing blood circulation.

B Tests have shown that this can increase an athlete's ability to use oxygen more efficiently.

C This product can improve performance partly by making you look more intimidating.

D Used immediately before exercise, this has been shown to increase stamina and performance.

E Not only will this aid the recovery of your muscles after exercise, but it will also replace lost nutrients.

F While this product is intended to boost the amount of oxygen taken in during exercise, there's little evidence that it works.

4 VOCABULARY **Find the words below in the text. Use the context to work out the meaning and match them with the correct definitions.**

<u>Anatomy</u> circulation fibres ligament
long-sightedness lungs passages
short-sightedness sweat swelling

1 _____ : an increase in size of part of the body, often caused by injury

2 _____ : tiny, thin pieces of tissue in your body

3 _____ : moisture which your skin produces when you are hot and/or exercise intensively

4 _____ : a short piece of tissue in your body that connects two bones

5 _____ : a condition in which you cannot clearly see objects which are close to you

6 _____ : the organs which transfer oxygen from the air to your blood

7 _____ : the movement of blood around the body

8 _____ : any tubes in your body for air, food etc. to move through

9 _____ : a condition in which you cannot clearly see objects which are far away

Professional sportspeople will go to extraordinary lengths to gain an edge over their rivals. Increasingly, this means using a bizarre selection of performance-enhancing tools to boost their speed, strength and stamina. But, for those who want to emulate the pros and boost their performance, what really works?

GETTING

1 Cashew nuts

Kelly Holmes, Britain's double-Olympic gold medallist, said cashew nuts were her secret weapon in warding off fatigue at the Athens Olympics. 'Cashew nuts are my little secret,' she said, adding that they helped to boost her powers of recovery so she was fully primed for her next race. A 50 g serving of cashews provides one-fifth of a woman's daily iron requirements and around one-tenth of a man's zinc needs.

Expert verdict: 'All nuts are a rich source of dietary protein – needed to enhance the recovery process of muscles after intense activity,' says Jeanette Crosland, consultant dietician to the British Olympic Association. Nuts also provide carbohydrate and essential minerals, including potassium lost in sweat, which makes them a very useful post-exercise snack.

2 Ice baths

Taking a dip in a bath tub filled with ice-cold water is among the most fashionable therapies in sport at the moment. Believed to alleviate muscle soreness and tissue swelling that occur after hard exercise, it speeds up recovery. Some England rugby players have taken the obsession to extremes by visiting a cryotherapy chamber (essentially a human deep freeze) at an Olympic training centre in Poland. They spend four minutes shivering at minus 120–160 degrees Celsius.

Expert verdict: 'Ice obviously cools the area it is applied to. Once the body senses the drop in temperature, it sends more blood to the area which boosts circulation and speeds up healing,' says sports physiotherapist Jill Hendry. 'Sometimes tiny tears occur to muscle fibres and ligaments after a hard workout, and ice can help to heal them.'

3 Fancy contact lenses

Developed over eight years, the MaxSight contact lens is designed specifically to improve the sharpness of an athlete's vision. The lenses are currently being tested by AC Milan players and use what the developers call 'Light Architecture' optics to filter specific wavelengths of light in order to 'enhance key visual elements' – such as a ball – at the same time as reducing sun glare. A vision consultant developed amber lenses for tennis, football and rugby, or grey for running, cricket and golf, which, according to the marketing literature, 'makes the eye look competitive' (i.e. freaks out your opponents).

Expert verdict: They have been approved by America's Food and Drug Administration for daily wear to correct short- and long-sightedness. 'They could offer an advantage over normal lenses for sport by reducing the glare of light and sun,' says Louise Sutton, principal lecturer in Health and Exercise Science at Leeds Metropolitan University.

AHEAD

4 Nasal strips

They look like sticking plasters and were developed to help people with health problems like excessive snoring, but in recent years Breathe Right nasal strips have gained in popularity among sportspeople who believe that they improve airflow through the nose and into the lungs. They can often been seen worn by professional footballers and other athletes.

Expert verdict: 'Although we breathe mainly through our nose when resting, during exercise when we begin breathing harder, the air coming in is predominantly supplied via the mouth,' says Sutton. 'It may improve airflow through the nasal passages, but there is no evidence that it reaches the lungs and boosts performance.'

5 Low oxygen tent

Exposure to thin, mountain air has long been known to benefit competitors in endurance events like cycling, running and triathlons because it helps the body to adapt to using oxygen more efficiently. A five-year study by the US Olympic Committee confirmed that people who live at high altitude and train for sport at low altitude perform better. Manufacturers have now developed hypoxic (low-oxygen) tents to simulate this effect.

Expert verdict: Stephen Day, an exercise physiologist at Staffordshire University, carried out tests on elite runners to see how effective sleeping in a low-oxygen tent can be. 'We assessed numerous parameters and found that one elite athlete's aerobic capacity improved by a massive 30% during several months of sleeping in a low-oxygen tent,' he says.

5 **VOCABULARY** Add the words from exercise 4 to the correct part of the chart below.

A parts of the body
muscles, bones, ...

B normal functions of the body
digestion, breathing, ...

C injuries and problems with the body
bruise, sprain ...

6 **VOCABULARY** Work in pairs. How many more words can you add to the chart in exercise 5 in three minutes?

7 Choose one technique from the text that you would like to try and one that you wouldn't. What are your reasons for choosing and rejecting those two methods?

8 **SPEAKING** Discuss your ideas from exercise 7 with your partner. Use the phrases below to help you.

I would/wouldn't be keen on trying X because ...

X would/wouldn't interest me because ...

I'd rather not try X because ...

X sounds as if it would be ...

I don't think I could be bothered to ...

1 Read the dialogue. Who is less keen to go to the gym, Ava or Bella? Do you agree or disagree with her reasons? Why?

Bella	There's a new leisure centre in Western Road. I'm thinking of joining so I can go to the gym and get fit.
Ava	Really? It's time I got fit. But I don't like gyms. Everyone's so image-conscious.
Bella	What do you mean?
Ava	They're all posing in front of the mirrors. They act as if they were contestants in a beauty contest.
Bella	Well, I'd rather they didn't have all those mirrors. But it doesn't really bother me.
Ava	I just don't feel relaxed.
Bella	Suppose we went together. You'd enjoy it more if you were with someone.
Ava	Yes, maybe. But running on a treadmill is so boring!
Bella	Stop making excuses. Imagine if we went to the gym every day after school. We'd both be so fit!
Ava	Oh, OK. I'll give it a go. Is it expensive to join?
Bella	No, it's really cheap if you're under eighteen. Shall we start tomorrow, then?
Ava	I'd sooner we left it until after our exams.
Bella	But they're weeks away! I'd better join on my own. You can decide later.

2 Read the *Learn this!* box. Find and underline all the examples of the unreal past in the dialogue.

The unreal past
We use the past simple after certain expressions even though the meaning is present or future.
It's (high) time we **went** home.
I'd rather my brother **weren't** here.
I'd sooner you **paid** for your own ticket.
Imagine (if) you **lived** here!
Suppose you **gave** me your phone number.
He acts *as if/as though I **were*** his servant!
Note that we normally use *were* instead of *was* in this kind of sentence.

3 Rewrite the sentences below using the unreal past and the phrases in brackets.

1 I'd prefer him to meet me at the arena. (I'd rather)
2 I think we should go swimming again. (It's high time)
3 She'd prefer me to stay at home this afternoon. (She'd sooner)
4 Please don't tell anyone about this conversation. (I'd rather)
5 I don't want you to pay for my ticket. (I'd sooner)
6 Why don't you try sending her a text message? (Suppose)

>>> GRAMMAR BUILDER 10.2: PAGE 133 <<<

had better/might as well
1 We use *had better (not)* or *might as well* to give advice or warnings and say what the best course of action is.
2 *Had better* implies that not following that course of action will have bad consequences. We often use *or + will* to talk about those consequences.
She'd better apologise for missing the class or she'll have to see the head teacher.
You'd better not forget my birthday!
3 *Might as well* implies that the course of action is unappealing but there is no better option.
We'll never find it. We might as well give up.

4 Study the *Learn this!* box. Then give advice or warnings to these people using *had better (not) ...* or *might as well*.

1 'Some of my brother's friends are planning a surprise birthday party for him.'
   You'd better not tell him about it.
2 'I've had this cough for three months now, and I think it's getting worse.'
3 'I've had these jeans for years. They're too small for me now.'
4 'This prawn salad smells a bit funny.'
5 'I didn't realise we had an exam today until I got to school.'
6 'I borrowed a friend's white T-shirt and got tomato ketchup on it.'
7 'We're so late, we've missed three quarters of the film!'

>>> GRAMMAR BUILDER 10.3: PAGE 133 <<<

5 USE OF ENGLISH Complete the second sentence in each pair so that it means the same as the first. Include the word or words in brackets.

1 I think we should travel by boat.
   I _____ by boat. (sooner)
2 Saying sorry for insulting her is the best thing to do.
   You _____ for insulting her. (better)
3 He seems to think he owns the school!
   He acts _____ the school! (as though)
4 I'd prefer you to come with me to the gym.
   I'd _____ to the gym. (rather)
5 We should buy a new car – ours keeps breaking down.
   It's _____ – ours keeps breaking down. (time)
6 The party's over, so there's no point in staying.
   The party's over, so we _____ home. (might)

6 SPEAKING Work in pairs, taking turns to be A and B.
Student A: Invent another problem or situation like the ones in exercise 4. Tell student B.
Student B: Listen to student A and give advice or a warning using *had better (not)* or *might as well*.

I can describe a photo and answer questions about it.

1 SPEAKING Describe the photo opposite in pairs. Use the words below to help you.

biceps   instructor   muscles   shorts   sweat   vest top   weights

> **EXAM TIP**
>
> It's easier to give a full description of a photo if you create a logical structure in your mind, rather than mentioning random details as they occur to you. For example:
> 1 overall scene and location
> 2 main focus of the photo
> 3 clothes and other props
> 4 expressions and actions.

2 🎧 3.26 Read the Exam tip. Then listen to two candidates describing the photo in exercise 1. Which description (1 or 2) follows the advice better, in your opinion? Is the structure the same as in the Exam tip?

3 🎧 3.26 Listen again. Complete the useful expressions for referring to things in the photo you can't see clearly.

Describing unclear details
Their faces are ¹_____ of focus …
The instructor is out of ²_____ …
I can just ³_____ out a few more faces …
… although it isn't ⁴_____ .
… although her face is partly ⁵_____ .
… because his ⁶_____ is blurred.

4 Read the examiner's three questions for the photo in exercise 1. In pairs, discuss the first question and make notes of your ideas.

1 Why do you think the people in the photo are using weights in an exercise class?
2 Do you think it's important to be physically fit? Why do you think so?
3 Tell me about some physical exercise that you did recently.

5 🎧 3.27 Listen to the first candidate answering the first question. Does she mention your ideas from exercise 4?

> **LOOK OUT!**
>
> If an examiner's question has two parts, make sure you answer both. If you have to give an opinion, you will get better marks if you justify your opinion.

6 🎧 3.28 SPEAKING Read the *Look out!* box. Then listen to both candidates answering question 2 from exercise 4. Which answer is better, in your opinion? Why? (There is no correct answer.)

7 🎧 3.28 Listen again. Which phrases do the two candidates use to structure their answers? Write 1 or 2 next to the phrases.

Phrases for structuring an answer
First and foremost, … ☐
For a start, … ☐
Secondly, … ☐
And thirdly, … ☐
Also, let's not forget … ☐
And most importantly, … ☐

8 🎧 3.29 Listen to candidate 2 answering the third question from exercise 4. In what order does he give the following information? What would a better order be, in your opinion?

a where it happened
b when it happened
c how you felt then
d an interesting incident
e your overall opinion of it now
f who was there

9 Do the exam task below in pairs. First, describe the photo. Then answer the questions 1–3.

1 Why do you think they are wearing helmets?
2 What positive effects, mental and physical, could rafting have, in your opinion?
3 Tell me about something you found difficult but managed to do successfully in the end.

WRITING ANALYSIS Description of an event

I can write a description of an event.

The only time I've been to a professional basketball game was last winter in New York. I was on a city break with my parents and my cousin Connor, who lives in Boston. Connor, who's a real sports fan, was desperate to see the Knicks play at Madison Square Garden. I wasn't so keen but I agreed to go along – and I'm glad I did because it was the best evening of the holiday! We arrived at Madison Square Garden about an hour before the start of the game and went straight to our seats. In the front row sat dozens of Knicks fans all dressed in the team colours. My cousin explained that it was a crucial game, one that the Knicks really needed to win. He was feeling nervous and so were thousands of other Knicks fans. When the match started, the crowd went wild. They were cheering every point. For most of the match the Knicks were neck and neck with their opponents, the New Jersey Nets. Ten seconds from the end, the Knicks had a free throw to win the game. When the ball went through the hoop, the arena erupted. The Knicks had won! And then it was time to leave. Into the cold night air we went, surrounded by ecstatic Knicks fans. The excitement and adrenaline rush meant we hardly noticed the freezing temperatures. All in all, it was an unforgettable experience and one I'd love to repeat some day.

1 **SPEAKING** Describe the photo. Do you think this is an amateur or a professional game? Why do you think so?

2 Read the task and the description below. How well does the description address the underlined parts of the task? Give examples to support your opinion.

Write a description of a sporting event, amateur or professional, that you remember for its <u>great atmosphere and excitement</u>.

3 In pairs, decide where the paragraph breaks should come in the text. In this text, there should be four paragraphs.

EXAM TIP

A description of an event needs a clear, chronological structure – for example:
A Set the scene – where? when? who with?
B The build-up to the event – atmosphere, feelings, etc.
C The event itself – focus on key moments
D After the event – how did it affect you?
Make sure your description matches the task and includes any specific information requested.

4 Read the Exam tip. Then look again at your answer to exercise 3 and check that the paragraphs match the plan.

5 **VOCABULARY** Match the two halves of these compound nouns from the text. Then choose three of them and write your own example sentences.

1	basketball	a	row
2	sports	b	colours
3	front	c	throw
4	team	d	game
5	free	e	rush
6	adrenaline	f	fan

6 **VOCABULARY** Read the information below. How many of these expressions can you find in the text in exercise 2? You can make descriptions more colourful by using extreme equivalents of simple verbs and verb phrases.

Extreme equivalents

want to do it	be dying/desperate to do it
shout	scream/yell
run	sprint
get excited	go wild/crazy/berserk
feel sad	feel heartbroken
be level	be neck and neck
beat somebody	thrash somebody
try	give it everything

7 Rewrite these sentences using more extreme equivalents of the verbs.

1 When the substitute ran onto the pitch the crowd got excited.
2 I wanted to play her at tennis because she'd beaten me the last time.
3 The two teams were level, and both managers were shouting at their players to try harder.
4 She felt sad when she lost the match because she had really tried.

8 **SPEAKING** In pairs, discuss the advantages and disadvantages of watching a sports event live rather than on TV.

1 You are going to do the writing task on page 110. Read the Exam tip below, then decide whether you are going to describe a real or imagined event. If real, are you going to invent some of the details?

EXAM TIP

If you cannot write a description from personal experience, it is fine to use your imagination and describe an event as if you had been there. It is also fine to invent details to make an authentic description more interesting.

2 Plan your description using the structure below. Write notes.

   a Set the scene – where? when? who with?
   b The build-up to the event – atmosphere, feelings, etc.
   c The event itself – focus on key moments.
   d After the event – how did it affect you?

3 Read the phrases below. Use one of them to write an alternative beginning for the story on page 110.

Phrases for starting a description of an event

It all happened (last summer, a few months ago, etc.) when I …

It was (last winter, six months ago, etc.) when I first …

I have very clear memories of that day (last spring, two months ago, etc.) when I …

(Last autumn, about a year ago, etc.) I watched a thrilling (football) match between …

One of the best (hockey) games I've ever seen took place …

4 Read the Exam tip below. Answer all the questions for the sport you have chosen to write about.

EXAM TIP

Make sure you use the right vocabulary for the sport you are describing. For the sport you've chosen:

• Where is it played? (*court*, *pitch*, *rink*, etc.)
• What players are involved? (*defender*, *goalie*, *forward*, etc.)
• What officials are involved? (*umpire*, *referee*, *line judge*, etc.)
• Do players score goals or points? do judges give them marks?
• Do the players pass, kick, catch, throw or hit a ball?

LEARN THIS!

Adverbial phrases

1 When we start a sentence with an adverbial phrase of direction, position, etc., the subject-verb word order which follows is usually inverted:
   In the middle of the room stood a policeman.
2 However, when the subject is a pronoun, we do not invert.
   Away ~~drove they~~. ✗ *Away they drove.*
3 When the verb form is *there is/are*, we miss out *there* instead of inverting.
   On the table were three envelopes.

5 Read the *Learn this!* box. In the text in exercise 2 on page 110, find two examples of sentences which start with an adverbial phrase. Which one includes a pronoun as subject?

6 Rewrite these sentences starting with the adverbial phrase.

   1 There was a tennis racket on the chair.
   2 The striker sprinted towards the corner flag.
   3 The umpire stood in the centre of the court.
   4 A small dog ran onto the pitch.
   5 All six swimmers jumped into the pool.
   6 There were six defenders in front of the goal.

   ⟫⟫ **GRAMMAR BUILDER 10.4: PAGE 133** ⟪⟪

7 Write your description. Follow the plan you made in exercise 2. Write 200–250 words in total.

CHECK YOUR WORK

Have you:

☐ started your description with a suitable phrase?
☐ followed your writing plan?
☐ written 200–250 words?
☐ included at least one extreme equivalent (from exercise 6 on page 110) to add colour and excitement?
☐ included vocabulary that is specific to the sport you are describing?
☐ started at least one sentence with an adverbial phrase to add pace?
☐ checked your spelling and grammar?

9–10 Language Review

Unit 9

1 Match an adjective below with each statement.

considerate heroic over-sensitive romantic ruthless

1 'I'm going to become leader of this political party and I don't care how I do it.' _____
2 'I'm going to dive into the lake and save that dog!' _____
3 'A dozen red roses for you, my darling. And here's a poem I've written about your eyes.' _____
4 'I didn't tell you about the party because I didn't want you to feel bad that they didn't invite you.' _____
5 'Why did that person look at me just then? Is my hair a mess? Does this top not suit me?' _____

Mark: _____ /5

2 Complete the sentences with the words below.

could hadn't needn't shouldn't wouldn't

1 Thanks for the food, but you _____ have brought so much. There are only three of us.
2 If I'd known how difficult this job was going to be, I _____ have started it!
3 These bags are heavy. You _____ have offered to help me!
4 I don't mind her winning, but she really _____ have boasted about it.
5 I wouldn't have known about it if you _____ told me.

Mark: _____ /5

3 Complete the second sentence so it means the same as the first. (They are all mixed conditionals.)

1 We're lost because you forgot to bring the map.
We wouldn't _____ map.
2 He doesn't like you because you teased him.
He would _____ him.
3 He screamed because he's afraid of spiders.
If he _____ screamed.
4 I'm tired because you woke me up at dawn.
I wouldn't _____ dawn.
5 I bought two DVDs because they're on special offer.
If DVDs _____ two.

Mark: _____ /5

4 Complete each wish or regret with the appropriate word(s).

1 I wish I _____ acted so foolishly.
2 If _____ I had been able to speak Italian.
3 I'd _____ you hadn't told anyone.
4 I wish I _____ have taken a year off.
5 I really _____ you had been there with me.

Mark: _____ /5

Total: _____ /20

Unit 10

5 Circle the correct preposition and complete the sports venues.

1 in / on a boxing r_____
2 in / on a football p_____
3 in / on a ski s_____
4 in / on a swimming p_____
5 in / on a golf c_____

Mark: _____ /5

6 Match the two parts of the sentences.

1 What happened was
2 Under no circumstances
3 What we did was
4 It was my cousin who
5 The people who I

a go to a café and watch the news channel.
b everybody had to leave the stadium.
c feel sorry for are the players.
d would they allow the match to continue.
e thought of videoing the events with his phone.

Mark: _____ /5

7 Complete the second sentence in each pair so it means the same as the first.

1 We need to buy our tickets.
It's high _____ .
2 There's no reason not to take the bus.
We might as _____ .
3 It would be a bad idea to carry your passport with you.
You'd better _____ .
4 I don't think you should invite the neighbours.
I'd sooner _____ .
5 How about leaving the car at home?
Suppose _____ ?

Mark: _____ /5

8 Complete the monologue with the words below.

also first foremost importantly start

'[1]_____ and [2]_____ , exercise is good for you. For a [3]_____ , it makes the muscles in your body stronger. [4]_____ , let's not forget that it has a positive effect on your mind and emotions. But most [5]_____ , it makes your heart more efficient.'

Mark: _____ /5

Total: _____ /20

Lead-in

1 Match the words below to make three famous sports events. Which event does the photo show?

Bowl   de France   Grand   Monaco   Prix   Super   Tour

Speaking

2 In pairs, take turns to do the speaking task below.

Imagine you can have free tickets to one of the sporting events in exercise 1. Which will you attend? Give reasons for your choice and say why you are rejecting the other options.

Reading

3 Read the text. Match four of the headings (A–E) to the four sections (1–4). There is one extra heading.

A   The early years
B   Wimbledon customs
C   The future of the tournament
D   A British Grand Slam
E   Playing for money

1   The Wimbledon Tennis Championship, held for two weeks every year at the end of June and the beginning of July, is one of the highlights of the British summer for sports lovers. For many tennis players and fans, it is still the most prestigious of the four Grand Slam tournaments (the other three being the Australian Open, the French Open and the US Open). It is the only Grand Slam tournament to be played on grass, and each year, around half a million spectators come to watch the world's top tennis players compete in singles and doubles events.

2   The Championship was first held in 1877, making it the oldest tennis tournament in the world. The women wore long dresses and the men full-length trousers. Until 1922, the reigning champion played only in the final, against whichever player had won through the other rounds. For many decades, it was a tournament for amateur rather than professional players. No prize money was awarded, but even so, the event was very popular with spectators and was televised as early as 1937.

3   The professional era began in 1968. At first, prizes were modest, with £2,000 being awarded to the men's singles champion and only £750 to the ladies' singles champion. Today, the prize money is over £1 million and since 2007 has been equal for men and women. And as with all modern sports stars, the champions can expect to earn far more from advertising deals than they get in prizes.

4   Although there have been recent improvements to the venue – like a retractable roof over Centre Court – tradition is very important at Wimbledon. The players still have to dress in white and the courts are not surrounded by advertising boards. The ball boys and ball girls, who collect the tennis balls during the matches, are all from local schools. And since the very first tournament back in 1877, spectators at Wimbledon have eaten strawberries and cream. These days, about 28,000 kilos of strawberries and 7,000 litres of cream are served during the fortnight.

4 Are these sentences true (T) or false (F)?

1   The Wimbledon Championship always ends in July.
2   Players regard it as less important than the other Grand Slam tournaments.
3   Between 1878 and 1922, the champion from the previous year only played one match.
4   Cash prizes were awarded when the tournament started being televised.
5   The men's champion gets a bigger prize than the women's champion.
6   Children apply from schools all over the country to be ball boys and girls at Wimbledon.
7   Strawberries and cream are one of the oldest traditions at Wimbledon.

Listening

5 🎧 3.30 Listen to parts 1–5. Why did the protest go wrong?

6 🎧 3.30 Listen again. Match one of the sentences (A–F) to each part. There is one extra sentence.

A   Daisy tells Stefan she is planning to record some video footage and post it online.
B   They're on their way to a famous place but Stefan does not know where.
C   Daisy blames Stefan for the fact that the protest is not going well.
D   They decide to go somewhere that Stefan has been before but Daisy hasn't.
E   Daisy is confused because things do not seem to be going to plan.
F   Daisy finds out that one member of her group is not what he appeared to be.

Writing

7 Imagine you are Stefan. Write a description of your day at Wimbledon. Use your own ideas and anything you remember from the Listening section.

⟫⟫ CHECK YOUR PROGRESS: PAGE 4 ⟪⟪

Reading

1 `Get ready to READ` **Which of the following adjectives do you associate with yoga? Give reasons.**

relaxing   hazardous   soothing   extreme   religious   modern   boring   demanding

2 Do the exam task.

READING exam task

Read the text. Mark the sentences (1–6) true (T), false (F) or not stated (N)?

Doing yoga as exercise is incredibly popular in the western world. There are now classes in most leisure centres in Europe and America, but what exactly is it and where did it come from? Yoga originated in ancient India as a physical, mental and spiritual discipline. It evolved as part of Hindu philosophy and religion. The original goal of yoga, or the person practising yoga, is the attainment of a state of perfect spiritual tranquility while meditating on the concept of divinity. The Sanskrit word 'yoga' has the literal meaning 'to join, unite or attach'. The idea is to unite the body, breath and mind into one quiet energy. It was used as a word to describe a system of meditation as early as the 2nd century BC. Someone who practises yoga or follows the yoga philosophy with a high level of commitment is called a 'yogi' for a man or 'yogini' for a woman. They vow to follow a plain and simple life of self-discipline in order to achieve the perfect state of harmony and tranquility.

There are several types of yoga. The one that we associate most with in the West is Hatha Yoga, which is sometimes referred to as 'psychophysical yoga'. 'Ha' means 'sun' or 'vital life force' and 'tha' means 'moon' or 'mental force', while 'yoga' signifies the union between the two. The Hatha Yoga school emphasised mastery of the body to focus the mind. It evolved in 15th century India, and instead of just sitting while practising meditation, Hatha Yoga developed a series of poses for the body. Yoga came to the attention of an educated western public in the mid-19th century along with other forms of Hindu philosophy. The first Hindu teacher to actively promote aspects of yoga to a western audience was Swami Vivekananda, who toured Europe and the United States in the 1890s.

In 1947 the first Hatha Yoga school in the US opened in Hollywood. In the 'Flower Power' hippie years of the 1960s, interest in Hindu spirituality reached its peak. Pop stars, such as the Beatles and many Hollywood actors, followed Hindu meditation and philosophy for a while to inspire creativity and as an antidote to the materialism of western culture. However, for us in the west, yoga has now become almost completely detached from its religious context and is typically undertaken as a form of exercise, with its powerful combination of controlled movement and deep breathing.

1	Yoga is now more popular in the Western world than in India, its country of origin.	
2	Achieving a calm and peaceful state is an important element of yoga.	
3	Hatha Yoga is physically more demanding than some other types.	
4	Prior to Swami Vivekananda's tour, yoga was unknown to westerners.	
5	The first Hatha Yoga school in the US was primarily attended by Hollywood stars.	
6	Although most westerners do yoga to improve their body, they have not lost sight of its spiritual aspects.	

Speaking

3 `Get ready to SPEAK` **Work in pairs. Divide the adjectives below into two groups: (1) feelings associated with winning, and (2) feelings associated with losing. Can you add any more adjectives?**

dejected   despondent   devastated   dismayed   ecstatic   elated   inconsolable   overjoyed   relieved   triumphant

4 Do the exam task.

SPEAKING exam task

Describe the picture. Then answer the questions.

1 Why is this man in such a strange pose?
2 Would you like to be a professional athlete? Why / Why not?
3 Tell me about an international sport event which you attended or watched on television.

1.1 Present perfect simple and continuous

Present perfect simple

We use the present perfect

- for recent events, particularly when giving news.
  Have you heard? The president has (just) resigned.
- for an action that happened at some unspecified time in the past. (If we specify the time, we use the past simple.)
  Have you (ever) seen a koala?
  I've been to New York.
- with state verbs, to say how long a situation has existed. (We use *for*, *since* or *how long*.)
  I've known Eva for years.
  I've never understood baseball.
- for recent events that have a result in the present.
  I've (already) bought the tickets. We can go inside.
  I can't go out, I haven't done my homework (yet).

Present perfect continuous

We use the present perfect continuous

- for actions that have been happening recently and repeatedly.
  We've been playing a new computer game recently.
  I've been working hard this term.
- with dynamic verbs to say how long an action has been in progress. (We use *for*, *since* or *how long*.)
  Jake has been watching TV for three hours.
- to explain a current situation in terms of recent events.
  I'm tired because I've (just) been playing tennis.

Additional points of contrast

- We use the simple form to emphasise that an action is complete. Compare:
  I've been reading The Hobbit. (I'm half way through.)
  I've read The Hobbit. (It was great!)
- If we specify an exact number of occasions, we cannot use the continuous form.
  We've been arguing a lot.
  (NOT ~~We've been arguing twice this week.~~) *We've argued ...*
- We can use the simple or continuous form with *just* and *already*. However, we do not use the continuous form with *yet*.
  I've just spoken to Jack./I've just been speaking to Jack.
  I've already worn it./I've already been wearing it.
  Has he packed yet? (NOT ~~Has he been packing yet?~~)

1 Complete the sentences with the present perfect simple and continuous of the verbs in brackets.

1 I _____ (search) for hours but I _____ (not find) my phone yet.
2 I _____ (visit) the USA a few times but _____ (never see) a baseball game.
3 _____ (you / see) my watch? I _____ (look) for it since this morning.
4 I _____ (just / talk) to Abby on the phone. Do you want a quick word with her?
5 I've _____ (eat) all morning. I'm so full!
6 '_____ (you / see) Martha?' 'Yes. She _____ (work) in the library. You can go along and see her.'
7 I'm tired because I've _____ (play) three tennis matches today.
8 We've _____ (watch) *Twilight*. Do you want to see the end with us?
9 Fantastic! England have _____ (win) the world championship!
10 Have you ever _____ (take) part in a sports competition?

1.2 State and dynamic verbs

Dynamic verbs describe actions and can be used in simple or continuous tenses.
Compare:
Dad makes dinner every Friday. (= regularly)
Dad can't come to the phone; he's making dinner. (= now)
Jake has watched TV every night this week. (= recently and repeatedly)
This evening, he's been watching TV for three hours. (= action in progress with *for*)
State verbs describe states, not actions. They are often connected with abstract ideas:

- **emotion** *care, envy, fear, hate, like, love, mind, prefer, want*
- **possession** *belong, own, possess*
- **thought** *agree, believe, disagree, doubt, know, mean, recognise, understand*
- **others** *contain, cost, depend, fit, matter, need, seem, weigh*

State verbs cannot be used in continuous tenses.
I hate cheese. I hate this song. (NOT ~~I'm hating ...~~)
I've known Eva for years.
I've never understood baseball.
(NOT ~~I'm knowing/understanding ...~~)
Some verbs can be state or dynamic depending on the meaning. Only the dynamic sense can be used in continuous tenses.

	Dynamic verb	State verb
think	I'm thinking about work.	I think she's at work.
feel	I'm not feeling confident.	He feels I'm selfish.
have	He's having a shower/ a piano lesson/lunch.	She has three cats.
look	What are you looking at?	He looks very calm.
see	I'm seeing Dan later.	I see what you mean.
smell	Why are you smelling that sandwich?	Does the sandwich smell all right?
taste	She's tasting the soup.	The soup tastes great!
appear	He's been appearing on stage in London.	She appears to be quite assertive.

1 Choose the correct tense.

1 'Stop it! You _____ (behave) selfishly.'
   'Why? I _____ (not understand) what you _____ (mean).'

2 'Why _____ (you / laugh) at my T-shirt?'
   'Because it _____ (not fit) you!'

3 'This bag that I _____ (carry / weigh) a ton!'
   'I _____ (know). It _____ (contain) all my books.'

4 '_____ (you / like) this play?'
   'Not really, but it _____ (not matter). I _____ (not mind) staying until the end.'

5 'We _____ (need) to go home. It's midnight!'
   'I _____ (not care). I _____ (enjoy) myself!'

2 Complete the sentences with the correct form of the verbs below. Use each verb twice, once in a simple and once in a continuous form.

have   look   see   think

1 I noticed that a man _____ at our car.
2 My great-grandfather _____ a clothes shop in London in the 1950s.
3 I _____ the doctor tomorrow about my cough.
4 I missed my stop because I _____ about dinner.
5 When we arrived, the teachers _____ a meeting.
6 It's raining, but I _____ it will stop soon.
7 I _____ that you've been eating my crisps!
8 That game _____ fun. Can I have a go?

1.3 Verb patterns

When we put two verbs together, the second verb is usually in the infinitive or -ing form. Sometimes it is an infinitive with *to* or a past participle. Which pattern we use depends on the first verb.

verb + *to* infinitive
agree, arrange, ask, beg, dare, decide, expect, fail, happen, hope, manage, mean, offer, prepare, pretend, promise, refuse, seem, want, wish, would like, would prefer, help (can also be infinitive without *to*)

verb + -ing form
admit, advise, avoid, can't bear, can't help, can't stand, carry on, consider, delay, dislike, deny, enjoy, envisage, fancy, feel like, finish, give up, have difficulty, like, imagine, intend, it's no good, it's not worth, justify, keep (on), mind, miss, postpone, practise, propose, put off, recollect, recommend, risk, stop, spend (time), suggest

- Some verbs can be followed by an -ing form or an infinitive with little or no change in meaning: *begin, continue, hate, intend, like, love, prefer, start.*
- A few verbs (*forget, go on, regret, remember, stop, try*) change their meaning depending on whether they are followed by an infinitive or an -ing form.
  I won't forget meeting the President. / I forgot to ask.
  He went on singing. / He went on to become a teacher.
  I regret to inform you that your application was unsuccessful. / I regret not telling him how I feel.
  I remember locking the door. / Please remember to lock the door.
  She stopped singing. / She stopped to tie her shoes.
  We tried shouting for help, but nobody heard. / I tried to speak but no sound came out.
- The verbs *see, hear, watch* and *feel* can be followed by object + infinitive without *to* to talk about a completed action, or object + -ing form to talk about an action in progress.
  I heard Ben answer his phone, then laugh.
  I saw Danny playing basketball in the garden.

verb + object + *to* infinitive
allow, ask, command, dare, enable, encourage, expect, forbid, force, get, inspire, invite, order, permit, persuade, remind, request, teach, tell, trust, urge, warn, want, wish, would like, would prefer

verb + object + infinitive without *to*
have, make, let, help (can also be infinitive with *to*)

verb + object + past participle
get, have, need, want

Grammar Builder and Reference

1 **Complete the sentences with the correct form of the verb in brackets.**

1 I can't decide whether to persuade a friend _____ (come) camping with me or risk _____ (go) on my own.
2 We'd agreed _____ (meet) outside the cinema but Jake failed _____ (turn up).
3 I haven't managed _____ (contact) my cousins in Peru, but I'll keep _____ (try).
4 I suggest _____ (stay) at my flat, if you don't mind _____ (sleep) on the floor.
5 She pretends _____ (like) him, but in fact she can't stand _____ (be) in the same room.
6 My brother admitted _____ (take) my camera and promised _____ (ask) next time.
7 I really dislike _____ (argue) and I can't envisage ever _____ (have) a relationship with an argumentative person.
8 He carried on _____ (play) the guitar even though everyone in the room wanted him _____ (stop).

2 **Choose the best verb form in these sentences.**

1 'I can't find my phone.' 'Have you tried _____ your own number?'
   a call   **b** calling   **c** to call
2 Liverpool were two goals down at half time, but they went on _____ the match.
   a win   **b** winning   **c** to win
3 When I saw a man _____ in our garden, I asked him what he wanted.
   a stand   **b** standing   **c** to stand
4 He's a dangerous criminal, and the police want him _____ as soon as possible.
   a to catch   **b** catching   **c** caught
5 This a great track. It will get everybody _____ .
   a dance   **b** dancing   **c** danced
6 Please remember _____ some photos for me to look at.
   a take   **b** taking   **c** to take

2.1 *used to* and *would*

- We use *used to* or *would* to describe habits and situations in the past that are now finished.
  When I was a child, I used to play sport at weekends.
  When I lived in the city, I'd go jogging in the park every morning.
  I didn't use to like ice cream, but I do now.
  Did there use to be a corner shop at the end of the road?
- We don't use *used to* or *would* when we say how long a situation or habit in the past continued; we use the past simple.
  He wore the same blue suit to work for ten years.

- We can't use *would* with state verbs. We use *used to*.
  My dad used to be a policeman.
  (NOT My dad would be a policeman.)
- *never used to* and *would never* are common negative forms.
  I never used to wear glasses.
  He would never return my phone calls.
- If we stress the word *would*, it implies that we found the habit annoying.
  I had to get rid of our cat. Well, it would leave dead mice at the bottom of my bed!

1 **Choose the correct endings: a, b or both.**

1 I love carrots now, but when I was a child, I
   a didn't use to like them.
   b wouldn't like them.
2 When I was at primary school
   a I would get up at seven o'clock every morning.
   b I used to get up at seven o'clock every morning.
3 I sometimes got angry with my brother because
   a he would interrupt my phone calls.
   b he constantly interrupted my phone calls.
4 For five years in the 1990s, we
   a lived in France.
   b used to live in France.
5 When Joe was a small boy
   a he never used to wear glasses.
   b he didn't use to wear glasses.
6 When we lived in London
   a we didn't own a dog.
   b we wouldn't own a dog.
7 My elder brother
   a used to be interested in planes and trains.
   b would be interested in planes and trains.
8 My uncle
   a would work all his life in a factory in Manchester.
   b worked all his life in a factory in Manchester.

2.2 Second conditional

- We use the second conditional to talk about an imaginary situation or event and its result. It can refer to the present or the future.
  If I were better at football, I would be in the school team.
  (present)
  If I failed my exams next year, I wouldn't get into university.
  (future)
- We use the past tense to describe the situation or event. We use *would* or *wouldn't* + infinitive without *to* to describe the result.
  If I had a lot of money, I would travel round the world.
  (situation)   (result)

- The *if* clause can come before or after the main clause. If it comes after, we don't use a comma.
  If he weren't homeless, he wouldn't be a squatter.
  He wouldn't be a squatter if he weren't homeless.
- In the *if* clause, we can use *were* instead of *was* as the past tense of *be*, singular. It is considered to be a little formal. The meaning doesn't change.
  If I was rich, I'd buy a house in the country.
  If I were rich, I'd buy a house in the country.

1 Complete the sentences. Use the second conditional.

1 If you _____ (work out) your total income, you _____ (know) how much you had to spend.
2 Your children _____ (manage) their money better if you _____ (let) them take responsibility for financial decisions.
3 You _____ (be able) to afford a holiday if you _____ (not spend) all your money on music downloads.
4 If you _____ (give) me a bigger allowance, I _____ (not be) broke all the time.
5 My dad says he _____ (not have) a credit card if interest rates _____ (not be) so low at the moment.
6 If my dad _____ (win) the lottery, he _____ (retire).

2 Write second conditional sentences.

1 I can't afford a holiday because I'm hard up.
  If I weren't hard up, I could afford a holiday.
2 He won't lend you money because he's stingy.
3 The painting isn't worth a fortune because it's a copy.
4 The restaurant is rather pricey, so we don't eat there often.
5 He's careless with his money, so he's always broke.
6 He doesn't budget well, so he gets into debt all the time.
7 I don't borrow money because it's difficult to pay back.
8 You waste your money, so you're always short.

2.3 Past perfect simple and continuous

Past perfect simple
We use the past perfect simple
- for an action that happened before a specific time in the past.
  After I had washed up, I watched TV.
- with state verbs (*know, be, like*, etc.) and *for* or *since* to say how long an action had been in progress.
  I'd only been here at home for a few minutes when my grandmother phoned.

Past perfect continuous
We use the past perfect continuous
- to show the cause of something in the past.
  His hands were dirty. He had been gardening.

- with action verbs and *for* or *since* to say how long an action had been in progress.
  I'd been playing the lottery for years before I won anything.

1 Complete the sentences. Use the correct past perfect simple form of the verbs in brackets.

1 He was in debt because he _____ (not be) careful with his money.
2 She was never short of money because she _____ (always keep) some back for a rainy day.
3 I didn't know where she was because she _____ (not tell) me where she was going.
4 They _____ (be) comfortably off before the stock market crash.
5 _____ you ever _____ (visit) Germany before you started to learn German?
6 She was late for work because she _____ (get up) late.
7 If I _____ (know) you were a vegetarian, I wouldn't have cooked meat!

2 Complete the sentences. Use the past perfect continuous and a phrase below.

sunbathe all day   cook dinner   not sleep well
walk in the woods   not pay attention   rain
travel for six hours   sit at my desk since nine o'clock

1 The path was slippery because it _____ .
2 Fran looked tired because she _____ .
3 When I got home, there was a lovely smell. Clare _____ .
4 When we finally got to Devon, we _____ .
5 Liam couldn't do the exercise because he _____ .
6 I had backache because I _____ .
7 Their shoes were muddy because they _____ .
8 My face was very sunburnt because I _____ .

2.4 Past simple and past continuous

- We use the past simple:
  a for an action or event at a definite point in the past.
  We played volleyball last Saturday.
  He joined the team at the age of sixteen.
  b for actions or events that happened one after another.
  I passed the ball to him and he scored.
  She got up, had a shower, got dressed and left the house.
  c with certain verbs that are not used in continuous tenses: for example, *believe, hate, know, like, love, need, prefer, want*.
  I believed his story. (**NOT** I was believing his story.)
- We use the past continuous for a description of a scene in the past.
  It was raining. Some children were playing rugby.

- We often use the past continuous and the past simple in the same sentence. The past continuous describes a background action or event; the past simple describes a shorter action or event that interrupted it.
  I was having breakfast when the phone rang.
  My friends were watching TV when I arrived.
- We can use the past simple or the past continuous with *when*, *as* and *while*.
  What were you thinking as you walked down the street?
  What were you thinking as you were walking down the street?
- We often use *as* with the past simple for two short actions that happened at the same time.
  As I left the room I tripped over the cat.

1 Complete the sentences. Use the past simple or past continuous of the verbs in brackets. Sometimes both tenses are possible.

1 The sun _____ (shine) and the birds _____ (sing) when I _____ (leave) the house.
2 The moment I _____ (see) him I _____ (realise) I'd met him before.
3 What _____ you _____ (do) when Joe _____ (call) you?
4 While we _____ (wait) for you, it _____ (start) to rain.
5 She _____ (walk) into the room, _____ (sit down) and _____ (start) to read the paper.
6 At the time of the earthquake, I _____ (live) in Tokyo. I _____ (move) back to the UK shortly afterwards.
7 Harry _____ (play) a lot of football while he _____ (live) in Oxford.
8 As I _____ (leave) the house the sun _____ (come out).

3.1 Indirect questions

- We can use an indirect question when we feel that a direct question might sound rude or aggressive. Indirect questions use the same word order and verb forms as affirmative statements:
  Where do you live? (direct question)
  Could you tell me where you live? (indirect question)
- We can use the following phrases to introduce an indirect question. Note that the first two do not require a question mark at the end.
  I wonder .../I'd like to know ...
  Could you tell me ... ?/Can you tell me ... ?/Would you mind telling me ... ?/Can I ask you ... ?
  Have you any idea ... ?/Do you know ... ?
- The phrases above are followed by the same question word (*who*, *which*, *where*, etc.) as in the equivalent direct question.
  Why is he sad?
  Have you any idea why he's sad?
- If the equivalent direct question is a *yes/no* question, we use *if* or *whether*.
  Are they in love?
  I wonder if/whether they're in love.

1 Change the indirect questions into direct questions.

1 I'd like to know how much this shirt costs.
2 Do you know whether the help desk is open?
3 Could you tell me where the bank is?
4 Can you tell me if you need any help?
5 Have you any idea what time she'll be back?
6 I wonder what the matter is.

2 Read the direct questions and complete the equivalent indirect questions.

1 Why are you laughing?
  Would you mind _____ ?
2 Are they married or just engaged?
  I wonder _____ .
3 What does this word mean?
  Can you _____ ?
4 How old are you?
  Can I _____ ?
5 Is there a fast train to Liverpool from here?
  Have you any idea _____ ?
6 Does your sister eat pasta?
  Do you know _____ ?
7 When does the film finish?
  I'd like _____ .
8 Do you prefer football or basketball?
  Could you _____ ?

3.2 Subject/object questions

- The following question words can be the subject or object of a question: Who ... ?, Which (one/ones) ... ? and What ... ?
- When the question word is the **subject**, it is followed by a normal, affirmative verb form:
  Who works in that office? (Jake works in that office.)
  Which car won the race? (The red car won the race.)
- When the question word is the **object**, it is followed by an interrogative verb form:
  Who do you know at this party? (I know everybody.)
  What did you buy? (I bought a T-shirt.)
- When the question includes a preposition, we use the **object** form. We usually put the preposition at the end.
  What are you looking at? (I'm looking at the moon.)
  Who did you talk to? (I talked to Sally.)
- In formal English, we sometimes put the preposition at the start, before the question word. If the question word is *who*, it becomes *whom* when we put a preposition before it.
  To whom did you give the money? (formal)
  Who did you give the money to? (less formal)

1 Read the statements. Then complete the questions for the answers that are given.

1 He gave his number to Grace.
  Who _____? Grace.
2 They won a brand new car!
  What _____? A brand new car.
3 My dad drove them to the airport.
  Who _____? My dad.
4 A faulty TV caused the fire.
  What _____? A faulty TV.
5 The Fiat won the rally.
  Which car _____? The Fiat.
6 Sandy always sits next to Noah.
  Who _____? Noah.

3.3 Comparison

- Comparative and superlative adjectives are formed with -er and -est or more and most, unless they are irregular:

(regular)	difficult	more difficult	most difficult
	hot	hotter	hottest
(irregular)	good	better	best
	far	further	furthest

- Comparative and superlative adverbs are usually formed with more and most, unless they are irregular.

(regular)	slowly	more slowly	most slowly
(irregular)	badly	worse	worst
	well	better	best

- A few comparative and superlative adverbs are formed with -er and -est, like adjectives: early, fast, hard, late, near, soon.
  We'll be there sooner than I thought.
  Who gets up the earliest in your family?
- Some determiners also have comparative and superlative forms.
  few fewer fewest
  little less least
  much/many more most
- We can use (so) much or far to make the meaning of a comparative form more extreme.
  It's far warmer than I expected.
  She drives so much more safely than she used to.
- We use even to express surprise.
  I'm tall but you're even taller!
- We can use a little, a bit or no to modify a comparison.
  It's a bit harder than I realised.
  They played no better than last week.
- We can modify a comparison with as ... as by using just, almost, nearly, nowhere near or nothing like.
  She's just as argumentative as her brother.
  Skateboarding is nowhere near as difficult as skiing.
- We can talk about a gradual change by repeating a comparative form.
  It's getting harder and harder to find apartments.

- We can use this comparative structure to show that two things change because they are connected.
  The more he spends, the poorer he gets.
- Comparisons often have a clause after than.
  Driving to London is slower than it used to be.

1 Complete the sentence so that it means the same as the first.

1 London is far bigger than Paris.
  Paris is nowhere _____ London.
2 I expected yoga to be difficult, but not this difficult!
  Yoga is even _____ I expected.
3 New York is almost as far south as Madrid.
  Madrid is only a bit _____ New York.
4 Greenland is much smaller than it looks on most maps.
  Greenland isn't nearly _____ on most maps.
5 The ice caps are shrinking due to climate change.
  The ice caps are getting _____ due to climate change.
6 If you drink more coffee, you won't sleep as well.
  The more coffee _____ you'll sleep.

2 Rewrite the sentences to include a comparative form followed by a clause. Keep the same meaning.

1 I didn't realise Mark was so rich.
  Mark is much richer than I realised.
2 This restaurant didn't use to be so popular.
3 This phone shouldn't be so hard to use.
4 I didn't plan to spend so much money.
5 This hotel didn't look so comfortable from the outside.
6 I didn't imagine Chicago would be such an exciting city.

3.4 Question tags

- We use question tags to turn a statement into a question. We usually add negative tags to affirmative statements and affirmative tags to negative statements.
  It's hot today, isn't it?
  You don't need a lift to school, do you?
- With affirmative sentences which have a negative meaning because they include a word like never, nobody or nothing, we add an affirmative tag.
  I've had nothing for breakfast, have I?
  She never says 'thank you', does she?
- If the sentence includes a modal verb (can, might, should, will, etc.) we use it in the tag.
  She can't sing, can she?
  It won't hurt, will it?
- If the sentence includes an auxiliary verb (is/are, have, had, etc.) we use it in the tag.
  They're leaving, aren't they?
  You haven't told her, have you?
- If the sentence includes a simple, finite verb form, we use do (or did) in the tag.
  This phone belongs to you, doesn't it?
  You went home last night, didn't you?

Grammar Builder and Reference

- Note these special cases:
  Be careful, won't you?
  Don't laugh, will you?
  Let's be friends, shall we?
  There aren't any questions, are there?
  Everyone's ready, aren't they?
  Nobody wants to give up, do they?
  Everything works, doesn't it?
  Nothing matters now, does it?
- We use a rising intonation on the question tag when we need or expect an answer.

  It isn't my turn, is it? (I think it might be.)
- We use a falling intonation on the question tag when we do not need or expect an answer.

  Of course I'll help you. You're my best friend, aren't you? (We both know that.)

1 Add question tags.

1 Nothing's ever as simple as it seems, _____ ?
2 It's rained a lot recently, _____ ?
3 Don't spend too much money, _____ ?
4 Nobody knows what you're thinking, _____ ?
5 You haven't been listening to me, _____ ?
6 Everything changed after he retired, _____ ?
7 Let's start at the beginning, _____ ?
8 Leave your bags by the door, _____ ?
9 Your parents used to live there, _____ ?
10 You're going to invite me, _____ ?

4.1 Talking about possibility

will

- We use *will* for making predictions about the future. We often use *I think* and *I don't think* with *will*.
  I don't think it'll snow tonight.
- We can use *shall/shan't* instead of *will/won't* with *I* and *we*, but *will* is more common.
  I think we shall visit Italy next summer.
- We also use *will* to make assumptions about the present.
  It's 4.40. Right now Jim will be on his way home.
  Helen will be getting on the plane.
- We also use *will* to express our assumptions about the present.
  It's six o'clock. Mum will be preparing dinner.
  I'm sure the football match will have finished by now.

must and can't

- We use *must* for talking about things which we can deduce are definitely true.
  He must be at work. He just called me from his office.
- We use *can't* for talking about things which we can deduce are impossible.
  She can't be abroad. She hasn't got a passport.

may, might and could

- We use *may*, *might* or *could* for speculating about things that are possibly true.
  Fred may be in town. Why don't you phone him?
  Don't throw that vase away. It might be valuable.
  Your friends are very late. They could be lost.
- They often refer to a future event.
  Be careful with those plates. You might break them.
- We can use the negative forms *may not* and *might not*. However, we cannot use the negative form *couldn't* in this sense.
  I've sent her a postcard, but it may not/might not arrive.
  (NOT I've sent her a postcard, but it couldn't arrive.)
- *couldn't* has a similar meaning to *can't* and expresses impossibility. It's often used with *possibly*.
  I couldn't possibly accept the invitation to Jan's party. I'll be away that weekend.

should

- We use *should* to say that something is likely to happen, in our opinion.
  I should be home by six o'clock.
  Tim might be a bit late for the meeting, but that shouldn't be a problem.
- We can use other phrases to express probability.
  be bound to (= it's certain)
  The score is 4–0 with two minutes to go. They're bound to win.
  chances are (that) (= it's probable [that])
  Chances are I won't hand in my homework on time. (= very probable)
  be likely (= be probable)
  Is it likely to rain tomorrow?

1 Complete the sentences with the correct form of *must, can't, may, might, could* and *should*. Sometimes more than one answer is possible.

1 I'm not sure what we're doing tomorrow. We _____ go to the cinema.
2 Fiona _____ be at the leisure centre. It's closed.
3 You shouldn't drive so fast. You _____ have an accident one day.
4 I can see people opening their umbrellas. It _____ be starting to rain.
5 Jake _____ be wearing his coat. It's on the peg over there.
6 It's five o'clock now and the bus takes twenty minutes, so I _____ get home just after five twenty.
7 I went past the new noodle bar in town. It _____ be very good – there was nobody in it!
8 'Where's Sid?' 'I don't know. He _____ be in town shopping.'
9 Barcelona are much better than Manchester United at the moment, so they _____ win.

2 Rewrite sentences 1, 3, 6, 7, 8 and 9 from exercise 1. Use one of these phrases: *be bound to*, *chances are*, and *be likely*. You may need to make other changes too.

> 1 I'm not sure what we're doing tomorrow. Chances are we'll go to the cinema.

4.2 Future continuous, future perfect simple and future perfect continuous

Future continuous
We use the future continuous

- to talk about an action that will be in progress at a specific point in the future.
  > At six o'clock tomorrow evening I'll be watching The X Factor on TV.
- to talk about planned events, or events that we expect to happen. In this usage, it is similar to the present continuous for arrangements.
  > I'll be going to the shops later. Is there anything you need?
- to make polite enquiries. Using the future continuous instead of the future simple to ask about somebody's plans makes questions sound politer and less direct.
  > Can you let me know when you'll be leaving?

Future perfect simple
We use the future perfect simple to talk about a completed action or event in the future.
> By the time we get to the cinema, the film will have already started.

Future perfect continuous
We normally use the future perfect continuous to say how long an action or event will have been in progress at a specific point in the future.
> By the end of this year, he'll have been learning English for nine years.

1 Write sentences about what George will be doing at the times given. Use the future continuous.

7.15	shower
7.45	breakfast
8.30	catch bus to school
8.55	arrive at school
10.30	maths lesson
12.30	football

> 1 7.16 He'll be having a shower.
2 7.50 _____ .
3 8.40 _____ .
4 8.55 _____ .
5 10.35 _____ .
6 12.40 _____ .

2 Complete the sentences with the future perfect simple or future perfect continuous.

1 By Christmas Mandy _____ (know) Roger for five years.
2 Next Easter my mum _____ (work) at the doctor's surgery for six months.
3 If Dave passes his physics exam, he _____ (pass) all his school-leaving exams.
4 I hope you _____ (wash up) the dishes before you go out.
5 By this time next year we _____ (live) in London for six years.
6 When William is sixteen he _____ (play) basketball for three years.
7 By the time we get to the stadium the race _____ (start).
8 'Kate is going to try and pass her driving test again.' 'Really? How many times _____ she _____ (take) it?'

4.3 Future forms: *will*, *going to*, present continuous, present simple

- We use *will* to make factual statements about the future, and to make predictions.
  > The sun will rise at 6.47 tomorrow morning.
  > Do you think you'll finish your homework before midnight?
- We use *will* for things we decide to do as we are speaking (instant decisions, offers, promises).
  > That's the phone ringing. I'll answer it.
  > 'This bag is very heavy.' 'I'll carry it.'
  > I'll ring you as soon as I get to London.
- We use *going to* or the future continuous for things we have already decided to do (intentions).
  > I'm going to visit my grandparents at the weekend.
  > I'll be visiting my grandparents at the weekend.
- We use *going to* to make a prediction based on present evidence.
  > Look at those clouds. It's going to rain.
- We use the present continuous for things we have already agreed to do, usually with somebody else (arrangements).
  > I'm playing football on Saturday afternoon.
- We can use the present simple for timetabled and scheduled events.
  > What time does your train leave tomorrow?
  > The concert starts at 8 p.m. on Saturday.

1 Choose the best form. Where more than one answer is possible, explain the difference in meaning.

1 Bye! I _____ you tomorrow.
  a 'll see   **b** 'm seeing   **c** 'm going to see
2 'Have you got any plans for this evening?' 'I _____ with Vicky.'
  a 'll go out   **b** 'm going out   **c** 'm going to go out

Grammar Builder and Reference

3 My flight _____ at five so we need to be at the airport a good two hours before that.
 a will leave b 's leaving c 's going to leave
4 'I'm going to spend my gap year in Africa.' 'Really? What _____ there?'
 a will you do b are you doing c are you going to do
5 Look! That car's going too fast. It _____.
 a 'll crash b 's crashing c 's going to crash
6 I'm sure you'll get into university, but what _____ if you don't?
 a will you do b are you doing c are you going to do
7 _____ James this evening?
 a Will you see b Will you be seeing c Are you going to see
8 By this time tomorrow I _____ my exams.
 a 'll finish b 'll have finished c 'm finishing
9 I _____ to town later. Can I give you a lift?
 a 'll drive b 'll be driving c 'm driving
10 This time next week we _____ in Spain.
 a 're going to arrive b 'll be arriving c 'll have arrived

5.1 Passive: all forms

- We form the passive with the correct form of the verb be and the past participle. The tense of a passive construction is determined by the tense of the verb be. For example:
  The hotel is used by 8,000 visitors a year. (present simple)
  It was built in 1875. (past simple)
  It is being renovated at the moment. (present continuous)
  It will be reopened next year by the Mayor. (future simple)
  A new dining room will have been added. (future perfect)
- We use by ... to say who is responsible for the action. This usually goes at the end of the sentence.
  The bus shelter was destroyed by vandals.
- We can use the passive with present and past forms of modal verbs.
  The paintings can't be found.
  They must have been hidden.
- Prepositions which belong with the verb go immediately after the past participle.
  Burglars broke into the school.
  The school was broken into.
- Most adverbs go immediately before the past participle. However, adverbs of frequency and the adverbs still, just, already and even go immediately before be or been in compound tenses.
  The school is being completely rebuilt.
  The library has already been knocked down.
  The gym will still be used for basketball.
- We don't use the present, past or future perfect continuous form of the passive:
  They have/had/will have been chasing him for weeks.
  (NOT He has/had/will have been being chased for weeks.)

1 Complete the sentences with the passive of the verbs in brackets. Use the correct tense.
1 My bike _____ (steal) three times since Christmas!
2 If we win the quiz again next week, we _____ (win) it ten weeks in a row.
3 They couldn't use the phone because the SIM card _____ (remove).
4 When we arrived at the zoo, the elephants _____ (feed), so we watched.
5 Scientists say their research _____ (not complete) for another five years at least.
6 I've moved into my cousin's flat because my flat _____ (decorate) at the moment.
7 The shop refused to exchange the dress because it _____ (wear) several times.
8 The Grand Hotel _____ (build) in 1905.

2 Rewrite these active sentences in the passive. Use by ... to say who is responsible for the action.
1 The Chinese invented paper about 2,000 years ago.
2 Ada Lovelace wrote the first computer program.
3 Marie Skłodowska-Curie discovered polonium and radium.
4 The Wright brothers built the world's first aircraft.
5 Sony manufactured the first CD player.
6 The computer giant IBM designed the first successful home computer.
7 Jack Dorsey created Twitter in 2006.
8 Google bought YouTube for $1.65 billion.

3 Complete these sentences in the passive. Use the modal verb and the verb in brackets.
1 Helmets _____ (must / wear) at all times on the building site.
2 Our car isn't where we parked it. It _____ (must / steal).
3 If the weather's bad tomorrow, the athletics tournament _____ (might / cancel).
4 That homework _____ (should / hand in) days ago!
5 These vouchers _____ (can / exchange) for cinema tickets anywhere in the country.
6 Are you sure your bag was stolen? It _____ (could / take) by mistake.
7 Don't throw that plastic bag away. It _____ (can / use) again.
8 My phone has run out of power again. It _____ (can't / recharge) properly.

Grammar Builder and Reference **123**

5.2 Using the passive

- We use the passive when we don't know or don't want to say who or what is responsible for the action.
  My phone was made in China.
  We can also use the passive for stylistic reasons, especially to allow the main focus of the sentence to be the subject of the verb.
  One of my favourite paintings is Van Gogh's 'Starry Night'. It was painted in 1888.
- With verbs that often have two objects (*ask*, *award*, *give*, *offer*, *owe*, *pay*, *send*, *show*, *teach*, *tell*, etc.), either object can become the subject of a passive sentence.
  They sent me a DVD in the post.
  a I was sent a DVD in the post.
  b A DVD was sent to me in the post.
  It is much more common for the indirect object (usually a person) to be the subject of the passive sentence (example a above).

1 Rewrite the sentences in the passive. Make the underlined words the main focus.

1 Panasonic are going to release <u>a new kind of TV</u> next year.
2 Scientists in Oxford are building <u>a quantum computer</u>.
3 Van Gogh painted <u>this picture</u> in 1890 and gave it to a friend.
4 J.K. Rowling wrote <u>all the Harry Potter novels</u> between 1996 and 2007.
5 Jim Carrey, the Hollywood actor, will host <u>the next awards ceremony</u>.
6 Henry Ford designed <u>the Model T</u>, one of the earliest motor cars.

2 Rewrite the sentences in the passive. Remember, it's usually the indirect object which becomes the subject.

1 My aunt gave me a games console for my birthday.
  I was given a games console for my birthday by my aunt.
2 The school awarded my brother first prize for art.
3 The hotel manager showed us our room.
4 My grandfather has told me that story many times.
5 They paid my friend £20 to hand out leaflets.
6 They offered me my money back, but I refused.
7 The police showed the suspect the CCTV footage.
8 Arthur Rubinstein taught my grandmother piano.

5.3 Future in the past

- When we're talking about the past, we sometimes want to refer to things which were still in the future at that time.
  We use *was going to* when the future event was a plan or intention.
  She bought eggs and flour because she was going to make a birthday cake.

- We sometimes use *would*, especially when the future event was a long way off or lasted for a long time.
  In 1964, she met the man who would later be her husband.
  It was a holiday she would never forget.
- We use the past continuous when the future event was an arrangement.
  I took boots with me because we were going for a walk after lunch.

1 Rewrite these sentences in the past. You may need to change some of the time expressions too.

1 Jack's on the diving board. He's going to jump.
2 I'm excited because we're going on holiday tomorrow.
3 I don't know my exam result, but I'll find out soon.
4 I've borrowed my brother's laptop. Will he notice?
5 We're at the station. The train leaves in ten minutes.
6 It's going to be a long winter.

6.1 Passive: advanced structures

Passive with *believe*, *know*, *think*, etc.

- Verbs like *believe*, *consider*, *expect*, *know*, *report*, *say*, and *think* are often used in passive constructions, especially in formal language.
- We can use an impersonal construction with *it* + passive:
  it + passive (present or past) + *that*...
  It was believed by many people until the 19th century that tomatoes were poisonous.
  It is now known that they are not.
- Alternatively we use a passive construction with an infinitive:
  subject + passive (present or past) + *to do/to have done* something.
  Tomatoes were believed to be poisonous.
- We can use an impersonal construction with *there* + passive (present or past) + *to do/to have done* ...
  There were thought to be 1,000 people at the demonstration.
  He is known to have been very wealthy.
- If the sentence refers to a present belief about a past event, we use the present simple passive followed by a perfect infinitive (*to have done something*).
  Tea is known to have originated in China.

Passive modals, gerunds and infinitives

- We can use passive structures with modal verbs.
  Homework should be handed in on time.
- Verbs that are followed by an infinitive or gerund can also be followed by a passive infinitive or gerund:
  No one likes to be criticised.
  I can't stand being kept waiting.

Grammar Builder and Reference

1 Rewrite the sentences in two ways using passive structures. Start with the words given.

1 They think that the burglar climbed in through a window.
   a It is … **b** The burglar is …
2 They say that she owns five houses.
   a It is said … **b** She is said …
3 They once believed that the earth was flat.
   a It … **b** The earth …
4 They reported that the ship sank very quickly.
   a It … **b** The ship …
5 They expect that the Government will raise taxes.
   a It … **b** The Government …
6 They now know that the car was stolen.
   a It … **b** The car

2 Correct the mistakes in these sentences.

1 Coats can to be left in the cloakroom.
2 They enjoyed to be taken to the cinema.
3 The washing-up ought have been done last night.
4 Put this cream on to avoid be bitten by insects.
5 My mum expects to being promoted at work.
6 Batteries must being disposed of with care.
7 Stand up for yourself. Don't let yourself to be bullied.
8 Can you imagine what it's like be followed everywhere by the paparazzi?

6.2 Articles

a/an

We use the indefinite article a/*an*

- when we say what something is or what it is like.
  What's that? It's a smartphone.
  My uncle lives in a small flat.
- when we say what somebody's job is.
  My sister is a flight attendant.
- when we mention something for the first time.
  I've got a new bike.
- when we mean any example of something.
  Is there a bank near here?
- to mean *per* or *for each*.
  My brother earns £100 a week.
  The bus was travelling at 50 kilometres an hour.

the

We use the definite article *the*
- when it's clear what we are talking about. This can be
a because we've already mentioned it
  I've got a cat and a dog. The cat is called Freddy.
b because there is only one of something
  What time will the sun set this evening?
c because it's clear from the situation
  Let's go to the beach. (= the beach that's near here.)

- with most nationality words.
  The Italians have a reputation for being friendly.
- with the names of rivers, mountain ranges, deserts and seas.
  the Nile, the Himalayas, the Sahara Desert, the Baltic
- with a few countries and most groups of islands.
  the United Kingdom   the United States   the Netherlands   the Czech Republic   the Channel Islands
- in various set phrases, for example:
  go to the theatre/cinema   listen to the radio/the news
  play the violin, the piano
- with an adjective to refer to everybody who has that characteristic.
  the poor/the rich

No article

We don't use an article
- when we are making generalisations.
  Cats eat mice and birds.
- with most countries, continents, towns, lakes and mountains.
  I live in Krakow, in Poland.
  Toronto is situated on the shores of Lake Ontario.
  My friend has just climbed Mount Etna.
- with some nouns following a preposition.
  to/at work/school   at home   at night   by bus
  in bed/hospital/prison
- with meals.
  have breakfast/lunch/dinner

1 Complete the sentences with *a/an*, *the* or no article (–).

1 'Shall we go for _____ walk along _____ river?' 'Not now – I've got to go to _____ work in half an hour.'
2 The bananas are €1 _____ kilogramme.
3 I love looking at _____ Moon and _____ stars.
4 Turn on _____ TV. _____ news is on in a moment.
5 'Shall we go out for _____ lunch?' 'No, let's eat at _____ home.'
6 Alexej is from _____ Budweis in _____ Czech Republic.
7 'Is there _____ public toilet near here?' 'Yes, there's one in _____ park.'
8 _____ Lake Superior is _____ biggest lake in _____ world.

6.3 Quantifiers

Quantifiers
- We normally use *some* in affirmative sentences and offers, and *any* in negative sentences and questions.
  We've got some tea and biscuits.
  We haven't got any tea or biscuits.
  Have we got any tea or biscuits?
  Would you like some tea and biscuits?

- We use *any* with uncountable and plural nouns in affirmative sentences where the meaning is negative.
  I came out without any money.
  There is seldom any snow in the south of France.
- We can use *any* in affirmative sentences to mean *it doesn't matter which*.
  Any friend of yours is a friend of mine.
- We use *no* (meaning *not any*) when we want to be emphatic.
  There's no point in complaining.
  No shops are open after 10 o'clock.
- We use *(a) few* with plural nouns and *(a) little* with uncountable nouns.
  I've only got a little money.
  A few of the trees have already lost their leaves.
- We use *few*/*little* instead of *a few*/*a little* to emphasise the smallness of the number or quantity.
  He has little money and few friends.
- We normally use *whole* with singular countable nouns.
  He ate the whole packet of biscuits.
- We normally use *all* with uncountable nouns and plural nouns.
  He ate all the biscuits in the packet.
  Have we used up all the butter?
- We use *both*, *either* and *neither* to talk about two things.
  Both shops are expensive.
  Neither shop is cheap.
  You can buy cheese at either shop.
- Most quantifiers can be followed by *of* and a determiner (e.g. *the, these, my*, etc.): *most of the ...* , *a few of his ...* , *several of those ...* , *all of us, each of them, many of*, etc.
  All of the teachers are in the staff room.
  However, *no* and *every* cannot be followed by *of*. Instead, we say *none of* and *every one of*. *None of* takes a singular verb in formal contexts.
  Every one of you must take the exam.
  None of the teachers are under 30.
  None of the teachers is under 30. (formal)

1 Choose the correct quantifier.

1 The teacher made **all** / **the whole** class stay in at break time.
2 **Any** / **Some** questions? Is everything clear?
3 I've just made **some** / **any** tea. Would you like **some** / **any**?
4 I hardly got **some** / **any** sleep last night.
5 There are **a little** / **a few** potatoes in the fridge but **a little** / **little** cheese.
6 The police arrested **both** / **either** drivers after the accident.
7 There's **no** / **any** time to talk now.
8 **Any** / **No** student caught cheating will have ten marks deducted.
9 Why are you walking about without **some** / **any** shoes?
10 In the exam you should answer **either** / **both** question 1 or question 2.

2 Complete the sentences with *of* or leave them blank.

1 Several _____ the apples were bruised so I took them back to the supermarket.
2 Most _____ pop stars are very well paid.
3 None _____ my old jeans fit me now.
4 Did you eat the whole _____ pizza?
5 Some _____ people can be really annoying.
6 Many _____ my friends are into sport.
7 Read each _____ question carefully before you write your answer.
8 None _____ his family live in London.

7.1 Reported speech

Tense changes

- When we report somebody's words rather than quoting them directly, we usually change the tense of any verbs.
  'I'm hungry,' he said. He said that he was hungry.
  The normal pattern of tense changes in reported speech is:

direct speech	→	reported speech
present simple		past simple
present continuous		past continuous
past simple		past perfect simple
present perfect simple		past perfect simple
present perfect continuous		past perfect continuous
past continuous		past perfect continuous
will		*would*
may/might		*might*
must		*must/had to*
can		*could*

- We don't normally change the tense when:
  1 the reporting verb is present or present perfect.
     'I like fast cars.'
     She says she likes fast cars.
  2 we are reporting a past perfect verb, *would, could, should* or *had better*.
     'You should go.'
     He said that I should go.
- We often omit the word *that* from the beginning of the reported speech clause:
  He said it was hot.
- There are often changes in words which refer to the people, time or place. These are dictated more by logic than by rules.
  'I'm coming here tomorrow,' she said.
  She says she's coming here tomorrow. (reported on the same day, in the same place)
  She says she's going there tomorrow. (reported on the same day, in a different place)
  She said she was going there the next day. (reported later, in a different place)
  However, these time expressions frequently change in the following way:

Grammar Builder and Reference

direct speech	→	reported speech
today		*that day*
tonight		*that night*
tomorrow		*the next/following day*
next week		*the next/following week*
ago		*before*
last week/month		*the previous week/month*
		the week/month before

say and *tell*

- The object of the verb *say* is always what was said. It is often a clause.
  'It's late,' said Tom.   She said she was thirsty.
- If we want to mention the person who is addressed, we must use the preposition *to*.
  'I'm going now,' she said to her friend.
- The object of the verb *tell* is usually the person who is addressed. We do not use the preposition *to*.
  Have you told your mum?   He told me he was tired.
- We also use *tell* in set phrases like *tell a lie, tell the truth, tell a story*, etc.

1 Change the reported speech into direct speech.

1 Caroline says she'll wear her new dress to the party.
2 Kate says she isn't coming dancing with us this evening.
3 Max told me that he'd like to study law at college.
4 Pam said that she had been to Italy the previous spring.
5 Jon complained that I'd kept him waiting for two hours.
6 Joseph told me his team hadn't won a single match before their victory last Sunday.
7 Martha explained that she didn't want to go out because she hadn't been feeling very well.

7.2 Reported questions

- When we report questions, we use affirmative word order and verb forms after the question word.
  'Where do you live?' she asked him.
  She asked him where he lived.
- To report a *yes/no* question (one that has no question word) we use *whether* or *if*.
  'Is it raining?' he asked.   He asked if it was raining.
  'Do you like milk in your coffee?' she asked me.
  She asked me whether I liked milk in my coffee.

1 Report the questions. Begin with *Harry asked me*.

1 'Why haven't you tidied your bedroom?
2 'When's Kate arriving?'
3 'Would you like a cheese sandwich?'
4 'Why were you laughing?'
5 'Could I use your rubber?'
6 'What do you think you're doing?'
7 'What have you been doing?'
8 'Will you be needing a lift home this evening?'

7.3 Indefinite pronouns

- We form indefinite pronouns with *some-*, *any-* and *no-*.

People	someone/somebody anyone/anybody no one/nobody
Places	somewhere anywhere nowhere
Things	something anything nothing

- We use pronouns with *some-* in the same way as we use *some*: in affirmative sentences and in offers and requests.
  Somebody has drunk my coffee.
  Can you leave the shopping somewhere in the kitchen?
- We use pronouns with *any-* in the same way as we use *any*: in negative sentences, in questions, in affirmative sentences where the meaning is negative, and in sentences where it means it doesn't matter who/which/where.
  I'm bored. I haven't got anything to do.
  Have you got anywhere to stay tonight?
  He must be freezing. He's hardly wearing anything.
  That's easy! Anyone knows that!

1 Complete the indefinite pronouns in these sentences. Use *some-*, *any-* or *no-*. Sometimes more than one answer is possible.

1 Does _____ one know the answer to this question?
2 Would you like _____ thing to eat?
3 _____ body wanted to go to the cinema with me, so I went by myself.
4 There was hardly _____ body I knew at the party.
5 I don't mind where we go on holiday. _____ where as long it's warm sunny!
6 I heard a noise outside. _____ one's outside.

7.4 Reporting verbs

We can use other verbs instead of *say* and *tell* when we report statements, e.g. *add, admit, agree, answer, argue, boast, claim, complain, confess, confirm, deny, explain, observe, predict, promise, reply, reveal, swear, warn*.
'This pizza is cold.'
He complained that his pizza was cold.
'It'll certainly snow tonight.'
He predicted that it would snow that night.
We can use other structures when we report offers, promises, requests, commands, suggestions, etc.

Grammar Builder and Reference

- **verb + infinitive with *to***
  agree, offer, promise, refuse, threaten
  He refused to wear a tie.
  To make the infinitive negative we add *not* before *to*.
  He promised not to be late.
- **verb + object + infinitive with *to***
  advise, ask, beg, command, dare, encourage, forbid, instruct, invite, ordered, persuade, remind, request, tell, urge, warn
  She reminded me to post the letter.
- **verb + gerund**
  admit, deny, mention, propose, recommended, report, suggest
  He admitted stealing the money.
  These verbs can also be used with a *that* clause.
  He admitted that he'd stolen the money.
- **verb + preposition + gerund**
  apologise for, boast of, confess to, insist on
  He apologised for keeping us waiting.
- **verb + object + preposition + gerund**
  accuse sb of, congratulate sb on, warn sb against
  She congratulated me on passing my driving test.
- **verb + *that* + *should*-clause**
  advise, demand, insist, propose, recommend, request, suggest,
  He insisted that she should leave immediately.
- In formal English we also occasionally use the subjunctive with these verbs.
  He insisted that she leave immediately.
  The minister proposed that all illegal immigrants be sent back to their country of origin.

1 Report the sentences. Use the reporting verb in brackets.

1 'I'll feed the cat,' said Andy. (offer)
   Andy offered to ...
2 'I'm sorry I was so late,' said Susannah. (apologise)
3 'You broke my new smartphone!' Brenda said to Zoe. (accuse)
4 'Stay away from the cliff edge,' said Denise to her son. (warn)
5 'Could you all put your pens down?' said the teacher to us. (request + should clause)
6 The doctor says it would be better if Sam took more exercise. (recommend + subjunctive)
7 'I think smoking should be banned in all public places,' said the minister. (propose + subjunctive)

2 🎧 3.02 Listen and report the direct speech. Use the verbs given followed by the appropriate structure.

I She admitted breaking the glass.

1 admit	3 boast	5 suggest	7 invite
2 beg	4 congratulate	6 refuse	8 insist

8.1 Talking about ability

can and *be able to*
- We normally use *can/can't* to talk about ability in the present. We can also use *be able to* although it is less common.
  Fran can speak Chinese. Fran is able to speak Chinese.
- We normally use *will be able to* to talk about ability in the future.
  I'm sure people will be able to travel to Mars before 2050.
  However, we often use *can/can't* to talk about future arrangements.
  I can't come to the cinema with you this evening.
- We use *be able to* when we need an infinitive. (*can* has no infinitive form.)
  I should be able to finish all my homework by ten.
- We use *being able to* when we need an *-ing* form.
  I hate not being able to watch satellite TV. There are so many good programmes on those channels.
- We use *be able to* when we want to use the present perfect tense. (*can* has no present perfect form.)
  Sue hasn't been able to walk since her accident.

Talking about ability in the past
- We use *could* for general ability in the past.
  I could read when I was four.
- When we're talking about one occasion, we use a different expression, such as *managed to do* or *succeeded in doing*. We can also use *was/were able to*.
  How did you manage to repair the DVD player?
  They were able to win despite only having ten players.
- However, we use the negative *couldn't* whether we are talking about general ability or one occasion.
  Carla couldn't swim until she was fourteen.
  I couldn't get to sleep last night.
- We use *could* with verbs of perception, like *feel, hear, see, smell, taste*, even if it's one occasion.
  I could smell dinner cooking as soon as I came in.

1 Complete the sentences with the correct form of *can* or *be able to*. Wherever possible, use *can*.

1 I hate _____ drive. I have to ask my dad for a lift all the time.
2 _____ you play the piano?
3 If we stop saving money, we _____ afford to buy a house.
4 I might _____ help you if you tell me what's the matter.
5 _____ you give me a lift to the station this evening?
6 Miriam should _____ ski – she's had quite a few lessons.
7 I _____ receive any emails since my computer went wrong.
8 I'm sorry I _____ come to the cinema with you tonight.

8.2 Relative clauses

Relative pronouns

	defining relative clauses	non-defining relative clauses
people	who/that whom (object, formal)	who whom (object, formal)
things	which/that	which
places	where	where
dates	when	when
possessives	whose	whose

Defining relative clauses

- A defining relative clause gives essential information about the noun in the main clause which it refers to. Without the information the sentence would be incomplete.
  She's the woman who I was telling you about.
  Shelter is a charity organisation whose aim is to help homeless people.
- It can go at the end or in the middle of a sentence. We do not use commas around the defining relative clause.
  The doctor who treated me was very kind.
  I met the young woman who's just started teaching at the local primary school.
- The relative pronoun which or who can be omitted if it is the object of the clause (but not if it is the subject).
  That's the man who lives round the corner. (who = subject)
  That's the man who I saw. (who = object)
  That's the man I saw. (who = object – omitted)
- We can replace which with that. In informal contexts, we can replace who with that.
  Coal is formed from trees that have been buried underground for millions of years.
  She's the girl that's going out with Kim's brother.

Non-defining relative clauses

- A non-defining relative clause gives extra information about the noun in the main clause which it refers to. The sentence makes sense without it.
- We put a comma before the clause, and also after it if the sentence continues.
  This is James Meredith, who is a friend of Sam's.
  James Meredith, who is a friend of Sam's, works at the hospital.
- The relative pronoun which or who cannot be omitted.
  (NOT This is James Meredith, is a friend of Sam's.)
- We cannot replace who or which with that.
  (NOT This is James Meredith, that is a friend of Sam's.)

1 Combine the two sentences with a defining relative clause. Use *who*, *which*, *where* or *whose*.

1 I know a lot of people. They are opposed to wind farms.
  I know a lot of people who ...
2 Tom works in a factory. They make solar panels there.
3 From here you can see the enormous wind turbine. We were protesting about it.
4 I met some eco-protesters. The police were trying to evict them.
5 I support a charity. It's campaigning against the use of fossil fuels in energy generation.
6 I found a piece of space junk. It hadn't burnt up in the Earth's atmosphere.
7 That's the nuclear power station. My dad has been working there for the past five years.

2 In which sentences in exercise 1 can we (a) omit the relative pronoun? (b) replace *who* or *which* with *that*?

3 Combine the two sentences with a non-defining relative clause, either in the middle or at the end of the sentence. Add the correct punctuation.

1 Fossil fuels are not a renewable source of energy. They are found deep underground.
  Fossil fuels, which are found ...
2 Shale gas is becoming an increasingly important source of natural gas. It is gas trapped in shale formations.
3 There are many types of renewable energy. Governments are investing in them.
4 People in industrialised countries should be the first to reduce carbon emissions. They have already benefitted from years of economic growth.
5 Farm animals release a lot of methane. Methane is a very potent greenhouse gas.
6 Nuclear power stations produce a lot of radioactive waste. It's difficult to dispose of.
7 The Intergovernmental Panel on Climate Change (IPCC) is an international organisation. Its aim is to assess the impact of climate change.

8.3 Shortened relative clauses

- In shortened relative clauses we omit the relative pronoun and the auxiliary verb *be*.
  The man (who is) standing by the door is my uncle.
- Shortened relative clauses contain either a present participle, which replaces an active verb:
  The charity protects animals facing extinction. (= which are facing)
  or they contain a past participle, which replaces a passive verb:
  Global warming is mostly caused by CO_2 emitted by power stations. (= which is emitted)

- The verb they replace can be in any tense.
  A cloud of smoke, rising from the factory, blocked out the sun.
  (= which was rising)
  We drove past a factory making cars. (= which makes)

1 Combine the two sentences. Use a shortened relative clause.

1 Was that your brother? He was talking to Sue.
   Was that your brother talking to Sue?
2 The police have arrested the woman. She was seen shoplifting on CCTV.
3 I've got a photo of my grandad. He's driving an old Mercedes.
4 The man was a climate change scientist. He lived next door.
5 I live in a farmhouse. It was built in 1855.
6 I can't find the address book. It contains all my friends' contact details.
7 The insurance company have replaced the vase. It was broken by the removal men.

8.4 *do* and *did* for emphasis

- We can use *do* and *did* to make statements stronger and to show a contrast. We stress *do* and *did* when they're used in this way.
  You do like arguing, don't you!   We did enjoy the ballet.
- We can use *do* in imperatives to make them more emphatic.
  Do be careful with that vase!
- We can use *do* and *did* to show a contrast.
  He's sometimes a bit rude but I do like him.

1 Use *do* or *did* to make the sentences more emphatic or to show a contrast.

1 You didn't get much sleep last night. Go to bed early tonight.
2 It's a very important meeting. Be on time!
3 I don't much like him, but I like his brother.
4 We enjoyed the play.
5 I like your new top!
6 Be quiet, will you!
7 I didn't cook the meal but I did the washing up.

9.1 *should/could/might/needn't have*

- We can use *shouldn't have* to express disapproval of past actions.
  You shouldn't have stayed up all night.
- We use *should have*, *might have* or *could have* to say what the right way to behave was, in our opinion.
  You should have gone to bed before midnight.
- We sometimes use *might have* or *could have* to tell somebody what they should have done. It is usually an exclamation.
  Really! You could have saved some pizza for me!

- We use *needn't have* to say an action that took place was unnecessary:
  You needn't have worried, I was at my friend's house.
- If we talking about an action that was unnecessary and didn't take place, we use a different structure. Compare:
  They didn't have to pay for their tickets. Children under eighteen get in free.
  They needn't have paid for their tickets. My uncle owns the cinema. (But they did pay for them.)

1 Choose the word which makes the most sense in these sentences.

1 I don't mind you borrowing my phone, but you **might / needn't** have asked me first!
2 We **shouldn't / needn't** have eaten those burgers; they were a week past their 'use by' date.
3 I forgot our homework was due in today – you **could / needn't** have reminded me!
4 I was only two minutes late. You **might / shouldn't** have waited for me!
5 We **needn't / shouldn't** have gone to Greece in March; the weather was terrible.
6 My mobile was switched off – you **needn't / should** have tried my landline.

2 Rewrite the sentences so they include *should*, *shouldn't*, *could*, *might* or *needn't have*. Don't change the meaning.

1 It was a bad idea for you to give chocolate to your dog.
2 She wore formal clothes, but it wasn't necessary.
3 Inviting your cousins to your party would have been a good idea.
4 I wish you'd saved some chips for me!
5 Leaving the front door unlocked was a bad thing to do.
6 It was unnecessary for you to buy me a present.
7 It would have been better if you'd stayed at home.
8 I wish they'd given us a lift to the station!

9.2 Third conditional

- We use the third conditional to talk about how a situation in the past could have been avoided:
  If she hadn't lost her temper, Jack wouldn't have left.
  (But she did lose her temper and Jack did leave.)
- The *if* clause can come before or after the main clause. We use the past perfect in the *if* clause and *would/wouldn't have* in the main clause. Be careful: *had* and *would* both have the same short form: 'd.
  She'd have been amazed if you'd asked her out.
  (She would have been amazed if you had asked her out.)
- We use *could have* in the main clause when we're talking about ability. It means *would have been able to*:
  If I hadn't had a heavy suitcase with me, I could have run for the bus.

- We can use *could have* or *might have* in the main clause if the result is less certain.
  If my dad had gone to university, he might have become a teacher.

1 Complete these third conditional sentences with the past perfect and *would(n't) have* form of the verbs in brackets.

1 If you _____ (not leave) the door open, the burglars _____ (not get) in!
2 We _____ (win) the match if we _____ (play) better in the second half.
3 It _____ (be) better if you _____ (not mention) our plan.
4 If my dad _____ (not come) home, the party _____ (go on) all night.
5 They _____ (go) on holiday in the summer if they _____ (not go) skiing already that year.
6 You _____ (not guess) my secret if your sister _____ (not give) you a clue.
7 I _____ (not write) a letter of complaint if I _____ (not be) so angry.
8 If you _____ (ask) to borrow my football boots, I _____ (say) yes.

9.3 Mixed conditionals

- Mixed conditionals are a mixture of type 2 and type 3 conditionals and refer to hypothetical situations. Remember that type 2 conditionals refer to the present or future, and type 3 conditionals refer to the past. Mixed conditionals occur when the time reference in the *if* clause is different from the main clause.
  If you had eaten your lunch, you wouldn't be hungry now.
  past (type 3)   present (type 2)
  If we hadn't fallen out with each other, we'd go on holiday together again this summer.
  past (type 3)   future (type 2)
  If I lived in London, I would have gone to the match.
  present (type 2)   past (type 3)
- The choice of verb forms in mixed conditionals depends on the time reference. If we're referring to the past in the *if* clause, we use the past perfect (simple or continuous) as we would in a type 3 conditional; if we're referring to the present in the *if* clause, we use the past simple as we would in a type 2 conditional. Similarly, if we're referring to the past in the main clause, we use *would have*, as for type 3; if we're referring to the present or future in the main clause, we use *would*, as for type 2.

1 Match the two halves of the sentences. Complete the second half with the correct form of the verb in brackets.

1 If you weren't my best friend,
2 If they hadn't closed the bowling alley,
3 She might have become a model
4 You'd never have stood in a queue for three hours
5 If there was a good restaurant in town,
6 He wouldn't have become a teacher

a we _____ (go) there tonight.
b if she _____ (be) a few centimetres taller.
c if you _____ (not be) British.
d I _____ (not tell) you what I really think.
e if he _____ (not like) children.
f I _____ (not buy) fish and chips.

2 Rewrite each pair of sentences as a mixed conditional sentence.

1 They're very argumentative. That's why they fell out.
  If they weren't so argumentative, they wouldn't have fallen out.
2 He isn't fit. That's why he didn't finish the race.
3 My grandfather owned a factory. That's why we live in a big house.
4 She worked hard last term. That's why she's disappointed with her exam results.
5 I don't speak Spanish. That's why I didn't apply for a job in South America.
6 It rained all night. That's why we can't use the tennis courts.
7 You were rude to Ellie. That's why she doesn't like you.
8 We're on holiday. That's why we didn't go to the barbecue.

9.4 Wishes and regrets

- We use the following structure to express regrets about the past:
  I (really) wish + past perfect
  I'd (much) rather + past perfect
  I wish I hadn't spent all my money.
  I'd much rather you'd sent me a text message.

1 Write a sentence using the word in brackets to express these regrets about the past.

1 I didn't revise for the exam. (wish)
  I really wish I'd revised for the exam.
2 you told Jacqui my secret. (rather)
3 you didn't wear smart clothes. (rather)
4 I didn't ask for her phone number. (wish)
5 my favourite team didn't win. (wish)
6 we stayed in a hotel. (rather)
7 you didn't give me money for my birthday. (rather)
8 I promised to help Louis with his homework. (wish)

9.5 Expressing purpose and result

- We can express purpose with a simple infinitive or the phrase *in order (not) to* or *so as (not to)*.
  She stood up in order to ask/so as to ask a question.
- We can also use the phrase with a view to or *with the intention of* followed by an *-ing* form.
  They renovated the hotel with a view to charging more for the rooms.
- We can also express purpose with *in order that*, *so that* or *so* followed by a clause.
  She sat down in order that/so that/so the people behind her could see.
- We can express a result with *so* (but **NOT** ~~so that~~)
  I was tired so I went to bed.
- We can also express a result using *so* + adjective or adverb or *such* (+adjective) + noun followed by *that* and a clause.
  I was so tired that I went to bed at 7 p.m.
  They played so badly that they lost 8–0.
  It was such a boring film that I fell asleep.
  They were such difficult questions that I couldn't answer any of them.

1 Choose the correct words to complete the sentences.

1 The supermarket was closed _____ she went to the corner shop.
  a so that **b** in order that **c** so
2 We spent so long at the museum _____ we didn't have time for the art gallery.
  a so **b** so that **c** that
3 She went to lots of parties in the first week of term _____ making friends.
  a in order to **b** so that **c** with a view to
4 He logged onto his email account _____ check his messages.
  a so that **b** in order that **c** to
5 They got a passport for their baby _____ they could travel abroad.
  a so **b** in order to **c** that
6 The film finished early _____ they went to a café.
  a in order that **b** so that **c** so
7 She took off her shoes _____ not to get them wet.
  a so **b** so as **c** in order to
8 They spent _____ little time in France that they didn't learn any French.
  a such **b** so **c** that

10.1 Emphasis and inversion

- We can make a sentence more emphatic by adding an extra clause to highlight key information.

Normal	Emphatic
You wanted to go to the beach.	It was you that/who wanted to go to the beach.
I'd like to meet Lady Gaga.	The person I'd like to meet is Lady Gaga.
He really wants to visit China.	One country he really wants to visit is China.
I'll never understand baseball.	One thing I'll never understand is baseball.
She just walked the second half of the race.	All she did was (to) walk the second half of the race.
The fire alarm went off.	What happened was (that) the fire alarm went off.

- After *All (I) did was …* or *What (I) did was …* we use an infinitive with or without *to*:
  What they did was (to) make a shelter in the woods.
  However, after *All that happened was …* or *What happened was …* we need a subject and a verb. We can put *that* before the subject:
  All that happened was (that) they made a shelter in the woods.
- We can also make a sentence more emphatic by putting a negative or limiting adverb (or adverbial phrase) at the front. These include: *never, not since, not only, no sooner … than, hardly, rarely/seldom, under no circumstances, no way*. After the adverb or phrase, the word order is inverted.
  Not since his childhood had he enjoyed a holiday so much.
  Rarely has there been such a popular event.
- For verbs in the present/past simple we use *do/did*.
  No way does he deserve a prize for that!
  Not only did he win, but he won by twenty points.

1 Rewrite the sentences with an extra clause at the start for emphasis. Begin with the words in brackets.

1 You always forget your keys. (It's you …)
  It's you who always forgets your keys.
2 I really hate tomato soup. (One thing …)
3 My parents met in Japan. (It was …)
4 The referee awarded a penalty. (What happened …)
5 Lisa spent a year abroad after school. (What Lisa …)
6 I asked my dad for some money, that's all. (All I …)
7 I enjoy talking to my grandfather. (One person …)
8 My uncle took me to my first sports event. (It was …)
9 We just need one more basketball player. (All we …)
10 You can't go to Antarctica on holiday. (One place …)

2 Complete the second sentence in each pair so that it means the same as the first.

1 I've never seen such an impressive firework display.
  Never _____ an impressive firework display.
2 You mustn't, under any circumstances, unlock the door.
  Under _____ unlock the door.

Grammar Builder and Reference

3 We haven't been to Scotland since our wedding.
Not since _____ to Scotland.

4 He certainly can't speak six languages!
No way _____ six languages!

5 She broke her arm and also damaged her knee.
Not only _____ damaged her knee.

6 The party ended as soon as we'd arrived.
No sooner _____ ended.

10.2 The unreal past

- We use the past simple after certain expressions even though the meaning is present or future.
It's (high) time I had a shower.
I'd rather you didn't tell anyone.
I'd sooner we travelled by plane.
Imagine you worked in New York!

- We can use the past or present simple after these expressions, without a significant difference in meaning:
Suppose we had/have dinner out tonight.
They act as if/as though they are/were married!

- When we use the unreal past, we normally use *were* instead of *was*.
I'd rather I weren't in the athletics team.

1 Complete the second sentence so it means the same as the first.

1 I don't want you to read my diary.
I'd rather ...

2 Why don't we invite the whole class?
Suppose ...

3 Wouldn't it be great to have a Ferrari?
Imagine ...

4 We should return these books to the library.
It's time ...

5 I don't want my parents to be friends with me on Facebook.
I'd sooner ...

6 The Government should allow online voting.
It's high time ...

10.3 had better/might as well

- We use *had better* followed by an infinitive without *to* to give advice or a warning. Even though *had* is the past simple form of *have*, we use *had better* to give advice about the present or future.
You'd better ask the teacher before you leave.
He'd better start behaving himself!
The negative form of *had better* is *had better not*
(**NOT** hadn't better)
You'd better not do that again.
To describe the consequence of not following the advice, had *better (not)* is often followed by *or + will* future.

He'd better not argue with the captain or he'll lose his place in the team.

- We use *might as well* to say what course of action should be followed. It does not imply a strong recommendation for that course of action, but rather that there is nothing to lose by following it, or that the alternative is no better.
That plant is dead, so you might as well throw it away.

1 Rewrite these sentences with *had better (not)*. Include *or + will* future if appropriate.

1 I'll be furious if you borrow my laptop without asking.
2 They should hurry up to avoid being late.
3 If she doesn't apologise, I won't invite her to my house again.
4 It would be a bad idea to wake my dad up.
5 You won't get a good mark unless you answer all of the questions.
6 I should go home now. If I don't, my mum will be worried.

2 Complete the sentences with *might as well* and an appropriate verb or phrase.

1 The weather is terrible. We...
2 That torch doesn't work. You...
3 Tickets for the lottery are only £1 each. I...
4 These crisps won't stay fresh now the packet is open. We...
5 You'll find out the truth sooner or later, so I...
6 There's nothing good on TV. We...

10.4 Adverbial phrases

- When we start a sentence with an adverbial phrase of direction, position, etc., the subject-verb word order which follows is usually inverted. We usually do this with verbs of place or movement (*climb, come, fly, go, hang, lie, run, sit, stand*, etc.) but not other verbs:
Near the door stood a man in a white coat.
By the window, two men were chatting. (no inversion)

- However, when the subject is a pronoun, we do not invert.
Away they drove. (**NOT** Away drove they.)

- When the verb form is *there is/are*, we miss out *there* instead of inverting.
On the floor were three large bags.

1 Rewrite these sentences starting with the adverbial phrase. Invert the word order which follows only if appropriate.

1 His aunt sat at one end of the sofa.
2 My sister is asleep in the top floor bedroom.
3 An empty wine bottle lay on the grass.
4 There are three cinemas in the town centre.
5 She ran out of the room, screaming.
6 There's a tennis court behind the football pitch.

1.1 Synonyms and antonyms

LEARN THIS!

Synonyms and antonyms
A synonym is a word which means the same as another word: *unhappy* and *sad* are synonyms.
An antonym is word which means the opposite of another word: *tall* and *short* are antonyms.
Some dictionaries include synonyms and antonyms.

1 Read the *Learn this!* box. Then match the adjectives in group 1 with their synonyms in group 2. Decide if each pair is positive or negative and write them in the chart.

1 ~~cagey~~ conceited condescending daring energetic friendly humorous intelligent irritable logical loyal relaxed timid unassuming

2 active adventurous amiable calm clever faithful grumpy modest patronising rational ~~secretive~~ shy vain witty

positive	negative
	cagey – secretive

2 Choose the best antonym for each word.

1 approximately (adverb)
   a very   **b** nearly   **c** exactly   **d** correctly
2 calm (adjective)
   a exciting   **b** excited   **c** boring   **d** silent
3 neat (adjective)
   a messy   **b** hard-working   **c** lazy   **d** reliable
4 truthful (adjective)
   a incorrect   **b** false   **c** different   **d** dishonest
5 adore (verb)
   a prefer   **b** hate   **c** love   **d** enjoy
6 despair (noun)
   a optimism   **b** fun   **c** excitement   **d** joy

3 Complete the sentences with the words you selected in exercise 2.

1 I'm embarrassed about my _____ handwriting.
2 Can you imagine how _____ you'd feel if you won the lottery?
3 A marathon is _____ 42.195 kilometres.
4 It's a crime to give a _____ answer to a question in court.
5 I simply _____ all forms of motor-racing.
6 He always looks forward with _____ .

1.2 Compound adjectives

LEARN THIS!

Compound adjectives
Compound adjectives are adjectives formed from two words. The two most common types are:
1 adjective + noun with *-ed* ending
   kind-hearted, long-legged, big-headed
2 noun + *-ing* form
   space-saving, meat-eating, time-wasting
3 adverb + past participle
   well-worn, thinly-veiled

1 Complete the sentences with six of the adjectives from the *Learn this!* box.

1 He gets so much praise from his parents that he's become quite _____ .
2 Keeping the ball in the corner of the pitch is a common _____ tactic in football.
3 _____ plants get their nutrition from trapping insects.
4 She sometimes comes across as grumpy, but she's actually very _____ .
5 Most high-jumpers are extremely tall and _____ .
6 This French film is actually a _____ attack on Hollywood.

2 Make compound adjectives with a word from each group. Match them with the correct definitions.

able absent cold densely ~~dimly~~ level mouth sure

blooded bodied footed headed ~~lit~~ minded populated watering

1 ~~dimly-lit~~: dark; without many lights
2 _____ : having a lot of people living in small area
3 _____ : forgetful
4 _____ : delicious
5 _____ : cruel
6 _____ : unlikely to fall
7 _____ : calm
8 _____ : fit and healthy

3 Complete these sentences with compound adjectives. Then invent two similar sentences of your own.

1 People who wave flags are ~~flag-waving~~ people.
2 Cats with short hair are _____ cats.
3 People with strong minds are _____ people.
4 Bread that has been baked freshly is _____ bread.
5 A gadget which saves time is a _____ gadget.
6 A man with one arm is a _____ man.
7 _____ .
8 _____ .

2 Vocabulary Builder

2.1 Money idioms

1 Match the idioms with the definitions.

1 get ripped off ☐
2 cost an arm and a leg ☐
3 come into some money ☐
4 dip into your savings ☐
5 live from hand to mouth ☐
6 make ends meet ☐
7 tighten your belt ☐
8 make a killing ☐

a make a big profit
b spend all your money on basic needs like food without being able to buy anything else
c be given some money, usually after a relative has died
d be charged too much money
e spend some money that you had put aside to use later
f spend less money than usual
g be very expensive
h have just enough money to buy what you need

2 Complete the sentences with idioms from exercise 1. Use the correct form.

1 'Was your new bike expensive?' 'Yes, very. It _____.'
2 We had to _____ to pay for a holiday last year. But we've still got a few hundred pounds left in the account.
3 Jim _____ when his grandmother died. He was able to buy a new car.
4 Many people on state benefits _____, with barely enough money for basics like food and heating.
5 I don't earn a great deal, but we manage to _____ .
6 You could have bought that computer for half the price on the Internet. You _____ .
7 My uncle _____ when he sold his business. But then he lost it all when he invested in the stock market.
8 Prices are going up and wages aren't increasing. So we'll have to _____ .

> **LEARN THIS!**
>
> **Time and money**
> We use the same verbs with time and money: *be short of, have time/money to spare, lose, make, run out of, save, waste.*
> *Hurry up and stop wasting time!*
> *Don't waste your money on sweets!*

2.2 Buying and renting a flat

1 Complete the adverts with the words below.

amenities balcony for sale fully-fitted top-floor
walking distance

3-bedroom [1]_____ flat with [2]_____ . Separate [3]_____ kitchen. Within easy [4]_____ of local bus routes and [5]_____ . [6]_____ : £200,000.

available central heating double glazing furnished
rent spacious

[7]_____ apartment, offered [8]_____ or part-furnished. Benefits from [9]_____ and gas [10]_____ . [11]_____ from 1 May. [12]_____ £500 per month.

2.3 Extreme adjectives

1 Match the adjectives in group A with the extreme adjectives in group B.

A angry beautiful crowded clean dirty funny hungry silly surprising tired ugly

B astonishing exhausted filthy furious gorgeous hideous hilarious packed ridiculous spotless starving

2 Complete the extreme adjectives that mean:

1 very big: e_____ h_____
2 very good: f_____ w_____
3 very bad: t_____ a_____

Can you add any more? Use a dictionary or thesaurus to help you.

3 🎧 1.15 **PRONUNCIATION** Listen carefully to the example. Then listen and reply to the sentences in the same way, using an extreme adjective. Copy the intonation in the example.

1 Are you hungry?

> Hungry? I'm starving!

2.4 Comment adverbs

1 Choose the correct comment adverbs. Sometimes there is more than one correct answer.

1 **Personally, / Apparently, / To my surprise,** I don't believe in ghosts.
2 **To be honest, / Foolishly, / Frankly,** I'm not very keen on Italian food.
3 I'm broke, so **ideally / obviously / unfortunately** I can't come out tonight.
4 **Hopefully / Ideally / Luckily** I'll pass my driving test before my eighteenth birthday.
5 He fell off his bike, but **fortunately / not surprisingly / hopefully** he didn't hurt himself badly.

3.1 Stages of life

1 Number the stages of life below in the order that we reach them.

childhood ☐

old age ☐

adolescence ☐

adulthood ☐

middle age ☐

infancy ☐

2 Match the words below with the stages of life. Draw a spidergram. Some words can go with two stages.

career elderly forties grey hair kid marriage
nappies OAP retirement seventies teenager
toddler twenties walking stick white hair wrinkles

3 Can you add any more words to the spidergrams? Use a dictionary to help you if necessary.

3.2 Phrasal verbs with *up* and *down*

1 🎧 1.24 Complete the sentences with *up* or *down*. Then listen and check your answers.

1 You're welcome to visit us on Saturday but I'm afraid we can't put you _____ .
2 He doesn't play as well as he can because he doesn't want to show the rest of the team _____ .
3 They often have terrible rows because they both refuse to back _____ .
4 When you talk to my grandfather about his health problems, he always plays them _____ .
5 At the time, his marriage was a huge scandal that took years to die _____ .
6 It's a comfortable hotel, but they need to do it _____ .
7 As the teacher started to wind _____ the lesson, the students put their books away.
8 He only took _____ skiing after he'd retired.
9 There was an accident on the motorway which held us _____ for two hours.
10 He turned _____ a job in a bank because he wanted to be a dancer.

> **LEARN THIS!**
>
> **Phrasal verbs (1)**
> 1 Phrasal verbs can be transitive (they have an object) or intransitive (they don't have an object).
>   *He sat down.* (intransitive)
>   *He put down his bag.* (transitive)
> 2 Transitive phrasal verbs are usually separable. This means the object can go before the adverb.
>   *I cut down the tree. We cut the tree down.*
> 3 If the phrasal verb is separable and the object is a pronoun, the pronoun MUST come before the adverb.
>   ~~I cut down it.~~ ✗ *I cut it down.*

2 Read the *Learn this!* box. Then match the phrasal verbs (1–10) with the meanings (a–j). Use the sentences in exercise 1 to help you. Is each verb transitive or intransitive?

1	back down	a	renovate
2	die down	b	provide accommodation for
3	do up	c	delay
4	hold up	d	refuse to accept
5	play down	e	change your position or ideas
6	put up	f	minimise the importance of
7	show up	g	bring to an end
8	take up	h	start doing (as a hobby)
9	turn down	i	become weaker or quieter
10	wind up	j	make look inferior

3 Write another example sentence for each of the phrasal verbs in exercise 2.

4.1 Elections

1 Complete the text with the correct form of the words below. Use a dictionary to help you.

candidate   coalition   constituency   general election
hung parliament   majority   member of parliament
prime minister   proportional representation   vote (n)

The British Electoral System

¹_____ in Britain take place at least every five years. The country is divided up into ²_____ (areas) in which the various ³_____ , who are usually members of political parties, put themselves up for election. Each candidate hopes to become the ⁴_____ for that constituency. The electoral system is not ⁵_____ , where the total number of ⁶_____ for each party across the country is taken into account, but 'first past the post', where the winner in each constituency is elected and all the other votes count for nothing. If a party wins a ⁷_____ of seats in parliament, they form a government, and their leader becomes ⁸_____ . If no party has a majority, then it is a ⁹_____ and the opposing parties may agree to form a ¹⁰_____ .

4.2 International organisations

1 Match the logos with the international organisations.

a European Central Bank
b NATO (North Atlantic Treaty Organisation)
c WWF (Worldwide Fund for Nature)
d the EU (European Union)
e the UN (United Nations)
f Amnesty International
g the Red Cross
h World Trade Organisation

2 Describe the activities of the organisations. Use the words below to help you.

Verbs campaign for protect regulate support
Nouns economic affairs environmental issues
freedom of speech human rights military alliance
political prisoner refugees trade

4.3 Suffixes *-ism* and *-ist*

1 Complete the chart. Use a dictionary to help you. Be careful, not all the words end in *-ist*.

Noun / person		Noun / person	
1	feminism / feminist	6	capitalism / _____
2	vandalism / _____	7	socialism / _____
3	atheism / _____	8	patriotism / _____
4	extremism / _____	9	nationalism / _____
5	pessimism / _____		

2 Match words from exercise 1 with these definitions.

1 the belief that God does not exist
2 a person who loves his or her country very much
3 a person with extremely strong political or religious opinions, sometimes prepared to use violence
4 the belief or feeling that bad things will happen
5 the belief that women should have the same rights and opportunities as men
6 a person who deliberately damages public property
7 a person who wants their country to become independent
8 an economic system in which businesses are mostly owned privately, not by the state
9 an economic system in which businesses are mostly owned and controlled by the state

4.4   Variable stress

1 🎧 2.07 Listen and repeat the words below. Is the word a verb or a noun? Then say the word again changing the syllable that is stressed.

> *con*flict. It's a noun. con*flict*. It's a verb.

1 conflict   4 increase   7 record
2 import   5 produce   8 suspect
3 permit   6 protest

2 Complete the sentences with the correct form of words from exercise 1. Then read the sentences aloud stressing the gapped word correctly.

1 The Government refuses to _____ teachers' salaries.
2 Usain Bolt first broke the 100 m world _____ in 2008.
3 The demonstrators were _____ against the big rise in the price of petrol.
4 The police have arrested a man whom they _____ of murdering his wife.
5 Britain _____ a lot of food from other countries.
6 China _____ over 50% of the world's manufactured goods.

5.1 Technology components

1 Match eight of the words below with the pictures (1–8).

aerial antenna axle battery blade brake bulb circuit board cog dial fan lead lens microphone microprocessor motor plug pulley SIM card speaker spring strap switch thermostat touchscreen

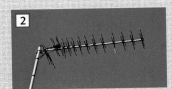

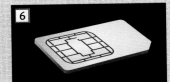

2 Divide all the words from exercise 1 into two groups. Write the ones you would find in a smartphone in box A; write the others in box B with one example of where you might find them.

A (smartphone components)	B (other components)
battery	axle – a car

3 In pairs, decide which components from exercise 1 the following objects probably contain.

1 electric razor
2 hairdryer
3 HD video camera
4 lawnmower
5 moped
6 microwave oven

5.2 Crime

1 Work in pairs. Complete the chart with the missing words. Use a dictionary to help you.

Crime	Criminal	Verb
arson	1_____	set fire to (a building, etc.)
blackmail	blackmailer	2_____
burglary	3_____	burgle (a house, office, etc.)
drug dealing	4_____	deal drugs
forgery	forger	5_____
6_____	fraudster	defraud (somebody)
hacking	7_____	hack (into something)
hijacking	hijacker	8_____
kidnapping	9_____	kidnap
joyriding	10_____	go joyriding
11_____	mugger	mug (somebody)
murder	murderer	12_____ (somebody)
13_____	rapist	rape
robbery	robber	14_____
shoplifting	15_____	shoplift
16_____	thief	steal (something)
trafficking	17_____	traffic
18_____	vandal	vandalise (something)

2 Complete the crime reports with the words below.

convicted jury pleaded sentenced verdict

Justin Jones was [1]_____ of kidnapping and [2]_____ to nine years in jail. Although Mr Jones had [3]_____ not guilty, the evidence against him was described by the police as 'overwhelming' and the [4]_____ took less than an hour to reach their [5]_____ .

acquitted alibi evidence found trial witnesses

At the High Court today, Karl Macintosh, who was standing [6]_____ for the murder of two teenagers, was [7]_____ after the jury [8]_____ him not guilty. Although prosecutors had argued that forensic [9]_____ linked Macintosh to the crime scene, several [10]_____ confirmed his [11]_____ .

accused arrest issued offences question

Police would like to [12]_____ a man about a series of [13]_____ in the Liverpool area. He is [14]_____ of defrauding more than ten elderly couples out of their life savings. Police have [15]_____ a description of the man and are offering a reward for information which leads to [16]_____ and conviction.

6 Vocabulary Builder

6.1 Informal food idioms

1 Match the informal idioms (1–10) with the meanings (a–j). Use a dictionary to help you.

1 a couch potato
2 be paid peanuts
3 in a nutshell
4 be out to lunch
5 spill the beans
6 go pear-shaped
7 be full of beans
8 butter somebody up
9 pie in the sky
10 have a lot on one's plate

a (of a plan) to go badly wrong
b be full of energy and enthusiasm
c to receive very little money
d be very busy, with a lot of things to do and think about
e something which someone talks about that is very unlikely to happen
f behaving strangely
g expressed clearly and in few words
h say nice things so that someone will help you or give you something
i give away a secret
j person who spends a lot of time sitting and watching TV

2 Complete the sentences with idioms from exercise 1. Use the correct form.

1 'Can I watch telly, Mum?' 'No, you've watched enough television today. You'll turn into a _____ !'
2 He keeps on saying the weirdest things. I think he's a bit _____ .
3 The kids are _____ . They've just played tennis and now they want to play football.
4 If you want to borrow his car, you'll have to _____ first!
5 He's sympathetic, supportive, generous, a good listener. _____ , he's a really good friend.

3 Replace the underlined words with idioms from exercise 1.

1 He talks about getting a new job, but <u>it'll never happen</u>.
2 Jake and Sue are getting divorced, but <u>don't tell anyone</u>.
3 I'd like to help you, <u>I'm very busy at work and at home</u>.
4 Her plan to sell her house and move to France has <u>gone all wrong</u>.
5 He has a very responsible job but he gets paid <u>very little</u>.

6.2 Food and nutrition

1 Complete the sentences with the words below.

additives   calories   cholesterol   fair-trade   fibre
GM foods   low-carb   organic   use-by date   wholemeal

1 _____ are used to improve the flavour of food or change its colour.
2 _____ contain plants that have been changed (genetically modified) in order to protect them from disease or to make them more productive.
3 _____ food has been produced without the use of artificial chemicals or fertilisers.
4 _____ bread is made from the whole grain of wheat. It contains lots of _____ .
5 If you follow a _____ diet, you eat less bread, pasta, rice, etc. and more foods containing protein or fat.
6 _____ goods help farmers in developing countries because the farmers receive a fair price for their produce.
7 The recommended daily intake of _____ in the UK is about 2,500 for men and 2,000 for women.
8 You shouldn't eat food that has passed its _____ .
9 Too much _____ , can cause heart disease.

6.3 Word formation

> **LEARN THIS!**
>
> **Verbs and nouns from adjectives**
> 1 We can add *-en* or *-ise* (US *-ize*) to some adjectives to form verbs.
> *short – shorten* (= make shorter)   *tight – tighten*
> *fictional – fictionalise*   *general – generalise*
> 2 We can add *-ness* or *-ity* to some adjectives to make nouns. Sometimes the spelling changes.
> *bitter – bitterness*   *ready – readiness*
> *real – reality*   *possible – possibility*

1 Read the *Learn this!* box. Complete the sentences by making a noun or a verb from the adjective in brackets.

1 Add some flour to _____ the soup. (thick)
2 _____ was down to 50 m in the fog. (visible)
3 I don't think it's a good idea to _____ cannabis. (legal)
4 The accident was the result of the driver's _____ . (careless)
5 Wait till the plums _____ before picking them. (ripe)
6 Shall I _____ your pencil for you? (sharp)
7 Thanks for letting me know what you think. I appreciate your _____ . (frank)
8 _____ is very important in business. (punctual)
9 The Government is planning to _____ the steel industry. (national)
10 Joe bears a striking _____ to his sister. (similar)

7.1 News

1 Match the words in A with words in B.

A	B
breaking	broadcast
citizen	journalism
live	flash
online	news
news	edition
news	programme

A	B
satellite	page
front	blog
eyewitness	correspondent
rolling news	phone
news	account
news	channel

2 Explain the meaning of these words. You can find them all in a newspaper.

1 article
2 headline
3 human-interest story
4 column
5 editorial

7.2 Headlines and news vocabulary

1 Read the newspaper headlines (1–6). Explain them using the information below to help you.

Headline language	
riddle = mystery	gems = jewels
bid = attempt	ban = make illegal
plea = request	vow = promise
quit = resign	pledge = promise
curb = control; limit	axe = cut

1 Riddle of missing gems solved
2 Doctors in bid to ban smoking
3 Royal couple in privacy plea
4 Manager vows to quit at end of season
5 Minister pledges to curb inflation
6 Government to axe 5,000 jobs

2 Which headlines are 'hard' news? Which are 'soft' news? Give reasons.

7.3 Phrasal verbs with *on*, *off*, *out* and *in*.

LEARN THIS!

Particles and meanings
Some particles can give a phrasal verb a certain general meaning. For example, *off* can convey the idea of:
1 going away, e.g. *take off, lift off, clear off*
2 starting, e.g. *kick off, set off, spark off*
3 becoming less, e.g. *wear off, die off, cool off*
4 resisting, e.g. *fight off, fend off, hold off*

1 Match the meanings below with the groups of phrasal verbs (A–D). Then translate the verbs into your language.

arriving   continuing   discovering/solving   ending

	Translation
A _____	
carry on	1 _____
go on (about)	2 _____
stay on	3 _____
B _____	
log off	4 _____
ring off	5 _____
call off	6 _____
C _____	
work out	7 _____
find out	8 _____
sort out	9 _____
D _____	
pull in	10 _____
get in	11 _____
check in	12 _____

2 Use the verbs in exercise 1 to complete the sentences. Use the correct form.

1 If you bank online, always remember to _____ when you leave the website.
2 _____ along this road until you reach the church. Then turn right.
3 Can you _____ if Danny has got an email address or not?
4 The football match has been _____ owing to the bad weather.
5 I'm going to _____ in this job until I've earned enough money for a new car.
6 We _____ at the hotel and took our cases to our room.
7 Before you take out a loan you should _____ exactly how much you earn and spend each month. Then you'll know if you can afford it.
8 What time did you _____ last night? I didn't hear you so it must have been after I went to bed.
9 He's always _____ about how much money he earns. He's such a bore!
10 The bus _____ to the bus station and stopped.
11 I'll make the food for the party if you _____ the music.
12 As soon as I answered the phone, the caller _____ , so I don't know who was calling.

8 Vocabulary Builder

8.1 Wildlife and endangered species

1 Complete the text with the words below.

breeding   captivity   conservation   extinction   habitat
poaching   reserves   threats   the wild

The population of gorillas
living in ¹_____ is in decline.
²_____ to their survival
include the destruction of their
natural ³_____ (the forests in
which they live are cut down
for fuel), and ⁴_____ (they are
hunted for their meat). In an
effort to aid gorilla ⁵_____ , a
number of ⁶_____ have been
created where the animals are
protected. There are also

⁷_____ programmes in zoos around the world, although
there is a much debate on whether it is cruel to keep such
intelligent animals in ⁸_____ . They are an endangered
species, but for the time being they do not face ⁹_____ .

8.2 Prefixes with particular meanings

anti- = against	*anti-clockwise*
ex- = former	*my ex-wife*
mis- = badly or wrongly	*mispronounce*
multi- = many	*multi-storey car park*
over- = too much	*overdo*
post- = after	*postgraduate*
re- = again	*rewrite*
semi- = half	*semi-detached*
under- = not enough	*underpriced*

1 Read the information above. Rewrite the sentences replacing the underlined words with a word or phrase that includes one of the prefixes.

1 Please arrange the desks in a <u>half-circle</u>.
  Please arrange the desks in a semi-circle.
2 I <u>failed to understand</u> what you said.
3 Last weekend we took part in a <u>demonstration against the war</u>.
4 He <u>used to be a policeman</u>.
5 You shouldn't <u>eat too much</u>.
6 This meat <u>hasn't been cooked enough</u>.
7 My dad was born in the <u>era after the war</u>.
8 The National Health Service <u>isn't funded well enough</u>.
9 If you didn't understand it the first time, <u>read it again</u>.
10 The children are <u>behaving badly</u>.

8.3 Words with similar meanings

1 Complete the dictionary entries with the verbs below.

damage   harm   hurt   hurt   injure   wound

¹_____ **1** to cause physical harm to sth, making it less useful
or valuable *The fire badly damaged the house.* **2** to have
a bad effect on sb's life, health, happiness *emotionally
damaged children*

²_____ to have a bad effect on sb/sth; hurt sb/sth *Pollution
can harm marine life.*

³_____ *(rather informal)* to have a bad effect on sb's life,
health, happiness *Hard work never hurt anyone.*

Damage, hurt or harm? Hurt is slightly less formal, especially
when it's used in negative statements. *It won't hurt him to
have to wait a bit.* It won't harm/damage him to have to wait
a bit. **Harm** is also often used to talk about ways in which
wildlife and the environment are damaged by human activity.

⁴_____ to harm yourself or sb else physically, especially in an
accident *He injured himself playing hockey.* • *Three people
were injured in the accident.*

⁵_____ *(rather formal; often passive)* to injure part of the body,
especially by making a hole in the skin. *He was wounded in
the arm.* • *50 people were seriously wounded in the attack.*
*Wound is often used to talk about people being hurt in war
or other attacks.

⁶_____ to cause physical pain to sb/yourself; to injure sb/
yourself. *He hurt his back playing tennis.* • *Did you hurt
yourself?* • *Stop it. You're hurting me!* • *My shoes hurt.
They're too tight.*

Hurt or injure? You can **hurt** or **injure** a part of the body in an
accident. **Hurt** emphasises the physical pain caused; **injure**
emphasises that the part of the body has been damaged in
some way.

2 Read the dictionary entries and then choose the correct verbs in the sentences.

1 CO_2 emissions from factories are **harming / injuring** the environment.
2 The bus was badly **harmed / damaged** in the crash.
3 Come on, Sally, eat your vegetables. They won't **hurt / damage** you!
4 He was **injured / wounded** in the arm in the knife attack.
5 My back is really **hurting / injuring** me today.

9 Vocabulary Builder

9.1 Adverbs

LEARN THIS!

1 Some adjectives ending -ly keep the same form for the adverb: *early, daily, weekly, monthly, yearly,* etc.
I took the early train.   She gets up early.
It's a monthly newspaper.   I get paid monthly.

2 Other adjectives ending -ly do not have an adverbial form: *cowardly, disorderly, friendly, jolly, leisurely, lively, timely,* etc. Instead, we put the adjective in an adverbial phrase:
He always behaves in a friendly way/fashion/manner.

3 Some adverbs have two forms: one with -ly and one without:

close	closely	just	justly
deep	deeply	late	lately
hard	hardly	near	nearly
high	highly	wrong	wrongly

The meanings are sometimes close and sometimes unrelated:
*They sailed **close** to the shore./It's a **closely** guarded secret.*
*She dived **deep** into the pool./The insult hurt her **deeply**.*
*She works **hard**./You've **hardly** touched your dinner.*
*The balloon flew **high** over the house./Crocodiles are **highly** dangerous.*
*I've **just** told you./Were they treated **justly** by the courts?*
*He arrived **late**./He's been doing that a lot **lately**.*
*Don't walk **near** the edge of the cliff./You **nearly** fell.*
*You've typed my number **wrong**./He was **wrongly** accused of burglary.*

1 Read the *Learn this!* box. Then complete the sentences using an adverb or adverbial phrase formed from these adjectives.

close cowardly deep friendly high late
leisurely weekly wrong

1 When he called the dog's name, it wagged its tail _____ .
2 His boss was angry because he arrived _____ for work on his first day.
3 These wild animals are _____ dangerous.
4 They walked _____ into the jungle.
5 Our plan worked perfectly at first but then everything went _____ .
6 The mugger chose _____ to target children and elderly people.
7 The Ferrari won the race, _____ followed by the Mercedes.
8 Sunday is the only day we have time to relax and eat lunch _____ .
9 The sitcom is broadcast _____ on MTV.

9.2 Adjective suffixes

LEARN THIS!

1 We can add suffixes to some nouns and verbs to make them into adjectives. (Sometimes the spelling changes.) Common suffixes are:
-able: *affordable, comfortable, dependable, washable*
-al: *accidental, exceptional, national, occasional*
-ful: *beautiful, fanciful, hopeful, useful*
-ive: *attractive, creative, expressive, responsive*
-less: *hopeless, jobless, penniless, pointless, useless*
-ous: *adventurous, dangerous, famous, mischievous*
-y: *breezy, squeaky, thirsty, woolly*

2 Some adjectives end in *-ible* (pronounced the same as *-able*). However, if you remove *-ible* from the adjective, you are not usually left with a complete word:
audible, legible, tangible

1 Read the *Learn this!* box. Complete the sentences with an adjective formed from the noun or verb in brackets. Use a dictionary to help you if necessary.

1 If he said something _____ (offense), I'm sure it wasn't _____ (intention).
2 Storing fireworks next to petrol and other _____ . (hazard) substances could be _____ (disaster).
3 They went hiking in a _____ (mountain) part of India.
4 The climate is usually _____ (rely) in June, but this year, it was very _____ (rain).
5 She's the chief executive of a _____ (globe) electronics company.
6 She has an _____ (envy) relationship with her parents, who are always _____ (support).
7 Many of these diseases are _____ (prevent) if you follow a healthy lifestyle.
8 The meat was cold, _____ (taste) and _____ (chew).
9 His poetry is very _____ (access) and extremely _____ (meaning) too.

2 Choose the correct spelling.

1 They find each other attractive, but they're aren't at all **compatable / compatible**.
2 The story he told the judge wasn't really **credable / credible**.
3 These boots aren't **suitable / suitible** for climbing.
4 This cycle helmet is virtually **indestructable / indestructible**.
5 His qualification is not **comparable / comparible** with a university degree.
6 Carbon monoxide is particularly dangerous because it's **invisable / invisible**.
7 Most infectious diseases are now **curable / curible**.
8 Don't drop this box, the contents are **breakable / breakible**.

10.1 Sports disciplines

1 Work in pairs. How many sports can you write which fit these patterns?

1 _____ball: basketball, handball, ...
2 _____ing: bowling, surfing, ...
3 _____ racing: horse racing, ...

2 Write the sports in the correct category.

aerobics   cricket   hockey   ice hockey   judo   karate
rock-climbing   snooker   squash   tae kwon do
water polo   yoga

A	participants compete in teams

B	participants compete as individuals

C	usually non-competitive

3 Match the two halves of the winter sports. Then write them under the correct photos.

bob	boarding
figure	jump
half	pipe
ski	skating
snow	skating
speed	sleigh

1 _____   2 _____   3 _____

4 _____   5 _____   6 _____

10.2 Noun suffixes

We can add suffixes to some verbs and adjectives to make them into nouns. (Sometimes the spelling changes.) Suffixes include:
-ism: *capitalism, organism, patriotism, professionalism, racism, sexism, tourism, vandalism*
-ment: *employment, encouragement, engagement, management, movement*
-ation: *consideration, examination, expectation, interpretation, presentation, transformation*
-ing: *dwelling, ending, failing, meaning, offering, recording*
-ings: *bearings, belongings, earnings, proceedings, surroundings*
-ship: *citizenship, championship, dictatorship, friendship, hardship, leadership, ownership, partnership, relationship*
-hood: *adulthood, childhood, falsehood, motherhood*

1 Read the *Learn this!* box. Which of the noun suffixes are usually added to (a) verbs? (b) adjectives? (c) nouns?

2 Complete the sentences with a noun formed from the word in brackets. Use a dictionary to help you if necessary.

1 In 1932, my great-grandfather spent all his _____ on a car. (save)
2 What is the _____ of winning the lottery the first time you enter it? (likely)
3 I asked the hotel receptionist if she had any _____ for restaurants nearby. (recommend)
4 His brother left the army and joined the _____ . (priest)
5 As people become more cynical about politics, _____ of political parties has dropped. (member)
6 Some groups have called for more _____ of websites like YouTube. (censor)
7 There was a minor _____ between two members of the same team. (disagree)
8 The main _____ for the job is a degree in engineering. (require)
9 He impressed the crowd with his dignity and _____ , despite losing the match. (sportsman)
10 Owing to a _____ , the hotel didn't have a room for us when we arrived. (misunderstand)
11 The scientists published their _____ in the journal *Nature*. (find)
12 Many people think there is too much _____ (commercial) in sport.

Communicative Activities

Task from Unit 6F

1 Work in pairs. Take turns to do the exam task below. Spend about a minute preparing your answer.

A large number of relatives are visiting you this weekend, and you need to buy a lot of food. Where and how will you buy the food? Choose one of the options in the photos. Justify your choice and say why you rejected the other suggestions.

2 Work in pairs. Take turns to answer the examiner's questions.

Questions for Student A:
1 Will online shopping put many high street shops out of business?
2 What are the advantages of shopping in supermarkets?

Questions for Student B:
1 How important is good customer service when you are shopping for food?
2 What are the advantages of shopping online?

Task from Unit 7F

1 SPEAKING Work in pairs. Describe the photo below. Then take turns to ask and answer the examiner's questions.

1 What do you think the girl is thinking? Why?
2 What do teenagers commonly argue about amongst themselves?
3 Tell me about an argument you had with a friend or a member of your family.

Task from Unit 8F

1 Work in pairs. Take turns to do the exam task below. Spend about a minute preparing your answer.

The Government is asking everyone to reduce their carbon footprint. What is the best way of doing this? Choose one of the options in the photos. Justify your choice and say why you rejected the other suggestions.

2 Work in pairs. Take turns to answer the examiner's questions.

Questions for Student A:
1 Some people think that we should ban cars from all city, town and village centres. To what extent do you agree with this opinion?
2 What can we as individuals do to help limit global warming?

Questions for Student B:
1 Should petrol cost much more to discourage motorists from driving?
2 What campaigns are there in your country to protect and improve the environment?